BREAKFAST IN HELL

A Doctor's Eyewitness Account of the Politics of Hunger in Ethiopia

Myles F. Harris, M.D.

POSEIDON PRESS • NEW YORK

Published by Poseidon Press,
A Division of Simon & Schuster, Inc.
Simon & Schuster Building
Rockefeller Center
1230 Avenue of the Americas
New York, New York 10020

POSEIDON PRESS is a registered trademark of Simon &
Schuster, Inc.

Designed by Irving Perkins Associates
Manufactured in the United States of America
10 9 8 7 6 5 4 3 2 1
Library of Congress Cataloging-in-Publication Data
Harris, Myles F.
    Breakfast in hell.

    1. Famines—Ethiopia.   2. Ethiopia—Politics
and government—1974–   .   3. Harris, Myles.
4. Physicians, Foreign—Ethiopia—Biography.
I. Title.
HC845.Z9F345   1987   363.8'83'0963   86-25504
ISBN: 0-671-63272-8

To my wife, Janet

ACKNOWLEDGMENTS

M A N Y P E O P L E helped me in the preparation of this book, but my thanks are due in particular to my wife, Janet, for the contribution her detailed memory of those awful events has made. Thanks also to Laura Lamson, who undertook the onerous task of reading and correcting the script so many times, and for her invaluable advice on the technicalities of writing it; to Doctors Neville Henry, Peter Stevenson, and Anthony Daniels for their criticisms and suggestions. I also owe a great debt to Michael Sanders in New York, who so expertly edited the manuscript of a very raw beginner. I would also like to thank Geoff Mulligan, Joanna Webb, and my agent, Deborah Rogers in London.

Last but not least, I would like to express my gratitude and appreciation to all those Ethiopians who worked so hard with me and who cannot be named because of the tragic situation that still exists in their country.

ON THE 17TH OF MAY, 1977, the Secretary-General of the Swedish Save the Children Fund stated that "One thousand children have been massacred in Addis Ababa and their bodies, lying in the streets, are ravaged by roving hyenas. . . . The bodies of murdered children, mostly aged from eleven to thirteen years, can be seen heaped on the roadside when one leaves Addis Ababa.

—*Human Rights*
Violations in Addis Ababa.
Amnesty International, 1978

The same government, that of Mengistu Haile Mariam, is still in power.

INTRODUCTION
BATI, WOLLO PROVINCE
ETHIOPIA 1984

IN THE AUTUMN OF 1984 the Red Cross set up a camp on the edge of the Ethiopian desert at a town called Bati in Wollo province. Bati, 250 miles north of Addis Ababa by road, stands at the entrance to a pass in the foothills of the great Ethiopian plateau, a plateau that rises over ten thousand feet to mountains that hold the remains of the ancient Kingdom of Abyssinia, now the Socialist Republic of Ethiopia. Through Bati came traders, missionaries, and the handful of European explorers who survived the crossing of a fearsome desert, the Danakil, that stood between Bati and the sea, a three-hundred-mile crossing alive with nomadic tribes who prized the testicles of their enemies as a proof of manhood. Few outsiders managed it.

In 1984 Bati was dying, its market empty, its people starving. In a valley outside the town, thirty thousand peasants from the surrounding countryside had gathered to die with it. Beyond them in the desert a sporadic war continued between the nomads and the Provisional Military Government, known as the Dergue.

I had arrived in Bati from the south of Ethiopia in November to work in a makeshift hospital in the camp. My job

9

was to supervise the rescue, from among the thirty thousand refugees crammed in that narrow valley, of those too ill to walk the last hundred yards for help. But today an outbreak of meningitis obliged me to go to the provincial capital to examine some specimens I had taken from two of the victims. Giorgis, an Ethiopian male nurse, stood in for me for the day.

I should have known something was going on as I drove away from my small country hotel near the camp; every few hundred yards along the road small groups of soldiers with light machine pistols lounged in the scrub or squatted on their haunches on the edge of the road. But I assumed it was just another rumor of a guerrilla attack. The week before the rebels had raided Bati and carried off a minor commissar. And this morning at breakfast the nurses had said that they had seen soldiers on the ridges between the hotel and the camp. These troops, I thought, must have been part of the same detachment.

When I got back that evening I heard what had happened from Tula, one of the Finnish Red Cross nurses. She said that Gabre Mariam, the camp administrator, had been jumpy all morning, constantly changing the chalked statistics in the briefing office, glancing at the tattered Ethiopian flag flying in the center of the feeding area, fiddling with a tie nobody had ever seen him wear before. The reason soon became obvious. About eleven in the morning, troops began to appear on the low hills surrounding the valley where we had set our camp with its tent hospitals, feeding stations, water wells, and blanket distribution center. Just after noon a convoy of vehicles, preceded by a half-track, began to sink down the hill toward a river known as *Mot*, or "Death," which marked the western boundary of the camp; it presaged a visit from a high official. Bringing up its rear were four green Soviet trucks filled with soldiers.

They were crack troops. The nurses said you could see it in the speed with which they spread over the camp. Within a few moments of arrival they were everywhere: inside the hospital; crouched in twos or threes at the crossways among the tent lanes; ranged along the walls of the outpatients. They even set up a machine-gun post among the mass graves on a hill to the north of the camp. The Red Cross flag, prohibiting the entry of armed soldiers within the area of its jurisdiction, hung limp above the gate.

It wasn't the first time this had happened; armed troops had already been in the camp a week before when they had taken away five thousand starving people. The European nurses staged a walkout. The Ethiopian nurses might have gone with them except that they would have incurred ten-year prison sentences.

Giorgis told me the rest. In the center of the convoy that brought the troops was a white jeep, which he assumed carried an important visitor. But when it drew up at the entrance to the feeding center its only pasenger was an army private who sat rigidly in the back seat, a decoy in case the guerrillas attacked. Then the steady ticking of a helicopter engine began to nag at the edge of the horizon. Five minutes passed before Giorgis saw it coming, not, as he would have expected, from the south over the mosque and the empty marketplace with its steel gallows, but low over the hills from the north, gliding and bucking in the hot currents of air that licked a dead dry earth even drier. It circled, fuselage tipped over to squint at thirty thousand pinched faces looking up at it from the dust, then swung in over the disused soccer field behind the feeding center. There it hovered, nose slightly in the air, while a small squad of troops deployed themselves below it. Only when they were in position, guns pointed at the starving crowd, did it slowly begin to descend in a fury of thick brown dust which parted occasionally to reveal the word AEROFLOT painted in white letters on its camouflaged fuselage.

The machine hopped twice then settled, and the pilot switched off his engine. In the silence that followed there was a rasping sound, a door opened, and a short aluminum ladder slid to the ground. One by one, five well-fed men in officers' uniforms with red flashes on their lapels, eased themselves down onto the dry gray earth, looked around, then turned to the door. There was a pause, then another figure emerged, ran down the steps, and, surrounded by the five staff officers, all of whom dwarfed him, began hurrying toward a small delegation of officials standing beyond the circle of soldiers.

The Emperor had arrived. Mengistu Haile Mariam, Strength of Mary Mengistu, Chairman of the Military Council of the Provisional Military Government of Socialist Ethiopia, Secretary General of the Council of Peasants and Workers of Ethiopia, President of the Armed Forces of the Democratic Peoples of Ethiopia, Chief of Staff of the Air and Land Forces, General in Command of the Bureau for Armed Struggle against Imperialist Aggression in Tigre and Eritrea, Head of the Security Advisory Committee.

It was a Napoleonic scene. The tiny Emperor surrounded by his field marshals surveying the site of a truly twentieth-century battlefield, a famine camp. A battlefield with an invisible enemy whose opening shots had been fired half a century ago. Once nature had used war to adjust the delicate balance of land to people, but today, with the population doubling every twenty years on what had already doubled twenty years before, famine had become her general.

The leader was shown inside one of the tents that served as a shelter for the seriously ill, packed so close that those who died in the night had to be left next to the living until morning. The party stood there for a moment among the smells and the flies—Mengistu's generals uneasy under the dull indifferent eyes of fifty dying children. Outside where once there had been trees, grass, grazing camels, oxen driven by small boys down red dusty lanes lined with sorghum and millet, the little Napoleon's ambitions, his insane military adventures, the tribute he was forced to pay to his Slavic colonial masters, and above all the mirage of socialist collective farming, had transformed the landscape into a desert.

Food alone would cure these children, although many were even beyond that. But here in Bati, 250 miles from the capital, there was little food, a wrecked hospital, one doctor, twenty nurses, and two packing cases of rudimentary drugs. Mengistu looked at the children, turned to Giorgis, and said, "Why do you not give them all blood transfusions?"

A unit of blood cost one hundred dollars, enough to feed all the children in the tent for a month. The nearest blood bank was in the capital and, besides, produced only enough blood for one person in every thousand in the country. In a radius of two hundred miles from where Mengistu stood there were eight million people starving to death. In any case, blood was not the treatment for malnutrition, although he could at least be forgiven for not knowing that.

Giorgis said to me afterwards, "Such men do not know the peoples." I stared up at his thin face. It was smiling apologetically at having such a fool for a king. I looked away . . . embarrassed to find myself near to tears.

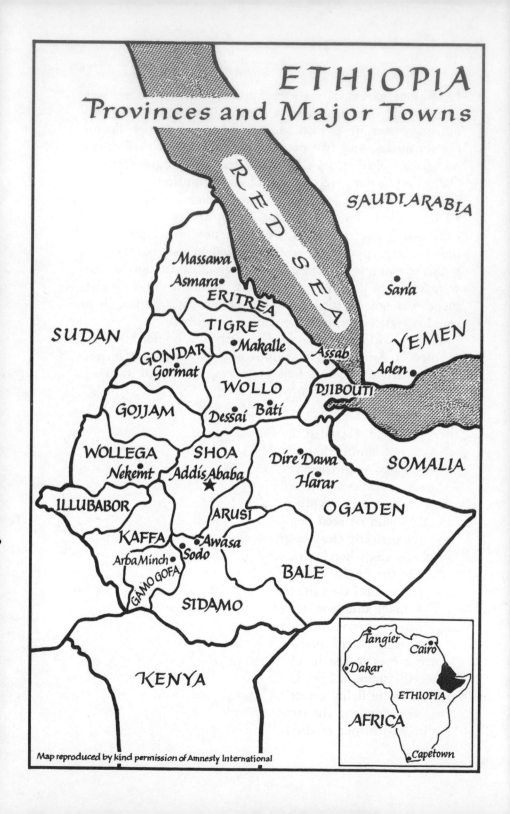

ETHIOPIA
Provinces and Major Towns

RED SEA

SAUDI ARABIA

SUDAN

Massawa•
Asmara•
ERITREA
TIGRE
GONDAR   •Makalle
Gormat
WOLLO
GOJJAM   Dessai• Bati•

Sana•

YEMEN
Assab•
Aden•

DJIBOUTI

WOLLEGA   SHOA   Dire•Dawa   SOMALIA
Nekemt• Addis Ababa• Harar
ILLUBABOR   OGADEN
ARUSI
KAFFA   •Awasa
ArbaMinch• Sodo•
GAMO GOFA   BALE
SIDAMO

KENYA

Tangier
Cairo•
Dakar•
ETHIOPIA
AFRICA
Capetown•

1

GENEVA

AUGUST 28, 1984. THE BEGINNING

My wife and I landed in Geneva from Melbourne at six
o'clock one summer's morning and took a taxi through the
neat suburbs with their carefully tended gardens to the city.
Already, fastidiously dressed men were leaving for work in
their Mercedeses, while through lighted windows their
women could be seen beginning the day's interminable pursuit of a perfectly clean house. But by seven we were in bed in
a slightly seedy hotel with unpleasant stains on the red carpet
opposite the English church that commemorates John Knox.
As I fell asleep I thought that the world I was going to would
not be much different from the Switzerland that Knox knew:
violently poor, ravished by plagues, and reft by dogma.

We woke about three, ate a late lunch under the disapproving eyes of the hotel restaurant staff, and took a stroll
along the shore of Lake Geneva and the upper reaches of the
Rhône. After flying directly from an Australian winter it was
hot, very hot, and the time was wrong. We were still living
ten hours in front of the hurrying crowds on the esplanade.

On the lake, steamers with tall funnels from the time of Kaiser Wilhelm, King Teddy, and the fiercely mustachioed generals of World War I plied tourists across the lake to where Lenin once wrote his strange mirror to *Mein Kampf*. I watched the lines pressing forward to board one of the boats and wondered how his gospels would translate in Ethiopia, the first Soviet colony in Africa. After a warm Coke in a terrace cafe I hailed a taxi and told the driver to take us to Red Cross headquarters.

We drove along the side of the lake past L'Institut Henri Dunant, a lovely baroque building set in the pebbled shore among giant cedars of Lebanon. Henri Dunant founded the Red Cross, but his name was for a long time an embarrassment to the Swiss and foreign bureaucrats who took control of it. After four years he was ousted from the organization he had founded to make way for the nineteenth-century equivalent of our modern corporate executives with their strange vocabulary of management.

"I understand your difficulty, Henri—may I call you Henri?—and I do think, believe me, that this meeting was a useful and ongoing contribution to our mutual problem, but I wonder, Henri, if relocation might not offer a parameter we could explore together?"

Or was the dismissal more nineteenth-century? A religious homily, a brutal critique, and then the knife?

Dunant was a Swiss businessman who on June 24, 1859, seeking the French emperor's support for one of his business schemes in North Africa, wandered by accident onto the battlefield of Solferino in northern Italy. He was so horrified by the suffering he saw that he immediately set about organizing the local peasants to rescue those of the wounded they could. He went back to Switzerland and founded the Red Cross, obsessed with the idea of an international, neutral organization for the relief of suffering in war. Neglecting all personal considerations he threw himself into its formation; but his obsession ruined him financially. Rival philanthropists seized his dream and, dethroned, he vanished for nearly twenty years.

At the age of sixty-seven he was discovered penniless in a remote Swiss village and, having adjudged him to be too old to be any further danger to society, they gave the proud, embittered old man the Nobel Peace prize, which he had the ill grace to immediately give away—some people never learn. The history of Henri Dunant, failed businessman and ruined philanthropist, is the history of the Aidgame.

My wife and I both knew about the Aidgame. It would be difficult for anybody who had worked outside of Europe not to. I had doctored and Janet had nursed in places as diverse as a beach hospital in New Guinea, a Canadian town just below the Arctic circle, a small island in the Caribbean, and, in our first contact with Africa, a mission hospital in the Kalahari desert. Senior Aidgamers were everywhere, jetting into makeshift, crumbling airports seeking, like Jesuits of a new order, recruits among the new middle classes of the Third World.

What did these recruiters want? They were looking for representatives, spokesmen for the poor to whom they could talk about a new equality. They had an idea that one day all people would be equal, that nobody would starve, and that disease would be wiped from the face of the earth. They even had a slogan—"Health for all by the year 2000." Nobody seriously believed it, but saying it was like a secular prayer, a magic formula that would open an impossibly locked door.

But Aidgamers are something much more than mere missionaries of a secular society. Aidgame represents the West's overwhelming desire to be loved and forgiven by the poor for being so rich. Like Hans Andersen's princess, the poor are the pea beneath a hundred mattresses that disturbs our sleep.

The difficult question is, who are the poor, who represents them? Who can be trusted to carry our request to them for love? Aidgamers, our representatives, often make mistakes in their choice. Sometimes they have no choice for, like us, they are victims of hopeless optimisms spawned thirty years ago.

It was then that the West abolished the idea of evil, legislated away differences between people, and, to set an example, began to abolish their own colonial empires. In their place came aid and the Aidgame. Its players were set to work in societies that, newly liberated from the straitjacket of colonialism, had returned not to a Victorian progressive optimism but to medievalism and feudalism dressed in modern military uniforms.

So for twenty years Aidgamers struggled in those parts of the world where the peasants are too weak, backward, or poor to resist such tyrannies. Desperately they have tried to flatter and cajole the new tyrants into doing some good. But flattery is two-edged. After a while you can come to believe that at least some of the tyrants are good, interested not in Swiss bank accounts but in the welfare of their peasants. That maybe it is a sound economy for them to drive Mercedes-Benzes past villages stunned by famine, and that, perhaps, huge and crippling bureaucracies are a sensible strategy for absorbing middle-class unemployment. You had to believe, for sometimes the reality was so awful you had to hide your head.

The end to this came around August 1984. Widespread famine struck the north of the continent. At first the news was concealed by mendacious governments or vanished inside the immense and secret chaos of the international aid bureaucracies. But slowly, then in a flood, pictures and stories of the death of a third of a continent began to flow into the Western press. At the time we were both working in a remote country practice in the Australian outback. One morning we were sitting on the veranda at breakfast listening to the parrots scold each other in the trees when the phone rang.

I knew the medical director of the Australian Red Cross through friends in New Guinea. I had long nursed an ambition to work in Cambodia and had asked him to keep me in mind if he heard of any hospitals there needing doctors or nurses. But he wanted to talk about Red Cross operations in Africa and invited me to Melbourne to discuss it. When we met three days later he showed me the films of the Ethiopian famine and talked about the secret massacres in Uganda. Would I be interested? I would. But I explained my reservations about the Aidgame. This time, the director said, things were different. This was a major emergency and minds in Geneva were wonderfully concentrated. They were looking for new blood and Australia would, for the first time, be in the forefront.

But would such small players as ourselves be new brooms or window dressing for the old methods? I suspected that this great tragedy, despite its billing, would end up like the opening run of a well-known and highly successful opera, but on a grander scale than anything staged before. Even if past their best, with some unmemorable performances behind them, many long-established singers would be used, and the treatment of the opera would be conventional to suit the deeply conservative tastes of an experienced audience. The critics would be there in force with their TV cameras, tape recorders, and notebooks, and, if it were a success, we could expect some guest appearances. A week later we signed contracts for six months in Ethiopia. Three days later, high over the Pacific, I fiddled with an airline breakfast and wondered if I had made a wise decision.

The headquarters of the various national Red Cross and Red Crescent Societies in Geneva is a large building shaped rather like a European coffin. It is extraordinarily clean inside with four floors of highly polished tile and that elusive smell of antiseptic and beeswax that you find in convents and hospitals in Europe. The impression you get of any place that is an annex to the end of the world must be fleeting, your mind too concentrated on the future, so that everything, even the weirdly clean toilets, only serves to remind you of the contrasts you are likely to meet within the next few days. Your mind is dominated by one thought: will I get back, and if I do, will it be in one piece?

The team assembled in the long briefing room behind double doors guarded by a disapproving bust of Dunant. I touched his forehead for luck as I went in. Each place was set with a pink folder, a packet of carbons, many envelopes with the Red Cross insignia, and a small pile of photocopied reports. Throughout the briefing, secretaries plied the pile with more as they came spilling off the copying machines that infested the building. These machines were everywhere, ceaselessly grinding, and working at a sort of bureaucratic midwifery, multiplying an endless stream of slightly scorched position papers.

There were four of us: three nurses—one Irish, one English, one Japanese, and myself, the team doctor. The Irish nurse was a nun. The English nurse was my wife, Janet. The Japanese nurse was making history. Until 1984 the Japanese had refused to send women nurses on their own to foreign countries. Yushi Koremitsu was the first Japanese nurse to travel to a disaster with a non-Japanese team.

The briefing was conducted by a tense upper-class-English young woman in her late twenties with a careful Oxford accent, a stoop, and a slight fuzz of hair on her upper lip. She bore a remarkable resemblance to Joanna Lumley's Purdy in the TV series *The Avengers*, but her diffidence destroyed the illusion after a few words. We seemed to frighten her, her accent and presentation becoming more and more that of an Oxford undergraduate presenting a thesis. I began to feel like a pedantic, rather dirty old don with a down on youth, but it might just have been a hot morning, or her layman's suspicions of the medical and nursing mafia. The morning wore on and Lumley was replaced by a handsomely tired Scandinavian who too frequently hooded his eyes, followed by a rather quiet, self-absorbed Englishman who introduced himself as the head of the East African department. At the end of the morning we adjourned to the World Health Organization headquarters for lunch.

The WHO restaurant was vast, institutional, and alive with the sounds of metal cutlery being slammed on cheap trays and the screeching of chair legs on tiled flooring. The noises echoed against the long gallery of tall windows that, making up one wall, were curiously and uneasily sloped away from the vertical. I felt oppressed by modernity, as if I had stumbled by chance onto a film set for Aldous Huxley's *Brave New World*. We ate among a clattering crowd of Aidgamers, men and women from every corner of the world. There were agronomists from Canada, intense sociologists from dull midwestern American universities, water engineers from Germany, countless administrators, doctors, nurses, nutritionists, experts on cattle-borne tick diseases, demographers, puzzled-looking statisticians.

For years this room had been filled with such people. Some were about to leave for long assignments in unpleasant, dangerous climates, others had come home, ill and tired, to report to comfortable headquarters executives, the eternal rivalry between staff officer and frontline soldier relived inside an international charity. Everybody in that room knew that most of their work had come to nothing, vanishing in a sea of misunderstanding or in the shifting sands of Third World corruption. Yet while all of them had experienced it, only a few would acknowledge it, not only to people at home anxious to hear the worst, but to themselves. They couldn't— they were inside the game.

I had avoided looking too closely at my new companions so far. There would be time enough in the next six months and I did not want to judge them too hastily; first impressions are like a fast dye to me, staining the mind. But something about the harsh light or perhaps the effect of the cheap Swiss red wine from the carafe set between me and the English director opposite compelled me to look.

Sister Prudence, the nun, was about forty-five years old with a lean Scottish face. She was spare, competent, and tense, dressed in cheap blue and gray prints with a large silver cross hanging at her breast. A pair of thick lenses lent a deceptive weakness to her face that contrasted oddly with her tough, angular appearance. She had an immediate charm that mixed delightfully with the gentle ego-bashing the religious practice without cease on everybody, including themselves.

We talked about our past experiences in the Third World. I knew from the tired Scandinavian director that Sister Prudence had been highly decorated for her work in Beirut during the Phalangist massacres of 1982. She had led a team of one hundred nurses, doctors, and medical auxilaries sent by the World Council of Churches. Within days of arrival, she said, some of them broke down and had to be sent home. Some took to drink, one tried to jump out of a window, another had continuous hysterics, and after it was all over, one delegate was arrested at Damascus airport for drug smuggling and sentenced to five years' imprisonment, the Syrians not sharing with the World Council of Churches a desire to forgive such a folly on the grounds of human weakness. It was noticeable, she said, that nearly all the ones who cracked had never been to the Third World before, and it wasn't the shelling and the street fighting that did it, but the normal frustrations of living in a poor country: the lack of simple conveniences, the long periods of inaction, boredom, and frustration interleaved only by clashes with officials who had replaced logic with wild medieval convictions.

In the middle of all this she had been tempted by the Gorgon-headed horror that lurks in all such places, the Conradian Heart of Darkness. She went to look at the results of the massacre in the Palestinian camps. I think she knew there were no survivors, though she may have gone in case there were. Yet that is never the reason, not for us. We are compelled, driven, to ceaselessly grope for our own breaking points, like a man feeling live electrical cables in a dark, wet cellar.

She told me of mothers skewered to the walls with their babies by Phalangist bayonets, people crucified in comical attitudes just as Josephus had described in the sack of Jerusalem by Titus's legion in the first century A.D. There is nothing new under the sun. But it had left her with nightmares, a feeling of terrible uncertainty and I wondered whether, when she came back, her church was able to help her. After all,

Vatican Three had drawn a veil over evil and stripped its marvelous liturgy of the old comforting magic. All they could do was to offer her a few kind words in English and that is no good when you have seen the devil himself.

Yushi Koremitsu, the Japanese nurse, sat next to me trying to grasp at half-understood bits of the conversation. You could feel her astonished incomprehension not just at the language but at the ideas and forms behind it. Ideas expressed in our straggling indisciplined script, loud argumentative voices and ataxic gestures. While we had waited to meet the director she had taken a small green square of paper from her bag and begun to fold it. The paper turned into a swan, delicate wings poised for flight over the glassy surface of the highly polished table. She smiled a great deal and said almost nothing.

The director asked me about my time in Botswana, and I sensed my wife tensing alongside me. We had spent three years in South Africa working in the Kalahari Desert at Livingstone's old hospital ten miles from the border with Botswana. It was a mission run entirely for blacks, completely cut off by the country's Canute-like pass laws from white South Africa. Laws that, as long as we worked in a black homeland, applied to us with as much force as they did to the Africans. But I knew that even voluntary isolation among some of the most oppressed of the continent's people would not escape the censure of those new witchfinders of the late twentieth century, the racial equality fanatics. And we were certain to meet some in a large international organization such as the Red Cross. I countered with some questions about life in Geneva, and Janet relaxed.

The lunch drifted to a close and we walked back to the coffin-shaped headquarters through a hot, late-summer afternoon. The director sent us upstairs to the medical center to have our vaccinations checked. We sat in a circle under some old, partly exposed oak beams and listened to an elderly nurse in sensible tweeds lecture on malaria prophylaxis. She had large, almost mannish hands reddened by much scrubbing.

To keep from falling asleep under the combined effects of the late-summer heat, jet lag, and the wine, I focused on a photocopied sheet I had been given that morning. There was a list of projected mortality figures for Ethiopia in the first three months of 1984. Two million. This wasn't just a minor tribe to be seen through a food shortage but the death of a nation, perhaps worse, the collapse of a continent. I looked at the old nurse chatting equably about malaria. Two million dead. It made her seem like an actress brought out of retirement to recite her lines to young troops on the edge of Armageddon. There were no questions when she finished, just a brief silence. Confused, she pushed a bell and a secretary showed us out.

Suddenly, interest in us waned and we found ourselves in an empty office, bored and slightly apprehensive, waiting until it was time to go to the airport. Around us on the shelves files of previous famines leaned against each other like old tombstones, each marked with a crude felt pen. "Ethiopia 1974." "Uganda 1975." "Congo 1958." Secretaries came from time to time and hemmed us in with parcels, mixing them with our own luggage on the floor. These we were to take with us to Addis Ababa, to be handed over at Red Cross headquarters there. They were all addressed to individuals, and I spent my time trying to imagine what these people would turn out to be like, which of them would become friends, which enemies.

One of the packages was ripped slightly at one corner and from it a poster protruded. I stared at the jigsaw of colors for about half an hour and then curiosity overcame me. Carefully I eased the poster from its wrappings. It was the picture of a chubby, cheerful Ethiopian doctor beaming at a small boy playing in the dust at his feet. Behind them was a round straw hut. I was to meet the doctor soon in vastly different circumstances.

"A tucul," Sister Prudence explained, pointing to the hut.

Prudence had been in Ethiopia before, in the 1970s' famine, but until now she had disclaimed any up-to-date knowledge of it, saying it was better to listen to the current briefings. But we pressed her about her experiences until, reluctantly, she told us. In keeping with a disciplined personality, it was an unsurprising and conventional view, telling of a country that, by an unhappy combination of events, suddenly and with absolutely no warning, had succumbed to a devastating drought. She drifted with, rather than held, the general view that it was due to a malign combination of Western bankers, the results of past colonial invasions, and a formless but pervasive Western greed.

I sat and wondered about what the nun had said. True, Africa was a continent of colonially created states ripped apart by tribes that owed only loyalty to family and tribe, tribes as old as the continent itself, roots to which each man returned in the end. But if the colonialists had never come, what difference would it have made? After all, scarcely had they left than a new tribe spread all over Africa. The Kenyans, liking puns, called them the Wabenzi. It means "Tribe of the Mercedes-Benz." They are rich, owe no loyalty to anyone, speak English, and drive Mercedeses. For the peasants it was nothing new. They saw the great power of the Wabenzi and how effortlessly they had stepped into the boots of the old colonial masters. These were the old masters with faces of a different color. Many thought them far worse. Great poverty came.

How did it happen? The way it always happens.

When World War II ended forty years ago, the colonial powers in Africa began to lose their grip on the territories around which they had drawn such arbitrary frontiers for two hundred years. Frontiers that paced the march of European soldiers, the reach of the copper-wired telegraph, or came up against natural obstacles that even the solid virtues of Victorian technology could not overcome. The lines ruled so confidently straight across the maps enclosed huge mining stakes, millions of acres of arable land, verdant forest, giant natural reservoirs. They became a vast source of wealth to their new owners and one which nobody thought they would ever give

up. Yet by 1918 a slow yet relentless weakening of their hold
on Africa began. Why this was, why World War II accelerated it, why anticolonialism became such an obsession among
young people everywhere in the late 1950s nobody knows. It
was no longer sufficient to see it as a reaction to naked exploitation. Many of those who wrote despairing angry letters
to the *Times* or *Le Figaro* from remote outstations in the bush
or the drab administrative offices of colonial governments,
warning of what would happen when the colonial powers
moved out, were selfless, decent men. For little pay and often
serious risks, they had devoted their lives to the administrative rule of Africa. Now there were roads and railways. Most
countries exported surplus crops, slavery had been put down,
the lot of women improved, an adversary system of justice
had been established, and the power of the private European
industrial combines curtailed. But it made no difference, colonialism was a bad thing, it had to go.

The colonial powers, sensing the inevitable, began to prepare an African ruling class. If you had stood by the side of a
customs officer at Tilbury docks in London in the 1950s, you
would have seen the seeds of this class arriving: young men
clutching soggy cardboard suitcases, wearing cheap suits and
sad, stiff peasant shoes, on their faces fear mixed with a slight
dab of arrogance, like a painter testing his palette with a
smudge of violent color.

As mission schoolboys in the '40s or early '50s each of
them had at some time bent over small green single sheets of
paper headed "Oxford University Matriculation Board. '0'
Level," to answer questions on such subjects as the accession
of Richard III of England, the War of Jenkins's Ear, the effect
of mixing something called hydrogen peroxide with sulphuric
acid, or how many chains there were in a cricket pitch. It did
not mean much, but they had good memories, and they knew
the correct answers might get them to England. Now, in the
rain, trudging down the Mile End road, their shoes already
parting at string seams, there was no sign of Jenkins's Ear,
King Richard, or cricket pitches made of chains. Just waves

of blank hurrying faces, eyes entombed within themselves. It did not take many days for every one of these new arrivals from pastoral Africa with its close family ties, its life interwound with the slow rhythm of open sky and land, to realize they were immured in Leviathan, a world of machines that in exchange for things made men cold and inward-looking, men who had neither kith nor kin, love nor laughter. From anywhere, but especially from a brown-walled London bed-sitter with a stained mattress, which is where many young Africans eked out their lonely Sundays deprived of love, it was depressing and puzzling, until as time passed they too became slaves to the machines.

But the young men found that not all the inhabitants of Leviathan were obsessed with machines. Some led complicated intellectual lives, read books of verse, and attended plays to which occasionally there were invitations for them. What message these spectacles, all of them seemingly staged in kitchens full of the latest electrical gadgets, and nearly always about young girls getting pregnant, were meant to convey it was not known. There were no electrical kitchens in Botswana or Kinshasa. If your daughter got with child in Africa, the neighbors came and danced with you, they did not shun you or whisper against you in the market. This part of the Leviathan, the theater, the strange, incomprehensible Shakespeare, the sad concerts full of slow music without drums, they would not take this back with them. Nor the customs of the courts where a man paid others to speak for him in front of another with a cheap rug on his head. Courts in which one man could take another man's wife and not be punished, while a man who took more than one wife could be sent to prison. Or governments that, owning the police, allowed the opposition to insult them in newspapers almost every day. It was not manly. It was not for Africa. In Africa, many children, much land, one's enemies in prison—these were the marks of strength and virtue.

The young men began to see that with machines they too could be masters in their own countries. But at first it seemed inconceivable that their owners would ever part with them. What after all did a poor African student have to offer in exchange? But soon the students discovered that the inhabitants of Leviathan all seemed to suffer some vast inexplicable guilt about their wealth. When words like colonialism, exploitation, mining interests, and multinationals were mentioned, they would start like a murderer reminded of the corpse beneath his lawn, and offer machines or money to be left alone. What man would not accept?

In the beginning everything offered was taken, but most of it broke down, rusted, or made people laugh. So in the end this currency of guilt stabilized into the Mercedes, backed by huge gifts of money that, it was learned, grew best, not in the difficult and fractious temper of political Africa, but in the cool white fluorescence of a Swiss bank vault.

That was all thirty or forty years ago. In Ethiopia a Mercedes, Leviathan's golden calf, now equals the income of nine thousand peasants. When all of Africa is a howling, sandblown waste a Mercedes standing on a plinth at its center should be its monument.

2

ADDIS ABABA

WE LEFT GENEVA at six in the evening. I watched the twenty trunks and parcels disappear down the moving ramp past the slim legs of a Swiss Air ticket hostess. We were her last customers of the day—an expensive handbag in black leather and a pair of white gloves lay on the desk waiting for her to finish. I tried to imagine the symmetry of her house, its polished floors and expensively conservative furniture, solid and unchanging, and wondered where we would be by the time she got up in the morning.

We flew south toward Rome and a five-hour wait for the Ethiopian jet. Below us the evening sun picked out streaks of dirty, late-summer snow still clinging to the Alps. There was a volley of snapping attaché case locks as the small platoon of businessmen around me began to leaf frenetically through their papers, pull nervously at the creases of their suits, and grin insecurely at the German-Swiss hostesses patroling the aisles. Looking at the businessmen's anxious, petulant faces, I wondered why I was not one of them, and what my motives were for this escapade. Few people know their own motives, and apart from earning a living on a short-term contract I was unable to decipher my own. Perhaps it is like a mountaineer, a grown-up version of a boy on a ladder. "Look Mummy what I am doing now!" "Why what a brave boy you are!" The corruption, dirt, and danger of the Third World is exciting, producing a dangerous craving for more. A world without evil, anarchy, oppression, and corruption would seem to be unbalanced. Perhaps I was going just to be reassured that it continued. If there is no evil there is no good.

It was raining and gray when we taxied into the terminal at Fiumicino, green trucks buzzing about the legs of the aircraft. Through the porthole I could see a queue of hopeful tourists standing immobilized on the steps of a Spanish jet. The briefcases gave another ragged volley and the Swiss businessmen rose to leave. We began to talk amongst ourselves about diarrhea as we made for the transit lounge and settled down for the evening. It was going to be a long wait. After eight the lounge began to empty slowly, the restaurants and lavatories closed, until the only other occupant was a man driving a mechanical sweeper round and round in circles on the black polished floor, leaning over to one side like a driver of a "dodgem" car. It felt as if the rest of the world, having discovered where we were going, had fled. The flight-arrival board rolled its figures and numbers like a one-armed bandit until only our flight number remained. Ethiopian Airlines flight 323 was going to arrive on time. At midnight our luck changed, the flight was delayed in London by two hours. We dozed, or paced about the long empty ramp.

I must have slept for about an hour. When I awoke figures had appeared in the lounge and were gathering around a small departure desk near the exit gate leading to the aircraft ramp. There were about ten of them, all Africans, all unspeaking; the men dressed in shabby hand-me-down suits, the women in vague reds and blacks. All of them were middle-aged. One of them, a small, compactly built man in a green plastic anorak, moved behind the desk. The tramplike people began to file past him, proffering worn passports and cheap paper visas overwritten by spidery Amharic cursives in purple ink. We joined the tail of the line. It began to rain again. While I had slept the aircraft had arrived, marked with the same script as on the visas, sinisterly antique on the fuselage of something as modern as an aircraft, unrecognizable, meaningless, and obscure.

We climbed up the gangway toward two slight-featured air hostesses dressed in white cotton gebis, guarding the door of the aircraft. The aircraft was new, brand spanking new. Off the peg it must have cost the Ethiopians twenty million dollars. Somebody had thought to offset this extravagance by ordering the most basic cabin decorations, a cheap brown carpet, bare walls, and as many seats as possible. There was a strange acrid smell, half spice, half musk.

An upper-class English voice began to bray. It came from an old lady of about seventy with wild neglected hair sitting in the second row among vague shapeless packages and copies of the *Tatler*. Her voice was so pitched and of such carrying power that even as the engines started you could still hear every word as clearly as if she were shouting in a deserted cathedral. She suddenly switched into what I assumed was Amharic, stumbling a little at first but then rapidly gaining in confidence. The hostesses were galvanized by her, thrusting glasses of orange juice into her blue-veined hands and wrapping her about with rugs. As the plane bumped out across the field for takeoff she turned slightly and caught me watching her performance. I got a brief dismissive stare that said "trade" before she turned back to the hostess. No doubt she was thinking that only some modern and quite frightful notion of equality had allowed me on the plane. I wondered if Karen Blixen might not have been very like her. Arthur Scargill's worried-looking face peered at me from the back page of her *Daily Telegraph*, as though ashamed that even his picture should be in such Tory hands as hers.

I woke sometime just before dawn to an impression of scattered solitary lights below me in the desert. As the sun rose, gray light began to seep across it, filling the wadis and craters and edging the huge jagged escarpments with light. The gray turned to yellow and then to red, picking out the sawtoothed ridges and huge pans of giant boulders. There was no water and no green, a medieval preacher's vision of hell. The old lady was awake, munching an apple and reading one of her *Tatlers*. Behind her the others in my party were asleep; Yushi's features collected even in repose; Prudence's thin shoulders and head leaning against her. Next to me, mouth open, Janet muttered nervously in her sleep. The sound of the aircraft motors changed abruptly. People stirred in their seats, a hand twitched at the floor of my stomach, and I wondered compulsively about Ethiopian maintenance engineers. Did they bother? I looked out fearfully, but the aircraft was only climbing to maintain its distance from the high Ethiopian plateau that was rising to meet us below. I relaxed, the others woke and stretched.

There were only two men in the unpartitioned first-class seats just in front. An Ethiopian man with massive wrestler's shoulders and a hard, bullying face, and a white man dressed in an expensive broad pinstripe of a vaguely unfamiliar cut, the sort of thing that Cagney would have worn in a '30s gangster film. What would the God Lenin have made of having a first-class section in a people's transport? The Ethiopian got up after a few moments and walked down past me into the tourist cabin, avoiding my stare with a hostile downward gaze. As people reached up from their seats anxious to shake his hands, I wondered about the uncertainties of being an oppressor in a totalitarian state. Eventually one overseas trip will turn out to be your last, you either come home to death or a life in jail, or if you are lucky, you get a message in time telling you never to come back, that your family are in prison or dead and that nothing remains of all your possessions.

Just in front of the old lady sat a thin, broken-looking man in a brown suit of startling cheapness. His yellow-gray hair was plastered in sticky strands to a sallow skull. With his high cheekbones and arresting pale blue eyes he looked Irish or Slavic. Probably a technician or clerk on his way to a Communist embassy in Addis Ababa. He sat nervously, slightly out of his seat, balancing on his knees a scuffed brown-cardboard suitcase. Down-at-heel slip-on shoes, looking as if they were run up from the same material as his case, hung from a pair of thin ankles. There were shiny patches of wear at his elbows and knees that I had not seen on a European since the early 1950s.

I glanced across at Prudence. Something indefinable about the nun, a slight wariness in her manner, fueled my suspicion that she was the one who would compete for the leadership of our group. We were going into a strange, dangerous country, and if I failed to ensure that mine was the secret nod of assent to what we did, then we could have trouble. At this stage we knew nothing about the two nurses who had arrived on the mission two weeks before. I looked out of the window at the biblical desert.

It was among grim scenery such as this that the early church had discovered the immense power it could give its priests by swearing them to chastity. It put them at once out of reach and yet made them the objects of obsessive confidences. Prudence's detachment from the sexual world automatically set her apart as the group's confidante. It would be a magnetic pull on lonely women in their middle thirties apprehensive of men. The problem was the explanation she had given in Geneva of events in Ethiopia in the 1970s. It worried me. It was true that the West had had a hand in creating the African disaster, but not through its banks or multinationals. It had been created through guilt. Paralyzed by an illusory picture of the past, we had ended up succumbing to the demands of the loudest-voiced bully—the history of Africa since independence. Such an attitude was not merely a political caricature. In Africa it could translate into the small exchanges of daily life. Silence in the face of petty bungling, smiles for the insultingly late, a turn of the head at surreptitious cruelties. Small bricks that built an edifice of suffering.

I looked at Janet. She was still asleep. Being a doctor's wife could be very difficult. People expected you to be manipulative, and it was worse if you worked in the same hospital as your husband. I wondered how the other women would treat her. They would be apprehensive, and to some extent she would be isolated. Medicine is hierarchical. People expect to take orders and relieve themselves with secret grumbling. They would not do it in front of her.

Below us the desert changed into a patchwork of gray rectangles, tombs of ruined irrecoverable peasant soil. At intervals a gray river flashed at us in the sun, no green along its banks. We passed the Rift, a giant wound in the earth like a stepped entrance to Hades. As the plane began to descend toward Addis Ababa green fields began to appear, interspersed with small forests and rivers.

We landed at about seven in the morning and taxied into the terminal under the eyes of camouflaged watchtowers surrounding the field, identical in design to the ones that surround the Soviet Union. Two Antonov transports with their old-fashioned rear gun turrets stood parked near the terminal, a sad, flat-roofed building with great flakes of cement peeling from its walls like an eczema. Prudence talked about the need for exit visas, saying it took sometimes a week to get one. I wondered out loud what would happen if you were ill. She shrugged.

The terminal turned out to be air-conditioned, not the real American type of air-conditioning but a tepid breeze fanning the patches of green-blue fungus growing up the building's cheap concrete walls. An uneasy crowd had gathered on the far side of the customs barrier, their heads slightly bowed so as not to draw attention to themselves. An air of taut, shuffling apprehension filled the place, infecting everybody. Airports, because they concentrate together two of the most dangerous species in a Communist state—foreigners and police—are not wise places to be seen in. It was in airports that people were led away.

As a gaunt-faced official in a crumpled green suit examined my passport, the air-conditioning gave a sudden death rattle and stopped. The old lady's voice filled the sudden silence. "Would you be so kind, officer, as to not throw my bags on the floor like that, they contain expensive china I bought in Harrods yesterday." Everything seemed to stop. Queues froze, heads turned, stamps uplifted to be banged down on passports were suspended in midair. Then the policeman began to laugh, gradually losing control of himself, wiping his eyes, laughing all the more. Waves of chuckles spread out from around the old lady until people at the edge of the crowd who knew nothing about the cause of the laughter joined in to be on the safe side. The old lady looked about, surprised, unable to understand it. The policeman waved her on and the tension crept back. The rest of us, half fearing the old lady's outburst meant a hostage would be taken from among us, edged our way past immigration, proffering visas, health cards, work permits, residence permits, travel permits, tourist permits. But nothing happened.

After half an hour it became apparent that there was something very unusual about Addis airport, something that made it seem not properly African. Nobody had asked for, or even hinted at, a bribe. We moved our twenty cases to the customs desk. The man behind it was hesitant, and very poor, with a down-at-heel, shuffling manner and a face pinched by years of aggravation. In England you might see him looking after a public lavatory, or sweeping the streets, every movement demanding to know how it was he had ended up at the bottom.

It took a long time, all the cases and boxes, even the ones clearly marked with large Red Crosses and the sign MEDICAL SUPPLIES, had to be opened and kneaded through like dough by this pursed, resentful face. Gradually, as he drew them out of the various bits of personal luggage, a pile of musical cassettes grew on his desk. *Rigoletto, The Bee Gees, Frankie Goes to Hollywood, Tristan and Isolde,* John Betjeman's innocent face stared benignly up at the flaking ceiling from the cover of a cassette reading of his poems.

"You got any more records, tapes?" the official asked.

He was going to blame me for the pile of cassettes, useless to explain that only half were mine. Perhaps this was the moment for what the Nigerians called special visa tax. Maybe if I gave him one of the cassettes . . . or two or three?

A voice behind me said suddenly, "They all have to be listened to for political messages."

I turned. A man of middle height in a pinstripe suit stood behind me offering his hand. "I am Ato Brihanu, Ethiopian Red Cross." Brihanu had small, regular features which made him look very young. These, with his perpetually serious face, gave one the impression of talking to a sixth-grader, rather than a man of forty with ten children.

He spoke rapidly in Amharic to the customs man, then turned to me and said, "I know this man, he is my wife's cousin, leave this with me."

The man gave a slight sniff of assent, tapped his right ear with a dirty fingernail, and said something in Amharic. Brihanu translated. "You will get all your records back this afternoon." I wondered what he would make of Domingo as Scarpia; it seemed appropriate.

I introduced Brihanu to the others. He seemed fascinated by Yushi, holding fast to her arm as he lifted one of her suitcases up onto the customs bench. The man in the cheap brown suit who had been on the plane edged past me and offered his tattered case to the mean-faced customs man. I craned over Brihanu's shoulder to look. The customs man snapped something at him in Amharic. The man nodded and very carefully opened the lid so as to prevent the hinges parting from fabric. Under a page of an old Italian newspaper were rows of toilet paper, cheap toilet paper, laid on top of some piles of gray-looking clothes. Nor was he

Eastern European, but Italian—his passport lay on the desk by the case.

As the dirty hands began to knead the underclothes, the European in the pinstripe suit from the first class walked casually up to the desk and held out a very small green book. The customs man started, took his hands from inside the cheap case, and picked it up with the tips of his fingers. It was a Russian diplomatic passport. Suddenly he was transformed from a down-at-heel hack to a master of diplomacy. Here he was an expert, a man of nuance, a subtle flatterer. This was a passport that had to be examined and yet not examined. Not to examine it would open him to an accusation of failing his socialist duty to defend the borders of the People's State, but to examine it too closely would be to imply that a representative of the country that had brought them the gift of socialism might be trying to conceal something, some irregularity. An unforgivable crime.

Carefully he laid the book on his desk, opened the first page, and gave a respectful glance at the photograph and Cyrillic preamble, closed it, paused for a fraction of a second, and then handed it back. There was the slightest of hesitations, as if the Russian was daring him to give permission to go, but the customs officer smiled at him and bent his head once more to the case of toilet rolls. The Russian holstered his passport and left, joining three similar-suited companions waiting for him on the other side of the barrier. The man with the cheap suitcase followed him out to where two priests waited for him. I had got things very wrong.

Slowly our group was passed through into the arrivals lounge, bits of luggage accumulating about our feet again. A Coptic priest in stained brown rags leaned on a T-shaped crucifix and watched us assemble. I was introduced to the medical director of the Ethiopian Red Cross Program. Brit Ulman was younger than me, about thirty-five, with a small face dominated by a 1950s hairstyle, a young woman disguised as an old one. We briefly swapped c.v.'s, probing each other's outer defenses. She had been four months in Ethiopia and before that a year with the boat people in Thailand. Much later she told me she worked for the Finnish State Opera Company as their doctor, touring with them all over eastern and western Europe. She was intensely reserved: when she was spoken to, her face would suddenly become totally impassive, so that words seemed to drop into it like stones into a still, silent pool. I wondered at first if she was deaf, but I found out later that it was the preoccupation of a personality that lived like a recluse behind several closed and shuttered mental doors. An outdoor Miss Haversham.

The man with her was dominated by an immaculate pair of tennis shoes. He was German, with immensely thick, straight black hair and plump features. Helmut Praetorius came from Munich. He had once been a burgomeister, had trained as an orchestral conductor and then as a reporter. Now he was in charge of the Red Cross finances. He caricatured German manners to a point where I later wondered if they were genuine or an elaborate piece of self-mockery. Bowing from the waist, shaking hands at each meeting, "Herr Doktor," "Gnadige Frau Doktor." But he was a cheerful man, efficient and kindly, who smoked too much and drove too fast.

Leaving the women with Brihanu I followed Helmut to the car park where he loaded me into his Volkswagen—it was inconceivable that he would have anything else—and began a breakneck run into the capital, Addis Ababa. The name means "New Flower" in Amharic. Its site has been changed often over the years. The old capital of Ethiopia moved as the available wood around it needed for building and fires was exhausted. Only the lands of the Coptic Church were immune to the royal axes, the forests surrounding their churches sacred. Even today there are few Ethiopians who will willingly touch them. Now new buildings rise among the blanket of slums that coat the hills surrounding the center. At first you are aware only of long walls of green-painted corrugated iron lining all the streets, but breaks in it reveal shanties sprawling along the rivers of mud and rubbish that pass for roads in most African cities. At intervals we passed huge billboards of Marx, Lenin, and Engels, bearded like Victorian gods, a white trinity made flesh to replace the pale-faced, sloe-eyed saints of the Coptic calendar. Underneath them the prayer: "Marxism-Leninism is our only guide."

Near the center we slowed in a wedge of wrecked taxis and trucks that somehow still managed to crawl along despite terrible injuries. Old Fiat trucks belched and staggered under enormous loads topped off with ten or eleven passengers clinging to their tarpaulins. One truck lay broken in two halves in the center of the road underneath a triumphal ply-wood arch that proclaimed "Forward with Marxism-Leninism!" It seemed so contrived that counterrevolutionary elements must have staged it.

A beggar, eyes totally whitened by blindness, thin and birdlike, an eyeless crane standing in the whirling traffic, felt his way to our car. He wore a single rag made of coarse sacking draped about him like a figure from a pious Victorian tract. Helmut handed a bit of cash into his thin fingers. He salaamed, turned, and tapped his way with his stick back to the shade of a withered tree. Helmut pursed his lips and ran a fat hand through his thick hair. Neither of us spoke.

Ahead of us six brand-new Mercedes limousines swung out of a side road like a shoal of expensive fish. They swam with our stream of traffic for a few minutes and then, with a flick of indicators, vanished down another side road.

"Cars for the Relief and Rehabilitation Commission," Helmut said jokingly. He pointed a stubby finger at a long new building to our left. It was vast. Expensive aluminum-framed windows looked in on empty offices. "The new Water Resources Offices."

"They look quite something," I said.

"They cost ten million dollars to build and so far not a penny to the villages for water-pumping equipment."

It was a United Nation's job. The same organization

planned a twenty-million-dollar international conference center in Addis and, once the expected protests by the international community had died down about the waste, they would go ahead and build it. We came down a short hill to a giant open space covered in asphalt. It was so large it gave the impression that the center of the city had been razed by bombs. Here and there on the edges were some offices, all in the leprous concrete of the airport.

"Revolution Square," Helmut announced, hauling on the handbrake.

The far end was dominated by a portrait of a young Negro, posed so that he appeared to be half looking over his shoulder. He wore an expression of faint surprise as if somebody had suddenly called his name from behind. Underneath the face the figure 10 was worked in elaborate decorations and wreaths.

"Mengistu," said Helmut.

I looked at the Emperor's face again. The impression of youth the billboard artist had worked for failed at a second glance.

I said, "He doesn't look Ethiopian. Is he African?"

Helmut waved a mocking finger in the driving mirror.

"Herr Doktor, if you want to stay with us more than a few days you must not say that. Here they take him very seriously. On the television they always read out his twenty state titles each time his name is mentioned, even if it is twice in the same sentence. The news is tedious enough, but that makes it worse. To call Mengistu an African or a Negro can earn you five years in jail for trying to undermine the head of state."

Two tanks in desert camouflage rumbled past below the portrait.

"You will be here for anniversary, Herr Doktor!" Helmut said with a laugh.

"What anniversary?"

"Next week, the tenth anniversary of the revolution."

I thought of the panic with which the Red Cross had summoned me from a country practice in Australia and said, "I hope we will leave tomorrow or the following day at the latest."

Helmut shook his head with a grin.

"Not possible, Herr Doktor. Nobody leaves the city till after the revolutionary celebrations. That would be disrespectful and, besides, all the permit offices are closed."

"You're not serious?"

"Oh yes, Médicins Sans Frontières have been waiting a month for their permits. Why should we be lucky?"

3

THE ETHIOPIAN RED CROSS

THE CHEERFUL GERMAN ACCOUNTANT was right. The Red Cross put us up in one of the most luxurious hotels in Addis, a late-fascist building of the 1930s built into the walls of the old Imperial Palace. We were to wait there for a week, which was not long in comparison with some of the rival aid teams. Young Frenchmen in stylish denims from Médecins Sans Frontières hung about the foyer arguing with gaunt-looking female doctors. One told me they had been there a month. Sister Prudence was not impressed. Over scrambled eggs in the slightly musty dining room she told me that the French team took three weeks off at the height of the 1976 famine to go scuba diving in the Seychelles. It was an absurd, almost apocryphal story, springing straight from the deeply felt fear the English have of the world's most successful civilization. I laughed at her, but she insisted on its truth.

At the bottom of the hotel gardens was a sewage-filled river spanned by a small bridge. Beyond it was the city. Always, night and day, the bridge was manned by guards armed with clipboards. Those who were neither rich nor white, which meant black men on foot, were stopped and questioned. If they insisted on entering, their names were

42

taken for investigation. The only peasants who came and went without fear were prostitutes.

Every morning ancient buses belching brown smoke from a morning ration of indigestible Soviet gas trundled into Revolution Square, which lay just beyond the bridge. Out of them spilled thousands of peasants, each one bearing a set of colored cardboard squares. After hours of marshaling and checking, they were led into a huge football stadium on the far side of the square to face three diminutive figures crouched, like soldiers around a mortar, on the roof of a building just below our hotel. These were Korean experts in *tableau vivant*. At intervals one of them would rise up from his crouch, wave a pair of semaphore flags at the stadium, and then sink back into a crouch again. Instantly a ripple would pass along the sea of heads leaving behind it the picture of a soldier, peasant, or worker, face suffused with the fever-bright cheeks of socialist realism. Sometimes it was the picture of a tank, a ship, or a fighter aircraft. Even the Emperor was portrayed, and in extraordinary detail. The cards his subjects held aloft kept the same half-innocent gaze directed over his shoulder that he had in more conventional portraits. Now and again a couple of jets would scream over the square curving in front of the only two skyscrapers in Addis. One day, late in the week, we were awakened to the grinding scream of tank tracks on cobblestones. Forty tanks in desert brown rumbled past followed by goosestepping soldiers.

To kill time we drifted about the shops, dusty places with heavy iron grilles on the windows that sold only tinned Bulgarian fruit or huge packets of salt. Security was tight in the biggest of them, everybody was body-searched on entering. One day a boy of about fifteen pushed some packets of yeast into Janet's hands and said, "Buy for me! Buy for me!" It seemed meaningless. Embarrassed, she tried to give them back, but people in the shop made gestures at us to help him. Hesitant and puzzled, she bought ten packets for him. Outside he gave her the correct money back. I asked him why he wanted the yeast.

"To make bread, then we sell. Government does not allow us to buy this stuff. Bread only made by government."

Three days passed. In the early hours of Sunday morning I woke to the sound of a strange nasal antiphony that filled the empty square, echoing against the metal barriers and sheet-iron roof of the huge stadium. It was inexpressibly sad, drifting and changing like wreaths of smoke. Dawn Mass had begun in the Coptic Cathedral.

I lay in bed and thought about the week. Where was the famine? It was as if, in speaking of it, people were describing events in another country, not here in Ethiopia. There were no signs of food shortages in the city. The shops, although threadbare, were no less poorly stocked than ones in Moscow or Leningrad, and there were no signs of famine in the streets. It was hinted, by those who had the courage, to be very bad in the country. But we were prisoners, forbidden to pass beyond the military barricades ringing the city. And where were the senior Ethiopian Red Cross officials? Each day we trudged over to headquarters to hang about the corridors waiting for news of our permits. Once, briefly, we were interviewed by a gnomelike little man pulling on a long brown cigarette holder. He was, it turned out, the secretary general of the Ethiopian Red Cross, but it was an interview designed to fulfill the needs of protocol, a way of placating Geneva, not one where valuable information would be carelessly given out to foreigners.

Then we heard a rumor that one of the most senior officials in the Red Cross wanted to meet us. And it was excitedly whispered to us that not only was he a senior official, but he had once been closely related to the old emperor, Haile Selassie. One morning we were summoned to headquarters with a promise of an interview with him, but it lingered through several cancellations and then expired.

Lesser officials gave us our mail, told us where the best places to eat were, arranged cars, but on the subject of the famine they were vague. Only two told us anything. One I was to meet again later when things got much worse, the other was Brihanu, the man in the neat suit who had met us at the airport. Brihanu was one of the most determined officials I was to meet in Ethiopia. It seemed there was no permit that he could not wrest from the Kafkaesque government bureaucracy.

Day after day he would visit different government offices on behalf of the Red Cross. He told us of officials never in their offices, one countermanding the signature of another. Often a permit needed three or four signatures at each step of the bureaucratic pyramid. Old scores between officials could be settled by blocking the paperwork. And it was not just one permit—we needed travel permits, tourist permits, extensions to our entry visas, petrol permits, residence permits. Each application had to be accompanied by identical photographs, as any with slight variations due to the use of a different camera or taken in a different place were not accepted.

One day, for a diversion, Brihanu suggested we go with him to get our driving permits; international driving licenses are not recognized in Ethiopia. We found the driving-license office housed in a sprawl of prefabs south of the city. Outside in the broken road were parked hundreds of ancient cars, most of them VWs. We assembled under a veranda outside an office packed to the windows with applicants. Peering in, I could see, between the bodies, about ten desks each manned by a harassed-looking clerk. We queued at the door while Brihanu went off to buy the now-familiar tiny revenue stamps with their inadequate cheap adhesive. They appeared on every permit we had and all over our passports. He came back with five application forms for each of us. As a supplicant left the packed office Brihanu inserted one of us in his place. I was second, but an angry-faced clerk shouted at me to go back outside. I was successful on the third attempt, easing my way between two truck drivers and a trembling peasant. Each clerk was engaged in filling in a huge ledger, then issuing a slip of paper which you carried to the next desk. Every half hour or so the chief clerk, the angry-faced man, would order the office to be completely cleared. But after a few minutes outside the applicants would begin to seep apologetically back into the room like water from a slowly leaking pipe. About two o'clock, as if at a secret signal, the clerks abruptly vanished. We waited. An hour later, as abruptly, they returned, just as bad tempered. The insane process resumed, the thump of canceling stamps, the shuffle of the queue, the outstretched snapping fingers of the clerks demanding the next set of papers.

Trouble came when we got to the next-to-last clerk, a young woman in black, indefinably better educated than the rest of the morose puddings who had dealt with us. Two of us had international driving licenses; these, she said, were not acceptable. To issue an Ethiopian driving license we had to surrender our national licenses. "No, copies will not do." Patiently we explained that you could not get an international driving license unless you had a national license. "No—these are the rules." Brihanu said not to worry, he gave his word we would get our own licenses back when we returned the Ethiopian ones. Janet hesitated. Driving licenses were virtual identity documents in Britain and Australia. What guarantee was there we would ever see them again? Brihanu got slightly irate. "Come on now, I tell you I give you my word." We argued hopelessly amongst ourselves for a minute, then gave in, as we had no choice. We stared gloomily at each other while she consulted a list, looking, it seemed, for as much trouble as she could for us. Licenses from Ireland were, she said, not recognized by the Provisional Military Government of Socialist Ethiopia. It meant that Prudence would not be able to drive. As if to emphasize our dependence, the clerk began to make trouble over the expiration date of my license, the year 2009. She took it away for consultation with somebody behind a sliding hardboard hatch. A senior official emerged and, coming over, asked me how were we allowed to drive in England for so long without being seen by an official. Everybody in Ethiopia had to come in person once a year to get a new license and be checked by the officials. Suppose you lost an arm or went blind? I shrugged and began to explain about private insurance, that if you had an accident and had concealed some new disability, the company would not pay. He looked at me, uncomprehending, so I let it pass, feeling a vague annoyance at not being able to confound the authoritarian logic of the left.

Even then it was not over. Brihanu and I joined a vast queue winding into the cash office where we had to buy a further stamp and have it canceled by separate clerks. After five hours I had in my hand a small red booklet. I also had a dreadful headache.

"You will not, even now, be able to drive the large cars," Brihanu said. "Look at the back of your license." Sure enough, there was a ludicrous weight restriction. "Nobody worries about that, it just means that the government insurance company does not have to pay if you have a crash."

Next day he was more optimistic about getting our travel permits, spending hours at the gray handset in his office. Late in the morning he took me aside and suggested that the next day I attend a meeting of all the nongovernmental aid organizations that was held monthly in the Red Cross headquarters. A government minister would be there.

The following morning a note was pushed under the door of our room. The hotel would be needed for important comrades and guests for the coming celebrations and we would have to leave. Our room in particular was earmarked for the Libyan delegation. In the hotel foyer groups of journalists, businessmen, and relief workers hung around waiting for cars to take them out on a search of the city for somewhere to stay until the end of the anniversary celebrations.

Brihanu had said the meeting of the nongovernmental aid organizations would begin at ten. At headquarters they were elusive, and a little resentful. Who had told me about the meeting? There was to be one, but they were not sure if it was to be today, this afternoon, or tomorrow. It depended on the RRC. The RRC was the sole governmental aid organization, the initials meaning Rehabilitation and Relief Committee. It had been set up in the last famine, but now, seven years on, its detractors accused it of being almost totally paralyzed by political meddling, sloth, and overmanagement. In Aidspeak a triad known as Evaluation, Planning, and Implementation. But a majority believed that it was the first genuinely efficient self-help organization in Africa and within the Aidgame a belief in it had become an article of faith. Whichever view was right, the RRC's job was to store and distribute food for the needy and to arrange the resettlement of people from drought-devastated areas. Accusations that it had been unable to do any of these things had led with each alleged failure to fresh organizations from the outside being brought in to do the work. Once established, such organizations tended to remain and there was, as a result, much bad blood between them and the RRC.

I was introduced to the planning coordinator of the RRC, a thin-faced, haggard-looking man. When I looked puzzled and asked him if he meant planning director, he began to make short thrusting gestures with his thin hands, like somebody searching through a cupboard of invisible clothes. Words like "director" (he paused to savor it for a second) were elitist. The new managerial skills indicated the need for a rethink of past attitudes. It was an old, very cracked record, playing on a windup gramophone. I stood uncomfortably in the hot, airless corridor, trying not to pay attention: Resource person, skills, needs. I thought about the power of words, words that themselves can intoxicate if taken with sufficient frequency, words without meaning that had become magical. Props that exist only in the believer's mind, shoring up whole tottering edifices of lost hopes and faded ideals.

We halted there, uneasy with each other, caught like two branches entangled in a stream until the drift of people toward the meeting unstuck us. I excused myself, hiding in a filthy, blocked lavatory for a good five minutes. When I came out he was gone and I walked down into the sunshine.

Outside, the courtyard was dominated by a huge limousine flying the Stars and Stripes. Next to it, somewhat diminished, was a Mercedes with the flag of the Provisional Socialist Military Government of Socialist Ethiopia. One of the Emperor's courtiers had arrived.

There were about a hundred people in the hall, a place vaguely reminiscent of the Boy Scout movement with wooden beams, dust, old flags in corners, and a coat of arms on the proscenium. A place for school plays and speech days. A man with a square, rugby player's face, a strong Irish accent, and a string vest under his shirt was speaking from a lectern. Two patches of sweat spread slowly from beneath his armpits. I glanced at the photocopied sheet on my desk. Brother Francis CB. I was brought up by the Christian Brothers, a distinction I share with many an African dictator. Replicas of Brother Francis used to lecture me on the evils of masturbation in halls identical to the one I now sat in. Next to him sat an Ethiopian in a very expensive three-piece suit. He had a childlike face with a rounded bald head upon which a few clumps of hair lingered like bits of tumbleweed.

I looked around. They were all here, every type and size of player in this game. Scandinavians with that tense, washed look leaning forward to patronize every word. Two men from the Foreign Office, both wonderfully chinless. American-Irish priests looking like white-haired prize-fighters. Fierce Irish nuns, slightly bearded, their glands shriveled by years of sun and prayer. Just in front of me sat the American embassy man, tall and thin with a donnish stoop and thick bifocals. He wore English clothes that were indefinably different. He had an aide with him, a beautiful, tense, driving American woman in an expensive tailored suit that spoke a salary of $70,000 a year and the same in expenses. Just in front of her sat a woman of about thirty, her pale Scandinavian skin faded and bleached by the sun. She wore her breasts naked under a semitransparent blouse. Next to her a Libyan struggled to keep his eyes to the front. The French, strung out in a corner, faces like thin horses, strained over the meeting's English. I heard an English upper-class chortle like water going down a blocked lavatory.

We all sat there waiting, turning round to adjust bags or

cases in order to get a better look at each other. I wondered
what *they* made of the balding, thin, and rather wild-eyed
Englishman sitting behind them.

An Ethiopian, the public relations expert from the Relief
Commission, rose from his seat and began to speak. It was
like listening to Moscow Radio, catalogues of production,
quintals of wheat moved, glorious workers slaving, thousands
of trucks moving. Feet began to shuffle in the audience,
chairs moved slightly, people coughed back and forth. This
was classic Aidgame play. As soon as he finished, Ernest
Hemingway's double, disguised as an American priest, got up
and asked why the Relief Commission would not send anybody to discuss the famine except their public relations man.
The bald-headed man on the platform leaned forward and in
faultless public-school English explained that it was a matter
of protocol. The Relief Commission was a government department and for it to come to a meeting of nongovernment
organizations would imply that it was not in charge of the
whole famine relief operation. It was clear that he was not
used to awkward questions. But he was in for more surprises.
The American priest then asked that being so, why is it
that the commission refused to call a meeting of the other
organizations? Because, said the Emperor's courtier, being a
government department it was not policy to allow other nongovernmental organizations to take part in their policy-
making. That would diminish national sovereignty. The last
two words he pushed at the meeting like huge denomination
chips at the poker game, so large the other players would
have to cast in their cards. I wondered about the priest's work
permit—if he was lucky the courtier would not have heard
his name.

The bifocaled American stood up, his thin frame leaning
like a tree into a strong wind. He wished to protest the fact
that gifts of grain, sent to Ethiopia from America, were being
held up for three to four weeks while the paperwork was
processed. Why did the government insist on the papers
being hand-carried the five hundred miles from the port of

Assab to Addis on the railway by an Ethiopian customs official? And why by rail, a journey that took two to three days each way, despite the American government's offer of an aircraft, car, or any other quicker form of transport? Worse, when the papers got to Addis it was often three weeks before they were cleared and each week that went past thousands of people died from famine. The courtier was plainly at a loss to answer this, and angry, not at the delays, but at the question. I could see his mind turning over this latest piece of insolence, storing it up for a later revenge. Other people in the audience shared the American's protest. I watched the British out of the corner of my eye for their predictable reaction. They would want so much to side with the courtier—he was after all the genuine article, a Third World bully—but something about the American anger made them silent. They neither protested nor agreed, avoiding the meeting with bowed mutterings to each other. The courtier announced he would look into it.

After that assurance the meeting sank like a piece of failed cooking. Words like "valuable" and "useful exchange" were pushed into it to try and make it rise again. The chief delegate to the Red Cross from Geneva, a thin retired colonel of the Swedish army, made a long speech about suffering. The public relations man from the Government Relief began another litany of statistics, but already people were leaving. There was a vote of thanks and then it was over. The cabinet minister's Mercedes, followed by the American limousine, swung out of the courtyard, leaving the nuns, priests, and relief workers gossiping uncertainly in the sun.

The thin Swedish colonel joined me. Christian Bjorn Svensen was sixty, a man of unexampled good manners and consideration. He was not to last long. In two months a palace revolution masterminded by Geneva would sweep him out of office. I was to meet him later, much happier, working on groundwater schemes in the north.

He was employed by the Red Cross headquarters in Geneva. His job was to act as a liaison between the Ethiopian Red

Cross and Geneva to see that the money donated by the West was actually spent on the starving. Because Ethiopia was a Marxist unitary state where the government had absolute powers of direction over everything including independent organizations, it was a job of appalling difficulty. The Revolutionary Government for all he knew, and we suspected, might have other plans for Geneva's aid. To oppose it would be treason.

Svensen had heard about our eviction from the hotel, and now he invited my wife and me to stay with him in his house in the center of Addis. It was a thoughtful gesture typical of him. Prudence and Yushi moved into a small agency flat in the center.

We moved there that afternoon. The house was a modern bungalow set in a large garden and hidden by high stone walls from the lanes surrounding it, lanes filled with beggars, excrement, heaps of rotting refuse, and one-room shanties made of cardboard and corrugated iron holding ten or fifteen people.

There was a wire bellpull on the wall outside. For some reason the beggars never pulled it, only crowded about the car, hands held out like somebody catching water from underneath a tap, thin faces like Modigliani paintings held to one side, lips muttering endless litanies of imminent starvation. I knew that none of these horrific figures must be allowed to become real. What if I began to speculate on what this old man at the gate had been like as a young man? He must have had a mother, father, brothers, sisters, a house, hopes. When he was young he must have dreamed of land, a woman, children. Now what was he? A shriveled wand of bones draped in a sack with a gray, pinched face dominated by two yellowed rotting fangs and a dead eye covered with flies. I looked down at his legs. Arthritic toes searched for a hold in the thick mud, an ulcer opened deep into muscle on one shin around the edge of which flies crowded like minuscule cattle at a water hole. His legs were so thin they appeared to have bowed even under his trivial weight. We had

had a meeting about him this morning—Mercedes cars had come for it—but I never heard anybody mention him, except perhaps the Swedish colonel.

The door opened on a huge baying dog held back by a gardener. We drove in and the gates closed on the nightmare. Once through its doors, Ethiopia with its slums, its poverty, its flea-ridden taxis and broken-down public transport system vanished. Before us was a lovely garden with marigolds planted in neat borders, a fan of red bougainvillea shading a veranda with a table laid for a midday meal. There were plates of Swedish fish, cold salads, meats, and cheese. Letters from home placed in a neat pile by each place, a bottle of wine. Somebody had just been playing badminton on the cropped lawn below a huge plane tree. Inside the house it was cool after the damp midday heat, with blue and white tiles and low Swedish furniture in polished pine. A spotless bathroom was laid out with thick expensive towels and fresh bars of soap. There was a flush lavatory that worked.

Helmut, the financial officer, arrived, bowing and shaking hands, thick, heavy hair flopping, complaining of the effects of a drinking session the night before with the outgoing German ambassador. Svensen was hopeful that sometime today we might have news of our permits, because although all the offices were closed for the celebrations, Brihanu had been optimistic of success when he had spoken to him that morning.

At lunch Svensen talked about where we were going. It was the first time that it had been more than hinted at. Three hundred miles south of Addis lay the district of Wollaita. It was a small administrative area by Ethiopian standards, about the size of greater London, supporting about one and a half million peasants. Lately things had been going very wrong. There had been no rain for six months and because of a policy of farm collectivization the government had forced on them, the disheartened peasants had no stocks of food set aside for such an eventuality. Relief organizations were not allowed to enter famine areas until a government team composed mainly of RRC officials had examined the area and certified the existence of a famine. Wollaita had been traditionally the bread-basket of Ethiopia. It had always been a vastly fertile region, self-sufficient even in the worst of the periodic droughts and in better times exporting food all over Ethiopia. Because of this the certification team had dragged its feet, fearing that reporting a famine might be interpreted as antistate sabotage. Finally, four months earlier, Wollaita was declared a famine area, and the Red Cross allowed in.

They found that for three months the peasants had had nothing to eat. The first to die were the babies, the ones just off the breast, displaced by newer children; then their older brothers and sisters followed them down under the red mounds grouped near each village. Then, as the weeks passed, lack of food began to rekindle the fires of tuberculosis in the adults. Soon they too were following their children. In all, it was thought that twenty thousand died.

The Red Cross had established an Ethiopian team in four camps, setting up feeding centers and organizing a mobile medical unit to visit them in turn. It had not been a success. There was trouble with the medical unit, and no proper control of who was getting the food. It explained the lack of cooperation at headquarters—our presence was a criticism of the local Red Cross. I watched Svensen's kindly earnest face, and wondered who had thrown someone as decent as he into this den of wolves.

He would now have to make the time-honored appeal to all of us to cooperate with the local government and its officials. Yet everybody around the table knew what to expect.

Svensen began to intone this prayer, and, over the half glasses of red wine, the scraps of uneaten food lying on the plates, we murmured the responses. But as I glanced up I could see his blue, watery eyes fixed on me. The believer always knows when a heretic is present.

Lunch took two hours. Afterwards Janet wandered around the garden with Svensen's Ethiopian housekeeper, exclaiming at the flowers while Prudence and Yushi tried a game of bad-minton, difficult at ten thousand feet. Svensen, Helmut, and

I drank coffee and exchanged pleasantries. Suddenly a pensive, rather staged look appeared on Svensen's thin face. He leaned forward and said in his singsong voice, "I have a difficult question to ask you. You will not mind, I hope?" For a moment I wondered if he was going to tell me that Janet and I would not be working in the same place; it could happen. But instead he said, "Brit Ulman is much younger than you, and we were worried that you might find it difficult to take orders from her."

Although relieved by its apparent triviality, I found it an odd, divisive remark. Brit and I had had no problems so far. I wondered if this was a layman's ploy to prevent the two team doctors from forming a combination. Brit would not, in any event, be very much in the field with me, as her duties as medical director kept her at headquarters or touring the country looking for pockets of famine—government officials permitting. But there was more—the remark about Brit only a softening up. The Ethiopian officials in the area we were going to, Svensen said, dropping his voice slightly, could be difficult. There had been problems. Helmut, picking at some cheese next to me, sniffed. If Svensen heard him he gave no sign, going on to say that although it was sometimes hard to understand what their priorities were it was possible to work with them. It just took time and patience. Experience told me that I was being offered a glimpse of a serious problem, but before I could find out anything further the gates opened to admit Brihanu's springless Peugeot.

Brit was with him. Because of the continuing shortages in the surrounding countryside, the war in the north, and the famine, the government was jumpy. Rumors that the city was about to be sealed off for the anniversary of the revolution continued to circulate. Somehow, despite all government offices being closed, Brihanu had managed to track down four officials in their homes and persuade them to issue permits for us to leave before the celebrations began.

Brit, fearing the permits might be canceled, wanted us to leave that afternoon. Not only did she want to see us safely installed in Sodo, where we would make our base, but she had to be back in Addis in two or three days to review the supplies coming from Europe. If we waited any longer we would all either be stuck in Addis, or she would be stuck in Sodo, 170 miles south, unable to return to the capital during the next two weeks until the revolutionary celebrations were over.

But before we left there was much to do. Extra supplies would have to be loaded from the Red Cross warehouse, and I would have to take delivery of a new diesel Landcruiser. Brit and I set off. She was tense, and when I asked her what the trouble was she told me of the resolute opposition there had been to bringing in a foreign team. In fact when she had first suggested it, the Ethiopian Red Cross had tried to have her sent back to Geneva as unsuitable, but as things got worse and worse in Wollaita, Geneva itself began to exert pressure on the Ethiopians to accept foreign help. It became in the end a question of no foreigners, no money. Brit did not think for a minute that the opposition had faded away—we could, she thought, expect difficulties. I wrote in my diary that night: "As soon as they have the money they will get rid of the foreign teams."

4

THE SOUTH

THE ETHIOPIAN RED CROSS had several large warehouses they shared with the International Red Cross, the Swiss-staffed branch that dealt in prisoner exchange, wars, and general violence. The arm to which we belonged, called the League, dealt only in the effects of natural disasters, such as famines, earthquakes, and epidemics. But the big difference was that the League delegates were expected to work under the umbrella of the local Red Cross Societies, staffed by Ethiopians, while the International Red Cross was completely independent. It made our job infinitely more difficult because we had to go along with the plans of officials whose real agendas appeared to lay deeply interred in a web of smiles, lies, quarter-truths, and evasions. For them the only safe assumption about us was that we were spies. I could imagine how insane it must have seemed to them for anybody to volunteer to come to Ethiopia. What good did we think we could do, people who could not speak the language, who came from a different climate, most of whom did not even believe in God, or Christ, let alone in the Coptic Church? And that was bad, because everybody in Ethiopia still believed in the Church, whatever the Party told them. I could see the question in all of their faces. It remained to be seen if we had an answer.

At the Red Cross warehouse we were met with the deepest suspicion, despite the fact they knew Brit well. Where, they asked, were our papers? We produced letters from the secretary General, requisitions from headquarters for camping equipment, drugs, and food supplies. The thin-faced warehouse supervisor laid them on his desk like a stamp collector looking for valuable flaws. After a good five minutes he gave a dissatisfied grunt and ordered his men to begin loading our vehicles.

Then he smiled and said, "We cannot give you any medicines, the pharmacist is sick."

"But he is always sick," Brit protested.

He ignored her and picked up the requisition for the Landcruiser. It obviously pained him to part with such an expensive item. I signed for it in three places and was given the keys. We followed him to the warehouse.

Grudgingly, our trucks were loaded with supplementary foods, blankets, cooking utensils, water carriers, ropes, and camping gear. In a corner cupboard were piles of boxes containing plastic bracelets used to identify children who needed special feeding. Somebody had forgotten to include them on the list. Brit asked the storekeeper if we could have some as well. He shrugged. If they were not on the invoices we could not have them. No, he would not telephone headquarters and get verbal permission. What, Brit asked, did he think we were going to do with them? Sell them? The storekeeper repeated that they were not on the list and he was not going to issue them. Yes, he knew who Brit was, a doctor in the relief, that made no difference—without the papers he was not going to give them to us. But he knew we could not possibly get back to headquarters in time to get the papers and then come back here, and we were leaving in the morning. The storekeeper turned to one of his staff—it seemed he was going to be helpful after all—and gave an order in Amharic. The clerk shuffled over and locked the cupboard con-

taining the bracelets, the storekeeper turned on his heel and
left us.

It was taking the car that had upset them. Most Red Cross
officials in Addis had a car, a commodity that was not so
much in short supply as subject to an ever-increasing demand. The one place where they were difficult to obtain was
in the field. Giving me one had probably dislocated a long
chain of borrowers. We could manage without the bracelets,
but it would have been better to have them. We were lucky to
have the Landcruiser. The effect of this loosened Brit's
tongue, and, as we drove back into the city, weaving among
flocks of goats, we talked of the indifference of the African
middle class to the plight of the peasants. They were like the
aristocracy in prerevolutionary Russia. They could walk down
a street crowded with beggars and see only people on it similar to themselves. The familiarity of the events at the warehouse depressed me. All it wanted now was a major apologist
for Mengistu's regime to step on to the stage for the picture to
be complete. That afternoon I knew that Ethiopia was not
serious about relieving its famine.

We passed a queue of angry-looking people standing in a
ditch that ran along the side of a ruined factory. The end of
the queue emerged from the ditch and vanished into a shop in
the side of the factory wall.

"Bread line," said Brit. There must have been nearly a
thousand people in it.

We stopped at some lights. One of the poles leaned across
the road as if it had been slapped about the ear. A cheerful
boy of nine approached the car. He was dressed in four or five
varieties of colored rag all held together with loops of furry
string. He gave us a radiant smile and announced through the
window, "Good morning, very happy Christmas, how are you
sir, money today?" It was afternoon and September.

Brit gave him some money and said to me, "The important
thing was sending a team from Europe, but now that we are
here they don't want us to do anything, in fact they dread it."

She then told me about the team that had been sent during

the famine in 1976. Like us, they were kept waiting, but for much longer, in Addis, something like a month and then, soon after they arrived at their camp, one of the delegates, a nurse, discovered that grain was being diverted to the port of Assab and exported to the Soviet Union to pay Mengistu's arms bill. She made representations to the Red Cross about it—it would be difficult to do anything else—and of course there was a fearful row.

Somebody, probably not the nurse, leaked the story to the press. The government wanted to deport the entire team, but they couldn't, realizing that it would have lent credence to the story. Instead they were allowed to stay on for six months working in another camp. But like Nebuchadnezzar's palace, the walls of buildings in Addis were filled with warning slogans. One of particular menace quoted the Gospodin Lenin. "Everything is remembered, nothing is forgotten." And sure enough, the Party did not forget.

Brit said, "Ask one of the others about that team." So I did later, I asked Prudence. She remembered them instantly. Her tone was forgiving. "They were," she said, "a very immature team, some of them fraternized with the soldiers in one of the camps, going to parties with them, that sort of thing, so of course they had to be sent home."

She added, "Of course they will never work for the Red Cross again." Association with the military is the cardinal sin in the Red Cross. The Party had not forgotten. Its punishment was always subtle and destructive.

She moved her head slightly so I could not see her eyes behind the cheap spectacles demanded by her vow of poverty. I asked her about the discovery by one of them that grain was being sold to Russia for guns. A strange look came into her face, as if she had bitten on an aloe. She mumbled something about having heard the rumor and changed the subject.

When we got back to the hotel, Helmut took me to the British embassy for some papers to be authenticated. Somehow the gate porter, an Ethiopian, had managed to acquire all the characteristics of a commissionaire outside a ministry building in England, a figure from Dad's Army; down at heel, gruff, with dusty, shifty eyes probing for the realities of social rank, betrayed perhaps by a worn heel, a pattern of shoe, a belt on a raincoat, an inflexion on a single syllable. Like a busy doctor in an outpatient ward, he ran his eyes over the major signs and served me with the exact portion of delay that I was due. No identity papers were needed or asked for. Did the British embassy run courses in social-class recognition like the Russians train their staff to recognize and report on all the military vehicles and aircraft they see when they are abroad?

Beyond the gate the embassy buildings lay concealed behind huge cedars in twenty acres of meadow, the only other legation having a similar spread belonging to the Russians next door. I joined a small crowd of Ethiopians in a brown waiting room. Pictures of cats and dogs with rabies snarled at us from warning notices on the walls. Piles of BBC brochures, some slightly yellowed editions of *Country Life*, and a few sprays of scarcely intelligible DHSS (Department of Health and Social Security) pamphlets gave the place the atmosphere of a down-at-heel dentist's waiting room. One almost expected grunts of pain from the visa office behind the counter. Next to me a well-dressed Ethiopian talked to a friend about the problems his daughter was having settling down at a private school in Gloucestershire. A half-caste woman of great beauty sat on the steps in the open door.

Everybody in the room was Ethiopian, including the visa clerks, but nothing jarred the intense Englishness of it. I sat and wondered how it was the English could be so naive as to allow Ethiopians to issue visas. No Ethiopian is allowed to work in a foreign embassy unless he is approved by the KGB. Perhaps the English were mocking the Russians. One of the clerks brought a cheerful young grammar-school man with the face of one of Trollope's curates to attend to me. He asked me as he stamped the papers if we would care to attend the weekly Ploughman's Lunch—there is an English film by that name which subtly mocks the rise of ruthless merit over idiot birth—at the embassy given for British residents. I explained, wondering to myself which chancellory aesthete had chosen the name, that we were leaving in the morning. We parted on terms of mutual regret.

I walked back down the hill where the Dad's Army doorman waited to open the gates on Ethiopia to me. Across the road a banner flapped the message: "Oppose capitalism with the broad might of the workers." Beggars crowded about the door of my car.

We got back to the hotel to find that the rumors Brit had heard about the road barriers closing were right. They were to be closed not tomorrow, but tonight, and would not be reopened for a week. By that time our permits would have expired and we would have to go through the whole tedious business of applying for fresh ones. Brit said we should leave directly. There were still four hours of daylight, and this was sufficient for us to reach a hotel at the halfway point to Sodo.

Two Ethiopians joined our party, a short man called "the Captain" with an immensely compact body that made him look like Sumo wrestler, and a tall man with a chubby babyish face named Amsalu. It was obvious why the Sumo wrestler was called Captain. He wore his clothes like a uniform and had a bluff, rather sinister, bonhomie that made me feel he would as easily shoot you as buy you a drink. Within in an hour of our meeting he told me that he had once been the captain of Ras Tafari's palace guard. It was an astonishing piece of information, so much a thing of the past did the old emperor seem. It was almost as if the smiling face in front of me had said he had once fought with Wellington at Waterloo. I asked him what the Negus was like. "Very tiny, so tiny that you could not see him when his bodyguard stood around him." He smiled at Yushi. "Once I went with him to Japan on a state visit." Ras Tafari's captain of guard laughed, "He liked Japan because the people were smaller even than he." He paused, frowned a little at the memory, and said to me, "All call me Captain."

The man with the chubby face was the chief field administrator for the Ethiopian Red Cross. He had an easy, smiling manner which, with his babyish face, the women found attractive. Amsalu of all the Red Cross officials, had the most confidence when it came to dealing with foreigners, something that none of them found at all easy. But while the West and its toys held a deep attraction for him, he found Western management methods with their open arguments and criticisms almost paralyzing, thrusting him into hours of brooding inertia. He was to be severely tested in the weeks to come.

We left Addis in a driving gray rain that seemed to wash away what little color there might have been in the acres of shacks and mud around the outskirts of the city. I drove the leading Landcruiser with Amsalu as my guide. Yushi came with us while Janet, Brit, and Prudence followed in the second car, driven by the Captain. I looked at the date on my watch. September the fifth. We had been in Ethiopia only a week. Just beyond the old Italian cemetery with its forest of black marble crosses we came to the police barriers. Long lines of overloaded trucks leaned half into a muddy ditch at the side of the road. Truck drivers hung hopelessly about in the rain, holding lists. Bus passengers stood among piles of soaking belongings while the police moved among them examining their permits. Nobody is allowed to travel in Ethiopia without a permit, but seeing either our white faces or the Red Crosses the police waved us through.

It was rumored that vegetables were in short supply in the country because the capital took nearly everything, so we stopped to buy some at a roadside store beyond the barrier. As Janet and Prudence slithered about in the mud and dung gripping plastic bags full of rotting carrots, Amsalu kept on urging us to be quick. There was, he said, very little time left before it got dark. I asked him if there was a danger of being attacked by terrorists, but he would only say that very few people traveled at night and we had to be in Shashemene by midnight when the curfew started. There has been a curfew in Ethiopia for ten years, from midnight to six in the morning, and in some areas in the north only sufficient to cover the hours of work, from eight in the morning to four in the afternoon.

The road out of Addis is a long curving descent from over ten thousand feet to the Kenyan desert five hundred miles away. For a while the narrow-gauge track of the Djibouti railway keeps the road company and then, as if bored, suddenly curves abruptly away to the east toward the Red Sea. We began to cross a huge and desolate alluvial plain. Almost at the horizon on either side stretched a mountain range. It marked the edge of a valley with a floor that must have been at least a hundred miles across. The absence of people, the scanty crops battered by wind and flattened by rain, the numerous wrecked trucks lying in the ditches, many of them with their cargoes still scattered nearby, made the place seem the home of giants, giants who smashed trucks like toys, trampled the crops, and needed such a huge valley just to stretch their legs.

We talked of trivialities. I tried to teach Yushi some English. She managed to explain to me that Brihanu had invited her for coffee that morning and asked her for something special. To my surprise, it was her solar-powered calculator. Her face wrinkled in puzzlement as she told me. Who, I wondered, taught the Japanese about the rest of the world? Did they learn about Africa from mad Victorian books written by half-crazy explorers from the last century, or from the even crazier texts of the last quarter century? I tried to find out, but her supply of English failed after a few minutes.

Slowly the countryside began to change. The open plains gave way to thorn trees crowding close to the edge of the road, the rain fell back behind us, huts and small plantations appeared. By evening we passed a huge lake about four miles to the east. The Captain driving behind me kept urging me to go faster by tailgating.

Yushi struggled with the name on her map.

"La . . . Klango."

Lake Langano was a weekend resort for the diplomatic

corps. It contained some hippos, a few alligators, and large numbers of fowl. To stay in one of the lodges for the night would cost a peasant his entire income for a year—sixty dollars. The engine started to miss and belch dense blue smoke. I stopped. Amsalu and the Captain became very nervous.

"We have to get on, Doctor," Amsalu said, looking up and down the road anxiously. I was unable ever to find out from him what it was that he feared. I never heard of terrorists operating in the south, or so close to the capital, as long as I was in the country. We opened the engine bonnet, but there was nothing obvious. The Captain thought it might be water in the fuel, and, as there was nothing we could do about it we got going again, but slowly. We reached Shashemene long after dark. Soldiers with Kalashnikovs and Uzis appeared briefly at the car windows as we stood waiting in front of the barrier. Nobody asked for our papers. After a few minutes, the boom was raised and we passed into the town.

5

THE SOUTH

SHASHEMENE LOOKED A WORSE MESS than Addis. It has one central feature that I was to get to know well, a long main street crossed halfway along by a river running at the bottom of a deep ravine. The road plunges abruptly down into the ravine, crosses a bridge, and leaps back up on the other side to continue as the main street. The bridge is narrow, and a temptation to the drivers of huge trucks who throw their vehicles down the steep gradient regardless of who is already crossing. It is seldom in doubt who the winner of such a mechanical joust will be, although in the valley below the occasional rusting truck bears witness to the victory of a David.

Shashemene was full of evil-looking hotels. Groups of low brown buildings huddled together like conspirators, their backyards open toilets. A large prison dominated the main road and nearby was a Soviet Army camp. Among the milling crowds of Ethiopians, the Soviet garrison troops stood out a mile away with their platinum-blond hair and pale skin, their wives dressed in cheap prints woven by old Lancashire cotton mills and exported to the Soviet Union in the late 1940s. At the other end of the town the concrete dishes of a new satellite receiving station for the international telephone system gazed hopefully at the sky. Among the crowds wove sagging *gharries*, horsedrawn, two-wheeled gigs made from old car wheels and seats. The seats were covered in old curtains, often with flowered patterns, so that from behind they looked like moving sofas. The horses were in tragic condition, thin, exhausted-looking beasts with pitiful, patient eyes and huge saddle sores rubbing underneath their harnesses. Sometimes the gharries would take on a Fiat truck, weaving and ducking in front of them as they tried to smash their way through the town, engines screaming at them to get out of the way. Sometimes they held them up for the length of the street, sometimes they lost. Fragments of crushed gharries lined the ditches on either side of the street.

We stayed that night outside of town in a new hotel with a large tree growing up through the floor of the bar. In its lower branches somebody had perched a TV set. It was, they said, the last TV before Nairobi. We sat drinking warm Coke and watching the news. The Ethiopians had obtained large quantities of footage about the British miners' strike, which they had dubbed rather crudely. Arthur Scargill, head of the miners' union, appealed his case for saving high-paid jobs to the hotel cleaners, poor men in frayed chammas—shroudlike cotton robes covering the head to just above the knees— standing in the shadows of the veranda.

We left late the next day, about nine, following the road out of Shashemene across a plain filled with round huts and camel herds driven by turbaned nomads, with mountains in the far distance. Herds of oxen crammed the road, guarded by tiny, serious-faced children with long sticks and swollen bellies.

Just before noon we came to a dried-out riverbed crossed by a stone bridge, each stone in it precisely cut and fitted.

"Italians," said Amsalu.

I had not realized that during the invasion of 1937 the Italians had come so far south. We stopped to eat, relieve ourselves, and stretch our legs. It was not a riverbed but a fissure caused by a violent earthquake. Here the thin crust of Africa had given way; trees, rocks, and soil had vanished into the depths of the earth. What was left hung expectantly in the hot silent sunshine waiting for the ground to heave open again and swallow it. Here and there towers of earth remained, a tuft of grass on each one like a bizarre crew cut. In time torrential rains would eat around their bases and they too would crumble into the riverbed. A peasant hut rotted in the shadow of the bridge overlooked by what once had been the farmer's sweet potato patch. Now the patch sagged over the edge of a fifty-foot precipice, barely a foot of earth coating a deep crust of granite. Above us a wind sang in the wires of two electricity pylons, standing like sinister metal spiders that had just emerged from the center of the earth.

We climbed to the farther side of the valley and saw that the wadi represented some horrible frontier. Beyond it was a rock-strewn plain with only the occasional thorn tree and some sad skeletons of donkeys and oxen, above which kites turned slowly in the midday heat. Columns of dust rose at intervals into the air like dervishes. In the far distance stood a group of dark blue hills, humped like whales.

"Sodo," said Captain.

"Is it like this all the way there?"

The old man showed his teeth, stared about the ravine for a moment, and then said, "Farmers not good in Ethiopia."

"This is due to farming?" I asked.

"They try to plant too many things too quickly, then the land dies, the wind comes, and poof!" Captain dusted his palms together in contempt adding, "No, Sodo is a very green place, very green, you will see." He walked away muttering, "Very green, very green!" to himself in little gasps.

We took another three hours to reach the base of the mountains. Closer, the central one looked like a huge tortoise. The road rose toward the side of its shell, skirted it to the south, and then began to climb into a long plume of cloud drifting from its summit. Torrential rain began as we rounded a bend. Ethiopian towns look as if they have been carelessly unloaded from a dump truck and then scattered by a bulldozer. Sodo was no different. It looked as if it had been dumped in a patch of jungle on the side of a mountain, bits of it subsequently rolling away from the pile and coming to rest underneath clumps of palm trees or among overgrown grass and bushes. The road, rapidly becoming a river, pointed down past crumbling ruins and thick vegetation to the police barrier. There was somebody in the police post, a pair of boots protruded slightly from the guard box. At the sound of our horn, one of the boots twitched slightly, a hand was waved dismissively at us from the side window, and the boots were withdrawn. Nothing happened. As we argued about which of us should get wet and take our papers over, the rain abruptly stopped, dripping slightly afterwards as it always does in the tropics like a slightly leaky tap after it has been turned off. The policeman emerged from his box, took one look at the convoy and opened the boom.

Ahead of us was the main street, a river of mud and potholes swilling with brown water. Shambling wooden houses lined each side behind deep drainage ditches filled with black filthy water. At the top of the hill, a few hundred yards from the barrier, was a gray breeze-block building set back in a crude forecourt. Somebody shouted, "The Dante!"

This was the hotel we planned to use as our base. It was reputed to be clean, the food tolerable if a little repetitive. It even had toilets in some of the rooms. The first owner had thought to make something of it in the way of tourism, Wollaita being on the edge of several game parks, but he was executed against its front wall during the Red Terror in 1977, the massacre that Mengistu visited on Ethiopia to consolidate his Soviet masters' absolute rule. Over ten thousand people were slaughtered.

I asked if it was haunted; I am half Irish and sensitive to ghosts. Amsalu laughed. "There are no ghosts in revolutionary Ethiopia."

6

THE HOTEL

THE DANTE MAY HAVE BEEN A GOOD HOTEL by Ethiopian
provincial standards, but only a week in the country and all of
that spent in a first-class hotel in the capital was no preparation for it. The restaurant, with its dirty white-tiled floor
smelling slightly of disinfectant, metal tables, bleak curtain-
less windows, and grimy concrete walls looked like an annex
to a jail. The length of our contract seemed absurd. How, I
thought, were we going to exist in a place like this? As I tried
to push away the panic that was nudging me, a young man
with a vacant friendly face shuffled up to us on worn black
shoes split along each upper. Everything about him was decrepit and dusty. He greeted us in Amharic. *"Tenastilin!"*

His name, he said, was Giorgis, and we were expected. He
took us to the back of the hotel. There was a small office with
two men sitting at a table. One was trying to put through a
call on an ancient windup telephone. The other, a younger
man, was filling in a ledger. The older man had a small
bad-tempered face cratered by smallpox. His companion
stared at us through a pair of red inflamed eyes that suggested
a bout of prodigious weeping. Ethiopia is full of such people,
their eyelids scarred and distorted by a flyborne infection

called trachoma. We explained who we were, and Red Eyes asked for our travel permits. As an additional check on free movement, nobody is allowed to stay in a hotel anywhere in the country without a permit signed by his local commissar. Red Eyes told us that the rooms were not ready yet, but there was some food if we wanted it. Giorgis would take our orders.

"Boiled meat with injera," Giorgis said behind us. Injera was a sort of fermented bread which most people had told me to avoid. We filed back into the dining room and took a seat at one of the metal tables. Giorgis covered it in a thick red cloth rather like the ones you see in Dutch cafés, but a recent washing had failed to remove stains in it so deep and solid it would take a knife to prize them loose. The whole hotel smelled like the tablecloth, a sweet smell of cheap disinfectant, strong curry, and raw undigested fat. "Injera wat," said Prudence, sniffing, explaining it was a type of curry powder used in a sauce of beans and lentils.

We sat down and stared out of the windows at the cold, damp rain. Something flicked at my ankles. I bent down to scratch and my eye came level with the cloth. Lice were moving slowly along one of its thick seams, like soldiers advancing along a redoubt. I looked at the small volcano on my shin. I had been bitten by a flea.

Giorgis flopped in with two unwashed gray soup bowls. They contained some gray lumps of meat swimming in a bright red sauce. It smelled like the hotel. I looked at it, my gorge rising, then at the rain and the gray prisonlike room, and forced myself to imagine I had just been arrested and imprisoned and this was the first meal of my sentence. What would I do then? I knew that whatever I was given, within reason, and possibly out of it, I would have to eat. My mind would have to be tricked into liking this offal by constant repetition of a lie: "This is really good." I began to chew the thick gristly lumps. It was ridiculous even thinking about the real reason for being in this awful restaurant, that we were here to combat a famine, because so far I had seen no evidence of one. For all we knew it was just a rumor, perhaps some piece of fathomless deception on the part of the Revolutionary Government. Across the table Janet, stonefaced, tore small pieces of injera from the gray pancake and slowly chewed, her mouth slack with distaste. Yushi stirred the red liquid list-lessly with an unwashed spoon. Prudence, head down, tucked in.

"Don't eat—don't live," I said to myself. I ate.

A small man in a neat two-piece suit came softly into the room. From then on, such men, the officials, would attend us constantly.

This one had a dome of a head ending in a pointed face which put me instantly in mind of Mr. Mole from Toad Hall, but this Mr. Mole not only lacked the whiskers, he had the rounded features and a neat mustache of a city Ethiopian. The official shook hands with each of us and sat down. He asked about our journey in a soothing conciliatory voice that filled me with alarm.

The cult of extreme manners in Ethiopia cripples reality. There, nothing is worse than to extend a conversation beyond that which flatters the hearer, praises his virtues, and makes light of his failings. To tread into the forbidden ground of argument and reality is considered to be not only unbeliev-ably coarse but incredibly foolish, for what does it achieve, except to reveal your own dissimulation? Ethiopians will weep if they are argued with, a dreadful sinister weeping which presages disaster. In the soil of such manners rumors flourish and malice puts down deep, ineradicable roots.

I listened to his anodyne inquiries about our journey and wondered how I was going to get on with somebody like this for the next six months. Everything he said made you feel like a patient with inoperable cancer. We obviously frightened him, but his fear had a bedrock of arrogance. It was as if he needed us, his persecutors, to repeat our wounding remarks so that he could savor the pain and better measure his revenge. We arranged a meeting for the next day—he and other offi-cials would brief us and take us around to the camps. I asked him about the camps: were they bad? Yes, but things were a lot better than two months ago; now they were feeding over three thousand people a day. The official seemed anxious to impress me with the intractable and chronic nature of the famine, implying that it would never end. The man with the red eyes, who turned out to be the assistant manager, came in to tell us our rooms were ready and that there was a telephone call for the official. The message seemed rehearsed.

The rooms occupied a single-story block that formed one side of a square. The block was made of cheap concrete, flat roofed, with a veranda looking out on a courtyard of over-grown grass and rocks. The rooms themselves were about ten by ten and almost filled by a cheap wooden double bed covered with a blanket and gray sheet. Between the bed and a filthy wall was wedged a wardrobe made of cheap splintered wood stained brown by means of boot polish. Each room led off to a lightless toilet from which emanated an overpowering smell. There was a handleless pail by each pan for flushing. Outside vultures gathered to watch from the top of a massively pruned tree in the center of the courtyard, the withered skin on their heads looking exactly like judges' wigs. Loud amplified music began to throb from across the street, the music of masenkos, the one-string viols of ancient Abyssinia playing the jumpy music of Wollaita.

Buying things assuages anxieties in the West, and there were shops in Sodo. I suggested that we try to find some disinfectant for the toilets. Outside the rain had stopped. Peasants resumed their pilgrimage to and from a huge market square on the side of the hill, beggars crawled out onto the red mud again, trucks started up in clouds of blue smoke, and herds of goats appeared, their stupid eyes wild with fear. Old men in chammas, the white cotton shroud of everyday wear in Ethiopia, drove stubborn donkeys down the street center loaded with shapeless sacks of charcoal or vegetables. Across the center of the street a plywood board had been tacked to the triumphal arch. A message marched across it in spidery Amharic with an English translation underneath:

"Marx, Engels, and Lenin, the only truth, the People's Party of Ethiopia. COPWE." On the school wall opposite, a bust of Lenin in careful colored chalks stared admiringly up at it.

The street looked like a badly executed cubist painting, irregular shapes of color piled haphazardly together and washed in a strange dusty light. It was lined by booths selling great piles of cheap shoes, pans, crates of dumped insecticide, witches' brooms, cheap flannel dresses, all unsalable anywhere else. At the hotel gate a beggar with a huge handsome head perched on a withered body folded in a a permanent crouch held out a thin tiny hand for alms. Yushi gave him some brass coins, and he smiled, a wonderful, entrancing smile, then swung away from us on two wooden blocks, one held in each hand, substitutes for feet. Small evil-looking children were pushed forward at us from out of the crowd by surly women beggars. A man on the other side of the street gave us a friendly wave of an arm disfigured by a huge open sore. He made no attempt to come over, but the gesture seemed a promise of his future attention.

The crowd of beggars followed us into a pharmacy, jostling, pushing, and fighting with one another. The owner of the shop seized a stick from behind his counter and rushed at them shouting, scattering them into the mud-filled ditch outside where they hung about ankle deep in filth, muttering and whining.

The owner returned breathless to ask me what I wanted. Somehow he mistook my English as a request for treatment, and I was led into a small cubicle at the end of the shop next to the inevitably smelly toilet. It took me some time to convince him that all I wanted was a bottle of Dettol and not some pills for myself. The Dettol was expensive; any kind of Western imported material fetched a high price by virtue of its reputation rather than any malign price-hiking by the manufacturers. As it turned out no disinfectant ever proved strong enough to combat the deeply laid smells of the Dante's toilets.

When we got back, the two nurses who had arrived two

weeks prior to us had returned from their day's work in the camps. One was from Denmark, the other from Finland. Scandinavia seems overrepresented in the Red Cross.

Inge Andersen, the Dane, was a tall, painfully thin blonde with a pale northern face. It was a face that gave no clue to her emotions, except perhaps one of deep self-punishing reserve. Instead, it was the way she held herself that told you her state of mind, a thin frame bent over an emotion. As we penetrated deeper into a nightmare she began to hunch herself more and more until it seemed that she was actually carrying something, some secret, unapproachable manifestation of anxiety, around with her. Her English was almost faultless.

On the step next to her sat a middle-aged woman with straggling hair. Where Inge was withdrawn, Tula Kianta was dominating and emotional. Although she had lived in London as a young woman and learned English, she had forgotten the difficult English sibilants, so that her voice rasped like a file over the vowels.

The curious forms and expressions that she used gave a hint of her ancestors, the Finns who migrated centuries ago from the depths of the Siberian steppe. She was highly imaginative and suffered for it. Occasionally and without warning the intensity of her feelings, a chance remark, or a misplaced joke would send her storming to her room.

Neither of them was new to Red Cross work. Inge had been with the organization in Thailand toward the end of the Pol Pot war; Tula had been with the Red Cross in Kenya on the Uganda border. Inge rarely, and then in colorless terms, described what it had been like. Tula, who had also lived for some years in Nepal and seen the thighbone flutes played in the high passes, often completely retreated into memories of past travels when times got bad. I was to find both of them incredibly hard workers.

The rain having finally decided to give up, Prudence suggested that we might take a look at the hospital. It lay outside the town on a hill, a rather crudely built brick building originally erected by American missionaries. I heard later that the government had ejected them two years earlier, making them pay heavy compensation to the local Party. It appeared that if you opened a mission, a hospital, or a school in Ethiopia you lay yourself open to being heavily fined by the government if the enterprise was a success. The Party would wait until the buildings were complete and a steady stream of customers established. Then officials would arrive and announce that the state was taking over in the interests of the people. Their first demand would be that a proper number of workers should be recruited for the job, about three times the existing number, and the unfortunate missionaries were obliged to finance their wages for the next three years or face even severer penalties. In a way it was a paradigm of every nonsensical leftist evil that you might hear about in the West, a sort of Marxist asset-stripping. Inevitably with three times the staff that it needed the hospital, school, or mission college declined rapidly under the weight of a tremendous bureaucracy and while ceasing to function remained just alive like a man on a respirator, a mockery of what it had been.

Sodo hospital was no exception. Outside, a few beggars threshed about in the sticky mud as we drove up to a square brick building erected around a courtyard. Inside was the same strong smell of disinfectant and curry that permeated the hotel. The casualty and outpatient wards lay deserted, so silent and empty it seemed that everybody had fled from some terrible disaster, except one old *sabanya*, a guard, asleep with his long biblical stick against a filthy brick wall. The courtyard had once boasted a well-kept garden and even now, two years later, some exotics still struggled to keep up appearances among the dense overgrowth of weeds, their branches festooned with dirty bandages and used dressings. Here and there bedpans lay half emptied in the bushes and by the door a decrepit trolley with two large wire wheels stood waiting, horribly stained. There were many flies.

Behind some swing doors we discovered a man in a white coat half asleep at a dusty table, by his elbow a chipped brown cup full of tea. It took us some time to explain to him who we were, but once he understood we were from the Red Cross his pudgy amiable face brightened and he offered to show us around. He was, he explained, the head nurse on duty that weekend.

We climbed a long dank concrete corridor used for bringing the stretchers up to the second floor. I tried to imagine the thoughts that would go through my mind if I found myself being wheeled up here. At the top, doors led off from a balcony. These, the nurse said, were the public wards. He opened the first door.

The sweet deathly smell of dressings that have been left unchanged for many days is unmistakable. It rolled at us as we stepped into a long tiled room containing about thirty wooden-framed beds. Only four of them had patients. There was another smell too, that of unwiped vomit, pools of it lay here and there on the floor, most of it dry. In one bed a young woman lay in the stillness of a deep coma. Next to her three visitors played cards with a male nurse. I looked more closely. She was about twenty with light features of considerable beauty. Her breath came in uneven, hesitating gasps, fluid gurgling and bubbling in the back of her throat. I imagined she was an inadequately treated pneumonia or TB who had reached the stage where little could be done. Opposite a child lay dying of starvation, a bowl of adult food standing mockingly near on his locker.

The door at the end of the ward opened and a fat pensive-looking man of about twenty-five wearing yellow leather shoes walked in. The sleepy nurse introduced him as the head doctor. Like many Ethiopians he was powerfully built, huge muscles like a stevedore filling his white coat. But it was his face that seized the attention, it was naggingly familiar, so much so that I could not take my eyes from it. Suddenly, looking away, I realized that he was the doctor on the poster that I had brought from Geneva, bending over a small child with a compassionate smile.

He introduced himself as Abraha. I had heard the name before in Addis. It was said that there had been trouble between him and the foreigners. He began almost at once a tirade about the famine camps which, he said, were full of people who should not be there. His anger was so infectious it blinded me to his case. Months later I was to realize that in that province at least, where the land lay begging to be farmed rather than collectivized, he was right.

Brit asked him about the mobile Red Cross team he had run. Was it any use? There was a moment's pause, then, almost imperceptibly, his whole body began to tremble like a bridge touched by some fatal harmonic and on the point of collapse. With an effort of his huge shoulders he controlled himself and instead of answering her question launched into an angry monologue on how many calories a starving child required. I looked round. Brit was smiling quietly to herself. The row must have gone very deep.

To avoid embarrassment, I suggested we would like to visit the private wing. Even in Socialist Ethiopia there is such a division. Abraha led us out of the ward and down another long corridor of brown doors. He opened one. "Private ward," he said contemptuously. Beyond the door was a small room, its walls almost black with filth, a gray torn mattress just discernible in one corner from the light of a single barred window. The stench was appalling. I tried to imagine who would want to pay for such a room. Even a healthy man would be sick after a few days in such a place.

I was to learn much later that while medical care in Ethiopia was in theory free, it was seldom accorded to the peasants, and especially not to those peasants who failed to please the local Party bosses. A week in the public ward of a hospital cost about eighty birr, equivalent to a year's wages. If you wanted free treatment you could apply for a certificate from the local collective farmers' association—that could take time, and did. In my experience, even in the most extreme emergency, it could take more than a day, by which time the patient was often dead. So with the cost of even basic care so high, the private wing was seldom used. The rich, and there are rich people in Ethiopia, go either to Addis or one of the still surviving mission hospitals. The fact of the matter was that Ethiopia could not afford medical care for her peasants, so it was rationed to Party officials and Party toadies. It was this system that we were to come up against at every turn.

The doctor showed us around the labs, and with some pride pointed out two surgical cases of his. Later I was to hear that things in the hospital had improved over the past year since he had arrived. Some surgery was now being undertaken, patients no longer had to be shipped in obstructed labor sixty miles to the last surviving mission hospital at Arba Minch. I noticed too that he was the first educated Ethiopian that I had met who was not obviously either in the secret police or a Party cadre. His clothes were different, and there was something about his independent fighting manner that set him apart from the security men. His was a tragic fate, forced to work in a filthy town with nothing to commend it, the hospital constantly running out of the most basic equipment as a result of socialist planning. Even more galling must have been the knowledge that Party aparatchiks frequently drove past his hospital on their way for treatment at Arba Minch, returning later to Addis to issue more statements about Ethiopia's self-sufficiency in medical care. We parted on terms of uneasy good will, making vague promises to meet again soon, something we knew both sides would work hard to avoid.

At the hotel we unloaded the vans, helped by a dwarf who rose from the long grass in the center of the courtyard. Each time we passed him he would effect a medieval bow, forehead almost touching the ground. Yushi hung some fresh orange peelings in her room as an antidote to the terrific stench from the toilets. By nine that evening depression and tiredness drove us to our rooms. For both Janet and me it was an uneasy night, willing our bodies onto the gray damp sheets and flea-infested blankets. About one in the morning I drifted into a doze.

At about two a.m. we were awoken by the metal door being hammered. An authoritative bullying voice shouted,

"Security Police!" I lay, instantly awake, in the darkness. Had they discovered we had once worked in South Africa? There was a pause and then the same voice, as if it had frightened itself, spoke in a tone of simpering false concern, like that of a persuasive rapist: "We have come to count the people in your room and check your papers."

Slowly I fumbled around the room—Janet now awake and sitting up in bed—and wrenched open the boxwood door. In the half light stood an officer and two peasant soldiers with machine pistols. The officer was nervous, unwilling to come into the light of my torch. He fumbled at my card, saluted, and backed into the darkness beckoning his men to follow. For a few minutes they banged unconvincingly on other doors and then mumbled away into the darkness. Ten minutes later two rifle shots somewhere in the street outside flattened themselves on my eardrums, then silence. We lay awake talking. Janet said, "It's like BOSS. Remember when they came to St. Michael's looking for the nurse with a copy of *Das Kapital?*" I did. They had turned the hospital upside down. We talked about home, what we would do when we got back. Janet would extend her garden. I dreamed of buying a word processor. We talked till three then slowly drifted into sleep. At six the siren ending the curfew awoke us.

An official, taller and slimmer than Mr. Mole, was slinking about the new Toyota diesel when I got up. He began a long involved explanation about the police raid which made me feel he was somehow in on it. Asked about the gunshots, his small eyes flickered away from mine. People, he said, frequently fired at marauders at night, it was normal. But I was never to hear it again in Sodo. He seemed to think that after our long journey from Addis we might be in need of a few days off and suggested a trip to the nearby lake for a picnic. There was, he said, a minor problem with the warehouse keys and it could be a few days before it was solved. Minor problems are almost never that in the Third World— they are the tips of huge mountains protruding from the sand. When I asked him to tell me more he countered by suggesting I should hand over the diesel to one of the drivers. It was, he said, unsafe for foreigners to drive their own cars in Ethiopia. He put a proprietary hand on the steering wheel. Remarking that the warehouse keys would have to be found, I joined the others for breakfast. Somehow I did not want to hear the details of where they were or who had them — none of it would be true.

Inge and Tula became voluble over their eggs about the officials. Most of their time had been spent waiting for one or other of them to turn up in the morning with the truck. The men in suits, they had discovered, loved riding in cars to meetings with higher officials and would keep the only ambulance for that purpose. So far neither of the nurses had been able to get much food released from the warehouse nor find out from the suited men why they wanted to keep it there. The camps, they said, were in chaos. None of the children had been measured to see if they needed feeding and the feeding tents were packed with healthy adults. There were some very sick starving children and adults, but they were getting nowhere near the food. The officials' plan seemed to be to keep both the warehouse and the food store filled up, one with food and one with people. Perhaps, I thought, like the components of an atomic bomb, they wanted to keep them apart, and the tension of that apartness would generate power for them in this famished land of the powerless. It was inevitable that they would wish the contents of either to dwindle or their power would dwindle too. The suited men planned, we learned later, to increase the clerical staff at their local office, and most importantly the number of vehicles under their control. Then they could extend their administration upwards instead of downwards toward the RRC office in Langano. Officials did not like visiting the camps. They were filled with people who had no power at all. It was a depressingly familiar litany that could be repeated in every small town in Africa. We would have to get control of the keys to the warehouse.

The disturbance during the night was only half alluded to

at breakfast; most of us had experienced this sort of thing before in other countries. There was little value in going over it unless we wanted to fuel the suspicions of whoever it was in the room that had been paid to listen to our conversation.

Mr. Mole arrived at nine, smiling, shaking hands, and bowing. He took a seat next to Inge and sat there sipping coffee, waiting for Amsalu. He arrived minutes later, ordered a plate of 'tibbs, fatty beef in curry, and sat down.

Prudence asked Amsalu about the warehouse. The chubby-faced administrator, his mouth full of fatty meat, nodded the question over to the little man.

But the latter was master of the two-rook, one-pawn defense. As quickly as we pinned him in one corner he would threaten one of our major pieces with an oblique move at the rear. He explained with a quiet smile that the warehouseman was also employed by the government relief organization. Should we insist on him being there each morning, it would interfere with the RRC work and that could cause problems with the local commissar and our permits. But, he said with a sigh, he could be only too glad to come with us. After all, it was his job to help us in every way he could.

Amsalu announced he had a meeting at the local government offices in half an hour so it might be a good idea if we spent the day looking at the stores. We could meet up later.

There was no difficulty in finding the warehouseman. Called Ato Salomon—*Ato* means "Mr." in Amharic—he was sitting on the veranda of a house half a block from the Dante, nursing a small cut in his left leg. He had a toothless face from fighting over women, or so he said. Mole got down to speak to him. After a few moments of hurried conversation they both climbed into the back of the truck. We set off for the warehouse.

The Red Cross housed their stores in two disused hangars on the outskirts of town near a scruffy, half-derelict airstrip. While we stood around waiting for Salomon to open the huge sliding doors, an aircraft flew over, its polished aluminum body winking in the sun. Tula said it was Russian, muttering something about seeing plenty of them in Finland. We waited for it to land, but the droning grew less and less. It abruptly ceased in clouds far to the south, somewhere over the Kenyan frontier. Salomon slid back the hangar door. In the cool dusty darkness smelling slightly of rat droppings and cockroaches stood four giant stacks: the nearest, of flour sacks; behind it, cartons of dried milk; the third, drums of cooking oil; the fourth, a pyramid of boxes on each of which a fat baby waved a cheerful spoon shouting something in German from a bubble coming out of its mouth.

Each sack was marked with a Red Cross and the words GIFT OF THE FEDERAL REPUBLIC OF GERMANY. NOT FOR COMMERCIAL SALE. There were four huge wooden boxes containing feeding kits from Oxfam, tents, water carriers, stoves, cutlery, even a bullhorn for controlling the crowds. Here and there, gathering a film of brown dust, lay tires, pressure lamps, and digging tools.

One box, solitary in a corner behind fifty boxes of soya oil, was labeled in Russian. Brit pulled off a loose plank. It was filled with slighty rusty tins. On each was a picture of an apple-cheeked girl wearing a kerchief. Brit translated "Tuna," and laughed.

Inge wanted to take some of the dried-milk powder with us. I went to ask. Mole peered in a parody of cooperation at some papers on a trestle table in the center of the hall and then, looking up, shook his head sadly, his soft eyes nervously probing the dark corners of the warehouse. It required the signatures of three of his kind to release the food: his own, an invoice clerk, and one other, a tallyman who had not reported for work this morning.

Instead he produced a form and began to fill in some preliminary details—my name, the date—this was, he explained, a request form which I would have to sign, and then from that an order form could be filled in. The request form was in quadruplicate. Who, I asked, was going to examine these forms, since all the stuff in the warehouse was to be given away? He looked at me in astonishment. Inventories had to be prepared, proper requests presented. In the clinics stock inventories were prepared each week for him to examine. When would the other man whose signature was needed be available? The official took me into his confidence. The man was unreliable and had been twice demoted for poor work. He hoped that he would be fired at the end of three months; in the meantime we would have to do the best we could. Gently he mentioned the lake and a picnic again, as he did so the warehouseman began to slide one of the doors across preparatory to closing up.

We were helpless. The contents of the warehouse had been given to the Ethiopian Red Cross by the League and we, its representatives, were now powerless to do anything about its disposal. The official was beyond our jurisdiction. We could only offer advice that nobody wanted to hear, much less follow. What we had to discover was what it was they wanted from us, and what it was we could find out about them to give us some power. According to Inge the camps were in desperate need of flour.

Amsalu arrived, smiling and joking, raising hopes that the matter could be swiftly solved with a couple of orders from him. But the fantastic and deluded paperwork of the Third World was not to be put aside with just a few words. Instead he suggested a meeting sometime later in the day. Inge produced a Michelin map of southern Ethiopia to show us where the camps were.

There were four, lying in a rough crescent about twenty miles long. While heavy rains would make the roads slow going it should be possible to get the two trucks out of them. Mole-face sucked at his teeth and shook his head. We would need fuel permits. He looked at his watch. It was doubtful if the permit clerk would be in his office now, it was already ten and he often went out. He would take the truck into town and see what he could do. Tula wandered slightly away pulling at my sleeves to follow her. If we did that, she said, we would see neither him nor our transport again for the whole day. We all went.

In town we were directed to a series of rusting, corrugated-iron shacks, some of them offices, some of them cafés, one of them a private house. A woman in the house shook her head: the permit clerk had gone to Shashemene for the day. The palms of her hands were deep brown from henna. She said "wait" in English and disappeared into her house to reemerge with a thumbed piece of a school exercise book. On it in Amharic, Arabic, English, and French was printed "Permits not required for diesel fuel."

We split up at the entrance to the town where incoming country buses were being searched for permitless passengers and smuggled coffee. Only the government was allowed to have coffee, most of which went to pay Ethiopia's arms bill with the Soviet Union. Prudence, Yushi, and Janet went with Captain. He would drop Janet at the nearest camp, Prudence and Yushi at the farthest. Brit, Inge, Tula, and I would go to Aro Giorgis five miles from Sodo. Later we would drop Tula at Bugu, four miles from there.

The road, built by the Americans in 1950, had not been repaired since. Now, after the rains, it looked like a vast smear of red porridge poured from a giant's bowl across the countryside.

The desert we had passed through the day before had vanished. We were now in a green valley bordered by blue-green mountains. There were numerous streams and, on the floor of the valley, a marsh. Round grass huts stood among gardens, children played near low smoke-blackened entrances. Some of the huts appeared to be on fire, smoke pouring through the thick walls, but Mr. Mole explained that this was the injera being cooked inside it, the smoke permeating the roof. Huge pine-clad mountains stood all around the valley, and in the distance a blue lake winked in the morning sunlight.

Morning in Africa has an exhilaration born of the clarity of light, a light that magnifies each color and edges every line with crystal sharpness. The road was alive with people and animals of every variety moving in long streams toward various markets. Mules dug their heels in as we passed, huge spans of oxen, heads lowered, lumbered over the stones. Here and there an anxious, hurrying donkey, its owner perched on top holding a small whip, trotted past, deeply preoccupied. Horsemen whirled and stamped in our dust on elaborately harnessed mounts, clinging to ornate saddles with gilded pommels, brass and silver facings, and bright blankets. The riders were always men, dressed in white cotton togas sometimes lined with blue so they looked like Roman senators. Then in the far distance a bus would appear, faintly honking; approaching, it would begin to weave from one side of the road to the other, like an animal searching for an advantage in the charge. Then, windows black with people, animals jumping and shrieking on its roof, it would roar past, music blasting from roof-mounted speakers.

The camp at Aro Giorgis lay back from the road down a narrow grass and mud track. The track passed an empty sweet potato garden, crossed an open meadow in the center of which stood a magnificent plane tree, and ended up in front of a stockade of sharpened stakes. Inside a Red Cross flag flew from a tall pole. A small crowd of women and children clustered around the entrance, arguing and shouting with an old man in a shapeless blue uniform with a battered army cap on his head and a long bamboo wand in his right hand. Captain blew the horn. The guard looked up, saw the car, and began to lay into the crowd, scattering them from the gate like fragments from an explosion. As he opened the crude gate each fragment, like a comic film in fast reverse, made a rush for the entrance, but the old man was too fast for them and only we got through.

We had stopped in a compound about half the size of a football field. Along one fence four large tents had been erected, each crammed with people sitting in lines. By the entrance was a large tucul surrounded by a crowd of about sixty people, most of them sitting quietly in the sun, while at the top of the yard was a collection of more permanent wattle and mud buildings, in one of which the flames and smoke of a huge kitchen fire could be seen.

In the center of the yard ten young Africans in white coats and sheepish schoolboy faces stood waiting to greet us.

There are two Africas—medieval-village Africa and twentieth-century-city Africa. Medieval Africa is small and complete, a village life balanced by the strict accounting of birth and death, season and the rain, a place of deeply felt but quickly forgotten joys and sorrows. City Africa is a place of fear, where men chase ghosts and trade in counterfeit notions imported from the West like beads brought by the slavers of the last century. Officials were city Africans, these men were not. They had faces untainted by the vast corruptions of the capital, faces to be betrayed or traded by anybody with a mind to do it. These men were going to lose.

We shook hands. One of them, who at first stood slightly apart, was the camp health assistant. Somebody with two or three years' medical training, a rank in the Ethiopian health service that did most of doctoring in the villages—half nurse, half barefoot doctor. He was very quiet-spoken, slightly built, with a sloping face. His name was Assefa. He led me toward a tucul near the entrance.

Stepping between the waiting people he unlocked the door and motioned me in. It was cool and dark inside with a large cupboard standing near a boxwood table. On it were tins of antimalarials, aspirins, some antibiotics, eye creams, and a few syringes. Assefa gestured like an Italian, with both hands palms upwards. It was not much, but he had the best house in the compound. We talked about his training. He had spent three years with French missionaries in the north and taken his exams in Addis. He would often come back to the subject of the French over the weeks, how good the surgeon was, how long the hours. He was a dreamer, his mind constantly on a self-edited past, or dreaming of a future in the capital.

In poor countries devoid of the capital for modern drugs, hospitals, and their expensive equipment, the medical clinic becomes not a place of healing but a court of appeal. The hopeless cases, already sentenced, wait quietly on their stretchers, hoping to hear the date and time of their death, while around the doors press the as yet unsentenced, murmuring and fearful, holding up strangely marked pieces of paper like scapulas. At intervals the crowd parts to let relatives carry out a spectral figure, wasted by a disease. They will take her home to a dark hut in a small village, and sometime in the early hours she will die, surrounded by weeping anxious faces. While death comes too soon for most it is rarely the lonely horror that we know in industrial societies, a death cut off from love by gadgets and strangers. In Africa, each death is a play, a remembered performance, the funeral a rite, not an embarrassed shuffling of feet at what amounts to a ceremonial refuse disposal.

Assefa stepped back outside to inspect the mortally ill laid under the eaves of the clinic. He began to walk down the line, looking for the worst case. A small round boy of about two in a bright red shirt lay quietly in the sun, flies gathering about his eyes, dreadfully pale, his breath coming in rapid gasps. At the angle of his jaw a pulse was visible, flailing wildly under the pale grayish-tinged skin. He bent down and gently pressed a thin finger into a fat leg, when he took it away the indentation remained. The child was in the last stage of heart failure. He motioned for him to be taken inside.

On a crude stretcher lined with dry straw lay a dreadfully wasted girl of about fourteen, the slight haze of moisture of her upper lip betraying a raging fever. I bent to listen to her lungs, but it was hopeless, both of them were full of fluid and pus. Her father, an old man in a tattered white chamma, leaned on his staff and watched our faces for a sign, despair pulling at the corners of his mouth.

Next to her a young woman with a vacant face wept over a wasted wrinkled infant of about four months, its eyes rolled up in its head, its body cold from a night without blankets.

As I bent down to look, an old man thrust his head between me and it, pointing with a filthy, crooked finger at a single yellow tooth in his cretinous jaw. Assefa said, "He wants you to pull it out."

The three patients were moved inside the clinic, and the door locked. The rest could take their chances. Assefa began easing the red shirt off the little swollen boy. The child began to whimper, then said something in a series of slow breathless gasps. Assefa translated, smiling. "He says, mind my shirt." Next to him stood his ten-year-old brother who for the past week had been carrying him to the clinic in the hope that something could be done, but up to now had failed to fight his way through the mob. It was a walk of about five miles in either direction.

The treatment was not difficult, it was whether we would be in time. He was dying of a secret silent hemorrhage, an African vampirism—worms. These, nesting in his gut, had drained him of his blood. In normal circumstances the child would be given a blood transfusion that in a matter of hours would transform him, but here there was no such possibility. We would have to rely on iron pills, treatment to kill the worms and, if we were lucky, some iron injections from the medical stores. Assefa helped his brother dress him. When they had finished the small figure offered a tiny hand for the three of us to shake.

The relatives of the girl said that three others in the family had died of the same thing in the past eight months. Coughing, blood, fever, death in the small hours. It was a history that made the diagnosis of TB almost a certainty. Assefa gave her an injection of penicillin. Hospital was suggested to the father, but the old face clouded at the word. Why should she have to die among strangers?

Assefa said softly, nodding toward the relatives, "They will not bring her again. They only want to know how long."

He bent to explain the situation to the old peasant face. The old man rose, thanked him, and gave orders to four villagers to load her back onto the oxhide litter. Then the four of them carried her out across the compound to the gates and vanished in the crowd.

The young mother with the vacant face was not much more than fifteen. She sat weeping sporadically on the wooden bench in front of us, her extreme youth and the mental subnormality that was now evident in her face making her hold her child more like a doll than a live baby. It had pneumonia and gastroenteritis. Between sobs she looked up, her childish face filled with fear, bewilderment, and unhappiness. Probably she had little idea of where the child had come from in the first place. We were treating two children, her and the limp, semiconscious bundle in her arms.

I left him with her and walked over to the kitchen. Cooks were ladling the bright yellow faffa porridge into red plastic bowls which were then laid, twenty at a time, on a long plank and carried into the feeding hut. Inside about three hundred mothers and their children sat in long rows under smoke-blackened rafters in front of small piles of eucalyptus branches to ward off the smells and flies. Health assistants and nurses moved among them checking that the sick children, not their healthy brothers and sisters, got the food. The noise was indescribable.

And there were more sick here, those who overnight had deteriorated from being just thin to being on the brink of death, and more admissions who had bypassed the medical hut. Babies lay in pools of diarrhea, some vomiting, some just silent. Propped against a pillar in one corner was a girl of about seven. She had that careful economy of movement that characterizes the seriously ill or starved, her face a living skull, the skin drawn drum tight across its bones. She weighed about fourteen pounds.

In one corner a four-year-old child lay dying, around its neck a collar of swollen glands so large they formed an obscene ruff parodying the ones you see on the statues of children on Elizabethan tombs in English churches. The mother, lined and raddled by thirty years of pregnancy, cradled its head on a pile of lice-ridden rags while her three other children spooned desultorily at the dying child's bowl of faffa. Around them, Macbeth-like, crouched a circle of old crones waiting for an end that could only be minutes away. One, older and even more withered than the others, suddenly leaned forward and with practiced gestures of her long arthritic fingers began to smooth its eyes and mouth shut. The other women began chanting, swaying slightly, each chant ending on a sharp upward note. A man walked across the room and snatched the bowl of faffa from the side of the dying child, took it to the center of the room, and standing, began to eat the contents. People shouted at him, one of the sabanyas, a guard, rushed at him with a wand. The man stuffed a final handful into his mouth, shook his fist at the women, and stamped out. When I turned to look again the child was dead.

Outside an official stood with a list, checking empty biscuit tins into the back of our truck. I mentioned the man with the child's food. The man stopped, sighed, and said, "These people, Doctor, they are only animals, only animals!"

I walked across to the supplementary feeding tents. They were still packed with people; Inge and Brit were trying to organize them into rows. Brit smiled over the noise and as I leaned forward to speak I felt something at my ankles. I looked down—an old man and an old woman were both in the act of kissing my boots. "Now that I hate!" Brit said, her Scandinavian accent intensified by anger.

Tula and Brit were trying to separate those children who were just hungry from those who were starving, those to whom food given now would mean the difference between life and death. Food was also given to the elderly, the pregnant, and the sick. It was easy to decide who among the adults needed food, with the children more difficult. The latter were weighed and measured and the findings checked against special charts. It provided some sort of comparison, a yardstick against which to make a decision. The very malnourished or ill were admitted to a special feeding regimen where they

were fed under supervision at least four times a day. The less
starved were fed three times a day or, if we had enough, sent
home on a ration. Many were turned away altogether. The
yardstick was a cruel one, and, because we had been denied
the special irremovable bracelets in Addis, the children needing food had to be issued ration cards, easily forged, time-
consuming, and clumsy to administer. In the villages, the
very weak, the very sick, and the very ill would almost certainly surrender their cards to those their families felt had a
better chance of survival. Peasant life is unsentimental. It is
far better to put food into the mouth of the strong than risk
throwing everything away on the weak.

After the weighing and the measuring the chosen lined up
in front of three Red Cross boys crouched by a golden pyramid of faffa flour. One had a scoop, one a scale, one a register.
One by one the people shuffled forward: young tearful
mothers, old gray men, crones with faces like dried figs,
small children abandoned or orphaned. Each handed his card
to the watching nurse, his eyes fastened on the faffa.

Through the open tent flap at the far end green untended
fields could be seen, some of them half ploughed, some given
over to groves of false banana trees growing wild and uncut.

At intervals a crone would rise over the sea of heads on
matchstick limbs and begin a long harangue through the flies
and smells. What was each one saying? Were they accusations, rumbles of revolution, or just the perpetual formless
discontent of the peasant? What was it like to be hungry,
really hungry, not just for hours, but for days, weeks, even
months? These people had seen hunger become almost a living thing, an embodiment—breathing, waiting, consuming.
Some said that in the end you no longer cared even for your
thin silent children, all you could think about was food, until
like a drug addict for his drug you would do anything, betray
even them for the smallest mouthful.

As the morning progressed to the howling of babies being
weighed in a sling, a strange facet of the officials' policy
began to appear. It was clear from the records that while quite

large quantities of food had arrived in the warehouse, very little had been distributed. What little distribution had been done had been done badly. Many of the poorer families had, judging by the desperate state of their children, received nothing. Were these powerful clerks, under orders, restricting the grain in order to force the peasants back to their fields? Something made me turn round, and I caught sight of a small figure, clipboard in hand, head slightly bowed, listening to one of the assistants explaining something from a red-backed ledger. It would be hopeless to even ask about the real agenda, a masonry of lies, circles, and half truths which would never approach the truth.

About twelve, the second Toyota appeared, driven by Yohannes, Amsalu's vacant-looking driver. In the back was an enormous blue bag that flopped and slapped against the windows like a giant piece of risen dough. He came to a halt by the water barrels. About twenty men began to haul and roll drums to the rear of the station wagon, while two fought with the metal valve at the end of the bag. Suddenly water began to spill in a clear gush into the first drum. They had been down to their last three or four gallons.

The official who was with us decided to return to Sodo, and left with Yohannes as soon as the truck was empty. He took with him two ledgers, one with mildew growing down the false leather spine, and a separate invoice for all the flour delivered the previous month. The more paper they carried the more serious and satisfied their faces became. The rest of us sat down to lunch in a small room just off the entrance to the intensive feeding hut. The cook a cheerful middle-aged women, offered soap to each of us and then poured water over our hands onto the compacted floor. A younger woman brought in an iron dish of chappatis made from wheat flour. We sat around on the beds and ate, Inge thin and nervous, her legs curled up under her waist like an insect, Tula loud and huge, laughing raucously, Brit quiet, withdrawn, scribbling in a small blue notebook. The assistants, shy and tense in our company, said little, only smiled and ate. Afterwards

Assefa smoked a cheap cigarette and told me how having turned down a scholarship to go to a military college in East Germany, he had been sent to Aro Giorgis as a punishment. The other assistants looked on blankly, their English far behind his, admiring his cigarette.

We resumed work about an hour later, checking on the morning's worst cases, tidying up the outpatient trivia. Many of the people had chest infections, all had scabies, many tonsillitis. Yet something about the camp seemed wrong, out of place. It might have been the fertile-looking valley outside the stockade, or the large numbers of well-fed children hanging about outside the camp, or the fact that life was going on normally in the village beyond the walls that alerted me to it, but it was something, something that I was determined to find out.

By four we were finished. The vacant-faced mother and her baby were put in a side room for the night, each wrapped in a Fincross blanket. The baby had had a feeding tube threaded down its nose into its stomach and linked to a flask of diluted milk. In this way it would receive a slow but continuous supply of food and fluid. It was slightly better, but it would be surprising if it survived. The mother, snuffling, made apathetic gestures for somebody to pull out the feeding tube. There was nothing to stop her doing it herself, when she did the baby would die; but perhaps that would be no bad thing, allowing her at least a temporary return to her childhood. To a child, having a baby can be a crippling blow. I left her there, hoping for what best I no longer knew.

We reached home at six to find Red Eyes waiting for us with a new ledger to sign. I washed in a bucket on the veranda and listened to the World Service of the BBC; the news meant nothing, the only thing different the new and more worrying burst of music introducing it. As I washed I tried to picture the news reader, and his route to the studio in Bush House. Up the steps of the underground at Aldwych, out into the street past the felt-pen scrawls of the Evening Standard Adverts, along the Strand to the temple-shaped building of

Bush House. I turned the dial to Radio Moscow. Somebody was abusing President Reagan in KGB English.

Captain's Toyota belched its way around the rear of the building to deposit Janet. Somehow he had managed to convert a single journey into two, bringing Prudence and Yushi back from one camp and then going back separately for Janet. She smiled as she crossed the compound, carrying a blue Singapore Airlines case with a Red Cross sticker over the airline logo. Her jeans and bush shirt were covered in a fine film of red dust. She got out the primus and we made tea with ten-minute boiled water to kill any amebic dysentery germs that might lurk in it.

She told me about Habicha Bantu. Brit would be going there tomorrow, but as things stood I would not see the camp for a few days yet. There were about twenty-five hundred people in the camp. Janet said they came daily from the surrounding villages and the whole place was in chaos. There were about seven Red Cross workers, a medical assistant, clerks, somebody with training in nutrition, a storeman—all working out of large Red Cross tents and a few outbuildings. The Ethiopians were, she said, incredibly protective from the very start, maybe because she was alone, maybe because she was a woman, or maybe because most of them were young enough to be her children. There was a man there they called "Strongman" because he could lift two sacks of flour over his head. Abebe, the medical assistant, had invited her to his house to eat with his wife and two children. He had a garden full of vegetables, which was pretty odd in a famine. In the afternoon she looked more closely at the fields and realized that most of them were fertile. There was also water, and many of the huts nearby had vegetable plots. The land seemed to have recovered remarkably quickly from the drought.

Prudence listened then said, "It seems the same in Chefisa, but in the tropics things grow quickly after the rains."

Tula yawned, rose from her seat on the veranda, and, calling out "bones!" to the rest of us, began to walk toward the restaurant. Red Eyes, standing outside the bar toilet buttoning his flies, watched her with lust in his eyes.

That evening we sat in the restaurant drinking coffee or beer until around nine. It was a pattern that was to repeat itself each night for the next two months. There was nowhere else to go, and the alien gray-brown shambles outside forced us in on ourselves, so that we became a curious type of family, with code words, silly jokes, and an antipathy for outsiders.

That night I began to read the first rationed pages of Waugh's *Men at Arms*. Crouchback in his Italian village praying for romance at the tomb of an English knight.

7

THE FUNERALS

THERE WERE NO OFFICIALS to be seen anywhere the next morning, and calling them on the hand-cranked phone near the hotel cash register produced no answer from their office with its packing-case tables and oil-drum seats. It filled me with a vague unease. Absent officials were far more sinister than officials hovering just a foot behind you. Then, glancing out the window, I caught sight of two of them, their heads framed in the open window of a café directly across the road from the Dante. It was to be their haunt for the rest of the time we dealt with them, their forays into the Dante confined to the stage management of guilt. I finished my coffee and wandered across, annoyed at having to seek them out in a parody of an audience.

The cafe was made out of flattened sheets of corrugated iron pinned on rough frames. It was greasy inside, dark, and filled with empty wooden tables upon the surface of which flies browsed on last night's injera wat. Seeing me coming, the two men had moved from the window to the farthest corner. One was fat and small, the other, who I had not seen before, strangely thin. A Mr. Rat to the absent Mr. Mole. I wondered if I had by accident stumbled on the fourth signa-

97

ture of the magic quartet needed to release goods from the warehouse.

The little fat official suggested a coffee, offering a cracked sugar bowl as a preliminary. It was covered with flies. The thin one leered at me over a plate of breakfast leavings. When I explained that today we wanted to go straight to the camps and leave the warehouse until tomorrow, the thin one cracked his long fingers and smiled, rose to his feet and said he had to visit the RRC that morning. The fat one ignored him, and the long thin figure slipped half bent under the low door into the sunlit street. The fat man repeated his offer of coffee. I gave in reluctantly, thinking of the raw sewage in the water. He paid for it and said with a triumphant smile, "That man who has just gone out, he is a very lazy man." Like somebody might say, "Smith is a brilliant physicist." My hopes of getting much out of the warehouse sank.

We left the Dante at ten, with time still in hand to visit the two camps, Bugu and Chefisa, beyond Aro Giorgis before curfew. The fat man was tense until we had passed the warehouses, nervously adjusting the hang of his neat suit, perhaps fearing a change of mind. Inge and Tula came with us. We were to put Inge down at Aro Giorgis and take Tula on to Bugu. The Captain was ferrying the others to the remaining camps in the Toyota. He would catch up with us later and take the official to the camp at Chefisa.

It had rained again, and the fields looked even greener and more mysterious than ever. There were children everywhere, five for every adult, driving cattle, playing in the dust, herding donkeys, climbing trees, wallowing in huge dirty pools of water. We passed schoolyards crammed with them, and buses whose windows were all children's faces. Yet, as we began to descend into a plain we saw that on either side of the road were fields of untended maize, many with stalks ten or twelve feet high. Here and there small meadows, sufficient for only a family, had been recently cleared to make way for the autumn planting of teff, a millet used in the making of injera. In some fields young shoots were already forming a slight carpet of green. But much of the land had been left fallow and lay untilled, covered in a dense mat of weeds. Africa's law that once the womb is seeded more land is put to the plough had been abandoned.

We began to see the funerals, passing three in the space of ten minutes. Two were small affairs, a few figures half-glimpsed hurrying down tracks in the maize carrying a mummy-shaped bundle on a crude stretcher made from eucalyptus poles. As we passed, the bearers averted their heads and veered away, as though ashamed to be seen.

But farther on we slowed for a crowd of about a hundred people spilling across the road. Not an ordinary crowd, but one gripped by a slow dreamlike dance painful to watch. It seemed as if the coffin, held aloft by four men and covered in a red pall, was floating on the heads of the dancers, rising and falling to the rhythms of the undulating dance. Each dancer seemed absorbed, unconscious of direction, yet they and the coffin were being slowly drawn toward a field just off the road that was filled with heaps of fresh red earth. The village pope, an old man in dusty medieval clothes and stovepipe hat, bent exhaustedly over a tattered book, pausing every few seconds to wave short impatient blessings at the coffin, as though he could not bear the sight of it, or the memories of hundreds seen over the past year.

We counted more than fifty new mounds in the cemetery.

"And they don't even mark the children's graves," Inge said, breaking into my thoughts.

"All adults?" I asked.

"Multiply the number by five for the children who have died," Prudence added.

We edged the truck through the procession, unseeing faces sliding past our windows, drove on for a few hundred yards then stopped. Tula already had her camera out. I searched for mine in the blue UN doctor's bag I had been given in Geneva.

The official's alarm at the sight of Tula's camera was one of the few genuine emotions I ever saw any of them reveal. He watched gray-faced as Tula began the slow deliberate movements of the amateur getting ready to take a picture. As she checked the lens he said in a hoarse trembling voice, the near-perfect English beginning to desert him, "It forbidden to take pictures of graveyards, it is leading to very serious troubles."

Tula muttered in my ear, "He doesn't want us to find out how many have died."

"Of course," I replied.

But Mole's sharp ears heard us. Instantly some color returned to his cheeks. If we had just ignored him, got out of the car and begun snapping away, he would have lost the initiative. But once we began to argue, like Lot's wife and the pillar of salt, we were doomed. Mole, like all his kind, was one of nature's Jesuits. With causistry and promises he could hold his own with anyone.

His voice became softer, even conciliatory. No, it was not that we were to be prevented from finding out how many had died, but it would be very bad to take pictures because it might be misinterpreted.

He baited a hook and held it out. "People might think you were not doing your job just taking photographs."

It was a shrewd cast. A gloomy silence fell inside the car. Slowly I engaged the drive and began to edge forward. What, I thought in rage, did he mean by suggesting we were not here to work? Why was the warehouse shut? But the man in the two-piece suit had won, striking at some deep insecurity that lurked in all of us. Something that made us plead guilty to any accusation of idleness however unjustified. For such accusations only echoed the steely, obsessional voice inside that constantly urged us to all work harder and, when we did, sniffed at the results. Now we would all stay in the truck, craving official approval and hating it.

Through the rearview mirror I saw Tula's mouth turn down. She began to mutter in Finnish, slowly winding the strap about the camera preparatory to returning it to its case. Her mouth formed a word, but she checked herself, slight tears in the corners of her eyes. For me it was a dreadful humilation, true Aidgame. I trod on the accelerator and the funeral vanished in a plume of white dust behind our van.

We reached Bugu ten minutes later. The camp had been set up in an open field, surrounded, like Aro Giorgis, with a fence of sharpened stakes. It was much bigger, however, enclosing a space about the size of two football fields. A giant African chestnut dominated the entrance.

Four men stood waiting for us in the center of the compound. Three of them dwarfed by the fourth who must have been at least six feet seven in height. He was wearing castoff clothes several sizes too small: a green anorak whose sleeves finished about four inches above his wrists, a red tie with a small dagger motif that hung halfway down his chest, and a pair of gray plaid trousers that ended midcalf. He had an enormous pair of feet, and a hangnail on the left big toe which somebody had dabbed with mercurochrome. His companions were equally bizarre; one wore a trench coat several sizes too big for him, one grinned at us from beneath a Davy Crockett hat made of mock leopard fur, while the third, although conventionally dressed by Ethiopian standards, held a beautifully rolled and very expensive umbrella in his left hand. Our official, a dwarf by comparison with all three, was uneasy, an uneasiness that we were to find often presaged a long campaign of obscure denigration.

The giant welcomed us with a series of short gutturals. There was a slight pause. Then, reluctantly, a man in a white coat with a contemptuous face stepped forward and snapped, "The chief bids you welcome," gave a glance at the giant as if he was some kind of idiot, and stepped back. The chief continued, unaware of the contempt. From the crowd the man in the white coat gave an impatient sigh and translated.

"The people have suffered greatly. He hopes you can assist them although you have come so far from another country."

We shook hands with them. The man with the contemptuous face introduced himself as the medical assistant. His name, like the driver and the hospital doctor, was Abraha.

The chief and his three companions falling behind, he led us toward some torn gray tents and sagging tuculs. This, he said, was not an interesting place; where he should be working was in the capital. Could I arrange his transfer? It was now eleven in the morning, the busiest time of the day, but the mud-brick building of the clinic was barred and shuttered, the only patient an emaciated girl of about fifteen lying horribly still under the eaves, her face crowded with flies. Two ancient peasants crouched over her, hunched in despair.

Abraha could barely suppress his rage, and launched into a long tirade about them being too lazy to bring the child until it was too late. He turned on the father and barked something at him in the same gutturals the chief used. Behind me the giant stirred slightly. The man in the Davy Crockett hat murmured something to the official. Tula asked him what they were saying. The little man shrugged. Their language was Wollaitinia, some peasant language, very crude. He smiled, but when I turned I saw that the chief's face was dark with anger.

The girl was semiconscious, her breathing coming in short painful grunts. Severe anemia, the harsh laboring sounds of her damaged heart, fever, and the tiny splinters of hemorrhage under her chalk-white nail beds, suggested bacterial endocarditis, a frequently fatal complication of rheumatic fever. Occasionally her eyes would open and stare confusedly around—at us, the hut, faces of her parents. Then after a few seconds they would lose their hold, begin to wander, then become fixed and vacant under her upper lids.

All Abraha had in his mud-walled office were a few tins of aspirin, a bottle of worming mixture, and a giant jar of antimalarial tablets. Tula had heard there was a Catholic mission just down the road, and, because there was obviously nothing that could be done for the girl where we were, it seemed a good idea to ask them for help. We spent two hours resuscitating her in the dark, mud-walled clinic, her father pathetically anxious to help, spooning water from a plastic cup between her lips, holding her sitting up to ease her breathing. While this was going on another patient arrived, a ten-year-old boy with a huge TB abscess the size of an egg poking from behind his ear. He too would need daily injections at the mission.

But when I asked the official to come with me, he became evasive. It was important for him to leave for Chefisa as soon as Captain arrived with the second truck, which he would do any minute. But he would find somebody to show me the way. After ten minutes he produced a thin schoolboy of a man called Berhane, with odd white sideboards and an expression of permanent watchful hurt.

We loaded the patients and left. Berhane's English was irregular but fluent. However, to questions other than how to get to the mission he merely nodded his head and smiled, his face preoccupied.

The clinic was about five miles away, just off the main road, a new building in dressed stone with a carefully raked gravel drive leading up to a veranda. A mile farther on, on a hill overlooking a river, stood a church flanked by two large buildings, one of them built in the style of an Italian farmhouse.

Nothing moved in the empty courtyard as we drove up. Leaving Berhane in the truck I climbed the steps of the veranda and knocked on a green metal door. For a while there was no answer, then a bolt was drawn and a hatch opened in its center. Protuberant eyes like those of an enthusiastic ferret peered at me through thick bifocals. The hatch snapped shut, a key turned, and the door swung open on a small nun of about sixty in a white habit with a fighting, slightly hairy face.

She introduced herself as Sister Frances in a Yorkshire accent that recalled George Formby. Later I was to realize that it even tinged the Amharic in which she kept up a continuous flow of orders, questions, criticisms, rebukes, and minor prayers. She had been in Ethiopia for twenty years, an entire life devoted to building up clinics and schools only to see them snatched away by the government and then run down.

She was not deterred. Here, unlike the clinics she had lost, everything was calm, clean, and orderly. The patients sat in rows on spotless benches, some talking quietly, others dozing or playing with their children, all of them waiting to be called to a small room at the end, where, through an open door, two Ethiopian sisters could be seen preparing injections and dressings. Even the familiar smell of old rags dipped in curry was hard to detect.

Berhane and one of the clinic guards edged through the door carrying the sick girl on their crossed hands, her thin arms flapping about their necks, her head lolling to one side in exhaustion. Sister Frances took one shrewd, rather frightening look at her, and turned away with her lips pursed. One of the thin Ethiopian sisters began to hover like a bird over the sterilizer.

To be helped—cure was impossible—she would need regular large doses of penicillin by injection and minute but powerful quantities of the heart stimulant digitalis. It meant coming every day in the ambulance for at least a fortnight, but I doubted if her relatives would bring her back again.

The small fat boy with the open sore the size of a large bird's egg tried to make himself invisible behind a pillar. Sister Frances gave him a ruthless smile, pushed him into the treatment room, and returned to talk to me about her clinic. Suddenly she stopped speaking, her small eyes fixing on something over my shoulder. I turned. In the corner an elderly peasant was enjoying a cheap cigarette.

Behind me the nun's voice began barking in the harsh gutturals that I had heard the chief use, interspersed with scraps of Bradford English. "How dare you smoke in my clinic! . . . How dare you, how dare you . . . I will not have smoking in my clinic, I will not have it . . ." In mid-sentence, just as suddenly as she started, she stopped, and said matter-of-factly, "That was Wollaitinia, a silly language they all speak around here."

I groped for the thread of our fractured conversation. It was frightening and unreal, something between being back at convent school and taking part in a music hall turn. The fat boy with the abscess came out of the treatment room with two silent tears on his cheeks and a fresh dressing on his neck. He no longer smelled and the flies had gone from the wound. I promised Sister Frances to get some more drugs from the government stores in Sodo — she would need a large supply to treat both cases. As a reward she took me around to the back of the clinic across a yard to a long single-story building with red tiles.

She fiddled under her habit, produced a ring of jailer's keys, and opened a door.

We found ourselves in a small delivery room with pastel yellow walls, the floor covered in brown and yellow linoleum. Over the bed a picture of Christ dripping blood from an incandescent heart gazed across the room at a small glass pot filled with vaginal speculae. A delivery table stood in one corner, covered with a chintz dust sheet. I looked out of the window to reassure myself. Across the road, staves upraised and hands folded below brown rags, a small group of peasants squatted around a bored-looking donkey. Suddenly it had an enormous erection. The peasants' staves rocked back and forth with their delight, the sound of laughter drifting across the road. The donkey gave a single bray and the curved black rope of its penis slowly shriveled.

I half listened to the little figure at my side outlining her plans for the room. She was keen for deliveries to be done at the clinic. A doctor and his wife were coming from Ireland in a month to take over the running of the obstetrics. The government, of course, had wanted to take the whole place over as soon as it had been opened — they had sent inspectors and even a minister from the capital to admire it. I asked what they had decided. The small, beady-blue eyes, slightly contemptuous, held mine for a moment. If they took it she would merely build another, and another. Perhaps to her clinics were only elaborate sandcastles. And the famine? They had a feeding center just down the road. From it they had persuaded many of the mothers to come to the clinic for mothercraft lessons. Many of them were so young they didn't even know how to feed or wash their babies, and by the age of twenty they often had four. I asked about the untended fields. The little nun smiled and rattled her beads.

She was about to say something when Berhane, grinning, detached himself from the doorpost against which he had been loafing and came forward.

She said to him in English, "Do you know the way to Chefisa?"

He nodded.

She said, "You will need a guide, the road is impossible."

We said goodbye at the door, promising to meet again at the mission one Sunday. I drove away glancing back more than once through my rearview mirror at the small figure in white on the veranda, then it turned and vanished through the green metal door.

Berhane said nothing on the long drive to Chefisa. I glanced at him several times. He looked about thirty-five, but his hair was gray, unusual in a Negro except in extreme age. And while he smiled readily enough, in repose his features became haggard, as if he had to bear the relentless gnawing of some chronic disease.

The short route across the valley was flooded, and to get to the camp it was necessary to follow a huge circle of low hills that rimmed the temporary lake. The road passed close to the mission buildings on the hill, then, narrowing, advanced eastwards through thick groves of eucalyptus trees that were all that remained in most places of a forest that once had covered 90 percent of the country. Now they were never left to grow to more than a quarter of their full height of a hundred feet. On the track we passed men carrying the semimature poles for house building or firewood, each felling contributing to the great red gashes that marked the ever increasing advance of soil erosion—gashes that looked like some awful eczema of the earth's skin: wrinkled, dried-out cracks with dirty water seeping along their bases. It was said the eucalyptus had been brought to Ethiopia by an Australian explorer in the late nineteenth century, and that the Emperor Menelik, encouraged by their speedy growth, had ordered them to be planted throughout his kingdom. But it was apocryphal; eucalyptus grows in profusion from the Cape to the Nile, but Ethiopians always tell the tale to Australians to flatter them. We were following a riverbed, one in which, despite the recent rains, no water flowed. The land to the north of it had sunk so far it had left the river stranded. The track passed village after village, many barely a few hundred yards from each other, separated only by scrub and a few rock outcrops.

Each village had a central green ringed by huts, each hut standing in a garden fenced with sharpened eucalyptus poles. In the gardens grew maize and millet, false banana or sweet potato. Some of the village greens were thick with a carpet of maize leaves, blowing about on the trampled grass among the cleaned bones of a freshly felled oxen, all that remained of a market held the previous day. As we approached, potbellied children, cheering wildly, would hurl themselves from their houses and race after us yelling something that sounded like *"chiasma-chiasma."* At this, Berhane, a thin nervous hand clutching the grab handle in front of him, would smile and point at the Red Cross on the bonnet.

The villages lay peaceful in the afternoon sunlight, unchanged in five thousand years. Medieval society is as bitter in its resistance to new ideas as we are enthusiastic in our surrender to them. To these people ideas are things to be talked about, wondered at, speculated upon, but set aside, like bottled snakes in a museum — interesting, but better dead. The inhabitants of this valley had thought the same thoughts, feared the same fears, wept the same tears, as hundreds of generations before them. It was a kind of immortality working upon an unchanging tapestry, repairing it, cleaning it, always restoring it to its original pattern. As my white-painted van with its red marks, once the sign in Ethiopia of a brothel, smashed and bumped through their lives, they must, behind the cheering of their children in our dust, have feared us greatly.

Before the revolution the missionaries had built a windmill at Chefisa. Its tower stood on a ridge dominating the country-side around. The windvane, creaking in the light hot wind, still advertising the company in Genoa that had built it. It was market day. The village square packed solid with people. We stopped on the outskirts of the crowd, climbing down to a circle of giggling teenage youths and small children.

Old women sat over bowls of strange liquid, spooning it out to aged men in small gourd cups. There were cattle for sale, humpbacked brahmin, slow and doe-eyed. In corners one or two were being butchered, standing for as long as the loss of blood from their cut throats would allow, then kneel-ing over for their owner to hack open their stomachs and spill out a mass of fat, yellowed entrails. In an hour, all that would be left was a head, a look of sad rebuke in its eyes, comical-looking in the grass, as if the ox had been almost swallowed up by a quicksand.

There were plenty of vegetables for sale. Maize, spread in heaps or piled in small white mountains on the grass, pep-pers, potatoes, coffee, huge baskets of carrots, tomatoes, and citrus fruits. Some women sold woven baskets, others just sat about and cackled toothlessly. Berhane and I edged through the dense crowd, unable to throw off the circle of pushing, giggling teenagers. A young man thrust an earth-caked po-tato in my face, pulling me toward a small pile on the grass. We had not had potatoes for days in the Dante, so I took out a one-birr note, worth about 45 U.S. cents. He shook his head and showed me three or four brass coins, worth about a penny. I noticed a flag over the heads of the crowd and made for it. There might be offices near it where I could change the note.

But as I got closer to the flag the crowd thinned abruptly until around its base for a hundred yards the ground was almost deserted. Below it, behind a crude folding table, sat

four men with hard, arrogant faces, coarsely woven suits—
not soft like the suits of our officials—and thick polished
boots. In front of each was a thick red ledger. A line of
peasants guarded by two scruffy militiamen queued in front of
the table. At intervals one of the men would look up and
shout something. Clutching a thin cotton chamma around his
wasted frame, a peasant would shuffle forward, one hand
holding out a small booklet. The man behind the table would
take the book and enter something in his ledger.

As I watched, one of the coarse-suits, a book open in his
thick hands, began haranguing a thin birdlike man standing
in front of him. The peasant flinched, then half knelt in front
of the table, arms extended in supplication. The suit ignored
him, threw the book in a box and shouted at the nearest
militiaman. He walked forward, produced a pair of handcuffs
and fastened them on the thin wrists, towing his victim away
to a gray Toyota truck parked in the corner. It had rails along
each side for transporting cattle. In it I could see three other
heads. Berhane, his face terrified, pulled me away, but he
need not have bothered. The suits, intent on their ledgers,
did not even look round.

In the safety of the crowd Berhane said in English, "These
men not pay money to the government . . . no money . . .
prison."

But the suits were far more than that most ancient curse of
the peasant, the tax gatherer. For a while Berhane's face
worked slightly under the twin effects of rage and a supreme
effort to form the right words. Suddenly he began to speak
English in a curious fluent biblical style, perhaps learned as a
child from a Protestant missionary.

He had been wronged by the men in suits and sent, like
the man in the truck, away to prison. He must have been
released on the surety of becoming a police informer, or he
would not have been with me. But what he had just seen in
the fortuitous presence of a *ferengi*, a foreigner and therefore a
government enemy, was too overwhelming a temptation. He
informed, not on the ferengi, but to him.

The men in suits, he said, were not only tax gatherers, they also fixed the price of food, bought it, and put it in a warehouse in Sodo. About September around the time of Mescal, the feast of the True Cross, trucks with soldiers would come and take the food away to Addis Ababa, where it was sold to the rich. Here in Sodo, the price of one quintal of teff was seventy birr, but his son, who had been in the army, told him in Addis it fetched three hundred birr. Seventy birr was not enough for the peasant, who had to sell to these men, buy seed, feed his plough oxen, and pay his taxes. And if he didn't pay his taxes? Berhane made a cutting action across his throat. They took his farm and animals and put him in prison.

Berhane's thin Arabic face smiled slightly, then clouded with fear and hatred. He pointed to the gray sideboards and said, "One year," before continuing.

The old rulers kept the peasants poor, chained to the soil by debt so that no heads were ever raised in defiance. But at least the feudal lords knew something of the land, how much it would produce, how much they would need for themselves, how much was needed to keep their peasant slaves alive. They needed them alive—to produce enough food for their tables, tithes for the emperor, and sons for his wars.

But the new men, they were from the city and knew nothing of the soil. They had dead eyes and spoke in riddles. They took everything the peasant produced and for a price so low it brought death and withering of the crops, fear, and whispers. And the new men heard everything and forgot nothing, even what a man murmured in his sleep. Many a peasant went to jail wondering what it was he had said and against whom. And some of these who were sent away were heard of no more, killed, some said, by the barber's chair with the wires, and their clothes delivered to the door of the prison on Sunday morning for collection by their wives who had come to visit them.

I started to ask him how much he had been in arrears with his taxes, but the mention of the word loosened his hold on

English; he continued in a mixture of Amharic and Wollaitinia which made no sense to me. What I had understood of
his story filled me with suspicion, but time and experience
showed that the thin foolish-faced man was not lying. He is
safe now, beyond the frontier at Kassala, in the Sudan, so that
the men in suits, when they read this, can search for him in
vain.

We drove into the camp and Berhane fell silent at the sight
of the suited figure of Mr. Mole standing in the middle of the
compound. He stood apart from all the camp activity with a
semicircle of assistants around him, his head slightly bowed.

I saw then that the officials were like those nightmarish
bullies that I remembered from among my schoolmasters,
whose power lay in a secret protocol of mad rules, which, if
broken, always produced the same triad. Sad surprise, followed by brooding withdrawal, then punishment. But worst
was the knowledge that penance and forgiveness would only
come when you discovered for yourself what it was that you
had done wrong, defined your own sin, and so forged your
own chains. The little man standing there in his soft suit had
laid a grip on that circle of faces with a secret catechism of
Marx.

Mr. Mole was so absorbed in what he was doing that he
failed to notice my arrival, and when I walked up to him, he
started as if in a dream, eyes blurred with the self-absorption
of power.

"It is the biscuit tins, Doctor," he said sadly, his mole eyes
watering.

"What about them?"

He shook his head slowly as if wondering about my stupidity, or even my complicity. Turning away slightly he offered
me a huge list of Amharic words.

"I can't read this," I answered. He turned over the pink
page to a yellow flimsy underneath. There, in a shaking
schoolboy hand, was a copy of the original in English. It was
an inventory of empty biscuit tins. "But these are only biscuit
tins."

The official gave a small hiss of displeasure. "All the cans must be returned to the central warehouse for counting, it is my practice. I have made it a rule."

"But what difference does it make once the biscuits are given out?"

He made no reply. Behind him the pile of tins, each about half a gallon in size, shone in the bright morning sunlight, even the ones that had been twisted and ripped had been collected. He came closer to me, fumbling at the pink flimsy, like a man at a woman's dress, and held it up. "All of this will be checked in Addis, all of it, everything."

He watched my face, waiting for a clue. "In this country everything is counted."

I thought of the great poster in Revolution Square shouting "Everything is remembered, no one is forgotten." The strange unfocused expression returned to his face and his weak puzzled eyes filled with fear, fear of murder and things thieved.

Beyond the tins lay the giant, deflated-mattress-shape of an empty water container. Without water the children would have to be sent home, some up to three miles in the midday sun. Some would die. He followed my glance and said, "It is the hyenas." At night they came and worried at the bags, trying to reach the water inside. Last night one had torn a foot-long gash in the bag. And the RRC truck, which was supposed to deliver water each day, had not turned up.

"What about the water tower? Can we not lead a pipe from there?"

"Too far."

"We could use the biscuit tins. Those children who are not sick could bring it."

The official stood with the clipboard in his hand, a slight wind flapping the pink list, and sighed. "They cannot be used like this, they have to be inventoried and checked."

After he went inside the small warehouse to count the flour bags, Prudence appeared, made a face at the little man's back, and saw to it that each child was given a tin and sent to the windmill. Within an hour they had brought enough water, slopping and splashing in the shining metal tins, to provide the camp with half a day's water. Afterwards they gathered in a crowd outside the kitchen and, while the men pounded the faffa porridge, began a song—small voices effortlessly harmonizing, bodies swaying to the beat of the pounding. When Mr. Mole emerged from the shed, it was to find himself defied. For a while he remained in the center of the field, holding his clipboard, listening. Then he vanished.

I watched the children singing and tried to imagine who they were. Coming from a society from which peasants had long since vanished, it was difficult for me to imagine them transposed to England or Australia. If there was a famine in England, who would be in the famine camps, the weak or the crafty? The dependent who haunt a doctor's surgery or the devious? But language and culture laid such an immeasurable gulf between us and the people we were supposed to help that they became abstractions, so many kilograms of weight into which so many calories of food must be pushed to bring them up to a theoretical minimum.

Prudence and Yushi had been busy. At the entrance the nun had placed some scales, seated behind which was a medical assistant with a ledger. Any child coming in had to be weighed, its height measured, and the sickest sent to the medical assistant. The inevitable gatekeeper armed with a bamboo cane kept an eager crowd at bay before the weigh station. Yushi was in one of the tents spooning yellow faffa into the mouth of a child riddled with TB. As she fed it, a long liquid stool in which a few worms threshed slid to the ground between its wasted hams. There were a lot of flies. Mothers surreptitiously licked their children's plates, or when they thought the nurses' backs were turned, slipped spoonfuls of the hot food into their own mouths.

Early in the afternoon, the official returned and started loading his truck with empty cans. The argument started up again, going endlessly over the same ground. He was sure that tomorrow the RRC would come with the water. But such an assurance, a mere slogan, meant nothing. If the Party said it was going to be there, it was going to be there, even if it wasn't. Faith, not the reality, mattered. If he left the cans he would be doubting the Party. We searched for some common ground, some haven we could drag ourselves into and compromise. In the end he took half the cans on the mutually understood lie that I would take the others when I had room in my truck.

Behind us as we spoke Captain lovingly polished my truck. The soldier in him hated the daily sight of my mud-covered Toyota. I would not have liked to have served with him in the emperor's guard.

Leaving Captain to load his truck with the cans, we set off together in mine for Sodo. Berhane would go with Captain back to Bugu. Somewhere, a mile from Chefisa, Mr. Mole said, "Our Abyssinian names are complicated."

Abyssinian is a term of contempt in Ethiopia, like aboriginal or native, but he gave no clue as to why he used the word, instead he began to explain the meaning of the various prefixes. *Wolde* meaning "son of," *Haile* meaning "strength," *Selassie* meaning "trinity."

"So *Haile Salassie* means 'Strength of the Trinity'?"

"Yes." He paused, then said, "*Gabre* means slave," adding, "The district commissar is called Gabre Jesus."

"Slave of Jesus?"

He nodded and, sighing, said, "These old Bible names!" There was a moment's silence. Then he said very softly, "The Slave of Jesus is anxious to meet you."

It was a shrewd lead-in to what he was after. Most people would be curious to meet a commissar called Slave, but Tula and Inge had already told me about the official's attempts to get them to meet him. The first day it was arranged, they waited two hours before a message came canceling it. The second time they waited three hours with the same result, and the third time they waited all day. After that they refused to wait at all. Inge thought it was just a ruse to keep us in town.

I shrugged and made some noncommittal answer. Taking

it for agreement the official told me a joke that was difficult to follow above the noise of the truck, a joke about a dog, a cat, and a donkey. It was probably funnier in Amharic, but even in translation there was a nasty bitterness about it, a bitterness that celebrated failure.

Amsalu was preparing to leave for Addis when we got back, his baby face cheerful at the prospect of travel. He was one of those people who became uneasy if forced to remain in one place, as if, like some fish that never rest, being stationary would suffocate him. The official fawned something in Amharic at him. His features suddenly became a mirror of respect.

Amsalu looked at me with the artificial concern of a car salesman calculating his approach. He was a man with supreme confidence in his own values; people who held different ones were not wicked or subversive, they merely lacked wisdom. He would have made a powerful salesman. He began to sell me the idea of visiting the commissar.

"You know, Doctor, the commissar is a very important man, we must show him respect."

I explained that we would at that time be out at the camps, and besides, did he not want to get back to Addis? He paused slightly, considered it, and then rose. "We will go there now."

Party headquarters was housed in an unspectacular building behind a gasoline station. Outside, it looked more like the forecourt of a bankrupt builder's yard than the place that held powers of life and death over two million people. Corrugated sheets nailed around the door, probably to prevent grenade attacks, gave it the impression of a hastily erected public *pissoir.* Behind them a badly hung boxwood door led into a dusty hallway that served as an office. A typist, surly-faced with power, pecked at a huge and ancient mechanical typewriter. Amsalu leaned over her and whispered something. Without looking up she waved to three splintered seats along the wall. We sat down. On a table in front of me lay a new book in a bright yellow wrapper. I picked it up and glanced at the title. It said, *The Collected Speeches of Yuri Andropov.*

It was heavy with expensive paper, the narrow face of the secret-police assassin staring from the dust jacket with a look of thoughtful forgiveness, like a priest contemplating a penance: What would be best? A year in Siberia, demotion, loss of pension, or the full plenary indulgence of a show trial in Moscow? The first page was in Russian, the rest in Amharic. I had seen the English edition before, a free copy left out for tourists on the Helsinki–Leningrad express. The waving ancient script would conceal a language couched in a style of injured but forgiving surprise at the lapses of the proletariat from the true path.

The door of the inner office opened and three peasants began to back ingratiatingly out. An invisible hand closed the door on them. For a moment they paused as if expecting it to open again, then, eyes averted, shuffled past into the sunlight outside. The surly typist rose, knocked, and disappeared into the inner office. We waited. Five minutes later she reappeared, face arranged in a smile, and beckoned us to go in.

The Slave of Jesus was a surprise. My idea of a commissar came exclusively from flickering black and white Russian movies, men in gray uniforms and peaked caps with hard Slavic eyes, directing jerking lines of soldiers into giant gray explosions. Instead there was only a short fat man dressed in a cheap blue linen suit sitting disconsolately at the end of a long table, the only Communist thing about him a square lapel badge portraying Lenin's head rising from a sheaf of wheat. As we entered, he rose, thrust out a spadelike hand to be shaken, and then waved us to a row of chairs down one side of the long polished table.

We sat down, and the typist brought in glasses of red tea spiced with cinnamon. As I took a glass, I glanced at Amsalu. His face was stiff with fear. His right hand gripped a pencil so tightly the knuckles were pale with tension under his light brown skin. For me, separated by quasi-diplomatic immunity and language, it was difficult to see what was so frightening about the Slave of Jesus. True, he had that slight aura that makes those in power seem not quite in focus, but otherwise he was nothing but a shrewd-looking peasant in a suit.

The wall behind the Slave's head was covered in scrolls, certificates, and cheap mass-produced glossy prints of the hierarchy, like the photos of film stars that were once displayed outside cinemas. Mengistu, his cabinet, Castro, Lenin, Brezhnev, several cosmonauts, Nyere of Tanzania, and a large colored picture of a Soviet heavy tank. In one corner, frowning, Yuri Andropov deprecated the entire display to an invisible audience.

After the greetings there was silence. My official writhed, Amsalu looked straight ahead. An expression of slight bewilderment spread over the Slave of Jesus's square features. I began to explain, Amsalu translating, what we intended to do, who was with me, and how long we expected the work might take. For Amsalu it was the equivalent of walking through a mine field to shouted instructions. He paused, stumbled, went back on himself, stuttered, and at times, panicking, froze completely. When he finished he rested his hands on the table in front of him. From them, twin auras of perspiration began to spread out across the polished surface.

Everybody began to sip his tea.

The Slave of Jesus tried a few sentences of halting English, vague assurances of goodwill. We leaned toward him as he stumbled through the phrases, willing him to say it right. But the tea outlasted his speech and we sat there trapped, the signals for leaving set simultaneously at go and stop, everybody avoiding one another's eyes. At last, perhaps at a hidden signal, the secretary opened the door. We rose, murmuring unfelt apologies for detaining him, which the Slave of Jesus countered with false expressions of regret at our having to leave so soon.

Outside in the sunlight Mr. Mole became almost jocular. I watched him closely in case he might disclose his battle order, but he caught my look and slid quickly back behind his usual insinuating manner.

I went back to the hotel to wait for the nurse. The bar, emptied by the rain the night before, was now filled with men in cheap suits: provincial administrators, teachers, health officials. I sat over a Coke and waited, looking at the three sepia pictures hung over the bar. One was of a rockhewn monastery at Lalibela; one of something that looked like Cleopatra's needle; the third of a lion standing near a lake. A fat girl with a sluttish manner dumped a cup of Ethiopian coffee in front of me. As I reached in my pocket to pay, Red Eyes gestured from behind his creaking coffee machine that it was on the house. He had heard where I had been.

Three women with awkward red Irish faces fell into chairs at the next table. The nearest one introduced herself and her friends. They belonged to Irish Concern, a Dublin-based charity that had been in Wollaita for six weeks. They seemed remarkably cheerful, sharing a bottle of beer and two coffees with smiling cynical faces and losing no time in telling me that they were only allowed the same wages as the Ethiopian peasants. It meant living rough, often starving, with only the occasional foray into a place like Sodo.

They lived in a couple of huts ten miles off the main highway between Sodo and the next market town. The worst time was at night because the peasants would not leave them alone, gathering at the doorless entrance to their hut to watch everything they did, even accompanying them into the darkened fields to watch them relieve themselves. Worse was to have just fallen asleep to be awoken by an anxious peasant, face inches away, pleading for medicines.

We began to be joined at intervals by the others—first Janet, looking slightly drawn, then Prudence, Tula, and Inge. Slowly, the talk around the table became a series of wary, competitive remarks, disguised initially as jokes, then outright challenges. The Irish talked about the dwindling numbers in their feeding center, their brogue outlining the shape of a new battle to come. For if it was true, as I was beginning to suspect, that for some inexplicable reason the government had given us permits only to an area where the

famine was over, any move to leave would be highly unwel-
come. There was a famine somewhere, I had seen the evidence
of it on film before I left Australia. The battle would be to
get to it. One of the Irish girls, Siobhan, said suddenly, "The
famine is over of course. You may have come too late." She
paused for effect, searching our faces over the rim of a bottle
of Red Stripe. Prudence's was torn between agreement and
instinctive secretiveness. Inge's gave nothing away, Janet
looked carefully neutral. Tula finished her beer, got up, and
walked out.

The next day the men in suits laid their first administrative
barrage into my lines. In the morning I found Captain busy
with a sponge and rag washing my truck, muttering to himself about the dirt. As I loaded my equipment into the back
one of them, Mr. Rat, came wraithlike down the drive toward
me delivering his good morning in a soft hurt voice. He
looked at the mud on the wings of the car and shook his head.
This car was new, and already it had been damaged. He was,
he said, going to put in a report to headquarters, and, when
they had made a decision, the car would be taken to Addis for
servicing. In the meantime he was asking them to send him a
new car with a driver, both of whom we would share. I could
see myself spending the next six months drinking coffee in
the hotel. I turned momentarily and caught a fleeting look of
malignant triumph on his face. Amsalu appeared, his timing
uncannily rehearsed.

"You know, Doctor," he said, his voice cracking slightly
with embarrassment, "this is a very complicated engine. You
would be better with a driver." He paused to weigh the value
of the insult. I looked at my watch. It was nine, an hour after
the two other cars should have arrived to pick up the nurses.
"Where is the other car?" "Waiting for gasoline permits," Rat
murmured. I knew it would be hopeless to ask why he had
not got permits the night before, or to point out that if we
lost the diesel to the Byzantine bureaucracy in Addis, we
would have deprived ourselves of the only vehicle that did not
require a permit. Such an idea would only appeal to him, for

each piece of paper forged an extra link in the administrative chain with which his organization sought to tie us down. I began to feel like somebody with a dangerous mental delusion. What on earth was this man up to?

"Where are the nurses?" he suddenly asked. "Sitting on the steps." The man smiled, as if they had come to Ethiopia to sunbathe. They were, of course, women, and therefore of no account in his scheme of things, poor weak deluded creatures. But when I went to look they were gone and not even Red Eyes, who knew every inch of our movements, seemed to know where.

Amsalu was taking a quiet swig of beer when I told him. He shrugged and asked if Brit was ready to go yet, they had to be in Addis that evening. But she had vanished as well.

Amsalu choked over his beer.

"Where?" he demanded.

I suggested he take Captain and the Toyota and start looking. I had to take the diesel to be repaired at the mission.

"But has no one told you? You cannot do that without authorization from Addis."

He looked at me, defying me to ask him why, as head of the relief administration in Addis, he could not make the decision on the spot. I smiled, made an excuse, and left the room. It was a time for fait accompli. Outside in the yard Captain stood waiting to take delivery of the keys, no longer just bits of metal that started an engine but symbols of who was in control of the feeding program. I forced a smile at him, climbed into the truck, and drove off.

Some Italian Franciscan monks from a monastery ten miles away near Tula's camp in Bugu ran a small engineering workshop in Sodo. Here they trained apprentices in repairing water-drilling rigs, tractors, trucks, pumps, and what few cars there were about the town. Some said the province entirely depended on the fathers for mechanical repairs. Today a yellow gantry stood in the yard, a pair of blue dungaree-clad legs protruding from behind its large front wheels. At intervals a large Roman hand would appear accompanied by a murmured request in Amharic, English, or Italian for tools or parts to a young black man crouched on the ground nearby. Seeing me the black man said something to the feet.

A stocky middle-aged Italian shot out from under the rig, blinked in the bright sunlight, focused, then scrambled to his feet, offering a forearm to shake to avoid his oil-covered hands. His name was Father Pietro. I explained about the car. He smiled, wiped his hands, and told the young man to take it away and wash down the mud. He would look at it in about an hour. They had a problem with the rig's clutch and it had to be ready for drilling this week. He must finish that first.

The priest shook a head of abundant gray hair and squinted at the top of the yellow gantry one hundred feet above us. The priests never discussed politics, or if they did, very circumspectly. But I had heard about the water-drilling program in Wollaita from a Canadian engineer who had spent two years on the project.

I had met him in the bar of the Ghion Hotel in Addis, glum and on the way home after two frustrating years in Ethiopia. He told me that two years ago the Canadians had struck an enormous natural spring about twenty miles from Sodo, a real gusher with a flow of about a thousand litres per minute. Successful capping and a nationwide appeal in Canada and Norway raised sufficient funds to buy a small prefabricated pumping station from Europe which, it was hoped, the mission would be able to install. It got as far as Addis Ababa. There the customs demanded 114 percent import tax.

There was an ugly row involving both the Norwegian and Canadian ambassadors, the Politbureau, even Mengistu himself. It was futile; the government insisted that it had an absolute right to levy over 100 percent duty on foreign equipment — the value of the pumping station was after all only a fraction of what the West "owed" to the military dictatorship of Ethiopia. It was only when the donors threatened to take the pumping station under bond on to Kenya across the land border at Moyale that the pump was released. But administrators do not give up that easily. They waived the tax, accepted the gift, and a month later a convoy of trucks appeared, loaded up the pumping station, and took it to Sodo. Two months later the donors learned that all the packing cases were locked in the RRC warehouse. They would remain there pending the outcome of an official inquiry into which subdepartment of the Ministry of Agriculture should uncap the well. That was two years ago. Every day the peasants walked past the capped-off gusher on the start of a ten-mile walk to a dirty trickle of water in an almost dry riverbed.

I guessed that the rig in front of me was part of the donated station. Perhaps someone somewhere in the administration had decided that honor was satisfied and it could now be used. Or maybe the possibility of the foreign press reaching Sodo and turning up the story had crossed their minds. It would be tactless to inquire from the priest. He had to live there, so he would not tell me. Pietro, as if reading my mind, gestured at the tall yellow gantry. "We are the only ones who know how to repair it."

He laughed, called one of the apprentices to take me over to the convent parlor where one of the maids would give me some coffee. I sat in the long, poorly furnished room killing time with a teach-yourself-Italian book I found in one of the shelves. An old cleaner brought me slices of hot, sticky chocolate cake and cold coffee. I tried what I had learned on a year-old copy of La Stampa. Pietro joined me after an hour, wiping his hands with a towel and shaking his head. He had checked everything but could not find out what was causing the trouble. He could not understand it. The car was new and even if it had been driven too hard, what of it? He shrugged.

"Maybe," he said carefully, "somebody put gasoline instead of diesel fuel in the tank at the port, in Djibouti." But if we were to find out, he would need some special tools from Addis. Sometime next week he had to go and get his work permit renewed in Addis. When he was there he would have a word with the Toyota garage.

I got back to the hotel to find Captain and his truck gone. Amsalu was where I had left him, but when I saw his face my heart missed a beat. It was not just haggard, but shocked, as if he had received some terrible news. My first thought was that something had happened to Janet, that she had been killed in an accident, or captured by guerrillas. We had heard that in the past such abductions had led to nightmare journeys in the desert for months. But it was neither of these—to Amsalu, it was worse. This morning, tired of being kept waiting for the truck to take them to their camps, Tula, Yushi, and Prudence had set out on foot, right through the middle of town.

Did I realize how dangerous that was? he asked. Did I not realize that walking in Ethiopia was an activity confined to the lowest peasants? That a public shaming had taken place? People would say, probably were already saying, that the Ethiopian Red Cross had no cars, and that it had ferengi doctors working for it who also had no cars. His voice became falsetto with anxiety. People would ask, what sort of people were these? Not good people. Ferengi doctors were, everybody knew, immensely rich. These must be cheap, useless doctors.

I asked where my wife was. For a moment he looked confused as if I had introduced a completely unrelated fact into the conversation. "She went early with Captain to Habicha."

He shook his head slowly in total disbelief and returned to the morning's catastrophe. "Why?" he repeated, "Why? There were plenty of cars in the Red Cross." He shuddered. Captain had found the women about two miles out of Sodo, walking in a line alongside the donkeys. He gave a sigh. He would have to put in a report about it.

The news that there was a prospect of getting the diesel repaired in Sodo pushed him further into gloom. Who, he asked, would pay for the repairs? I explained that the fathers would do it for nothing. Amsalu hunched his shoulders, darting suspicious looks across the table.

"Captain must check the repairs. People who charge no

money for repairs are not to be relied on."

The news came as a relief. The limit of Captain's ideas on how a car worked was the belief that clean cars ran better than dirty ones. The matter could be stalled off now until the priest went to Addis and got advice and the right tools. I could feel myself being drawn into this mad inversion of values, ignoring the reality of the camps for a symbolic struggle over cars. The danger lay in falling for the same values as the officials, seeing control of a car as the ultimate goal, not as a means to an end in our campaign to distribute the piles of food in the warehouse.

8

THE MISSIONARIES

BRIT TOOK ME TO HABICHA BANTU, the only camp I had not yet seen, the next morning. She planned to leave for Addis with Amsalu in the afternoon and this would be a last opportunity to introduce me to the Ethiopian team. With the coming tenth anniversary of the revolution celebration in Addis, the provincial authorities were jumpy at the prospect of being forced to gather so many of their subjects in one place and there were fresh rumors of an impending travel ban.

We passed under a recently erected plywood triumphal arch. Under a halo of tiny red pennants was written, "The Tenth Anniversary of the Socialist Democratic Ethiopian People's Government. Smash Imperialism." We had the Mole-faced official with us that day sitting next to me. He said softly, "Such rubbish." Neither Brit nor Janet sitting in the back reacted. I thought, Not all who say Aba Aba. We drove on in silence for ten minutes. Then Brit pointed to a narrow track on the left.

I can, like a lover, remember even now every foot of the track which took me to a place that seemed like the very beginning of the world, and one that at first, although it seemed very familiar, I could not place. Only when the last piece of the jigsaw, the curse of foreknowledge, was there, did I recognize it.

The track was now no more than ruts gouged over the past weeks by the passage of previous trucks. In places it clung to the side of riverbeds, in others crossed them to wind through eucalyptus groves.

The ruts we followed crossed and recrossed established paths where we had to slow for crowds of people on their way to market. It seemed that the entire countryside was on the move, whole villages filing past each other, each file heading for its traditional market, held, as it had been for centuries, on the same day in the same place each week. The women came first, carrying bundles of firewood, baskets of maize, or injera wrapped in great green leaves, carried on their heads like a cartoonist's headache cure. Then their men, grave-faced, measuring their steps in the red dust with long, thin, polished staves. Oxen, startled by the noise of our engine, would break loose from the little boys leading them to docile deaths at the market, and, fear flattening their ears, would speed along the track in front of us scattering the villagers to right and left until they found a gap in the hedge. Once through and in safety they would stand pawing the red earth, awaiting with silly eyes the comforting whistles of their executioners.

We came on the camp from above, mounting a ridge to see a Red Cross flag fluttering among some trees about a mile below us. Brit said, "Habicha Bantu." The flag marked a point about halfway down the side of a valley. A mile below it a gray, flat cloud covered the floor making it look for a moment like the surface of a lake. The valley was part of the Rift, an enormous fracture in the earth that I had seen from the Ethiopian airliner five hundred miles north of Addis. But here there was nothing more than spectacular wooded scenery, its depth and the arid brackishness of its lakes concealed by clouds, greenery, and softness.

The track began to switchback down toward the flag, mounting huge rock outcrops then sliding sideways down into thick red mud. We came at last, through a gap in the trees, to a schoolyard with a tree in the middle, surrounded by low mud and wattle buildings with corrugated iron roofs. At the entrance an old woman without teeth came to the door of her hut and waved, something she did every day for two months. It was the last thing I saw when I drove away never to return. Should I go back tomorrow or in ten years, she will be there, waving. At the bottom of the steep schoolyard a group of figures waited. I eased the truck toward them, slowly, like an old lady going sideways down some steep steps. As we came closer I saw a small, very dark man with a square face in a square head, a teenager with a nervous, worried face, a tall man, and a thin girl whose cheap cotton dress concealed her femininity, and four or five others, willing smiles clamped on slightly anxious faces. We pulled up.

Mole-face said unnecessarily, "Turn off the engine."

We sat briefly in the silence. A man of about twenty-five appeared from around the corner of a hut marching in the exaggerated manner of the mad, as if stepping to some childish music. He was dressed in a ragged Queen Scout uniform and a pair of huge shiny boots without socks. He came to attention in front of the truck and saluted, the torn yellow epaulettes on his shoulders flapping in the wind, shouting, "Teferi Benti Guard!"

The official muttered, "What are they doing? This man is simple, not right in the head."

I looked more closely at the scout. Vacant mad eyes peered from a face too fat to be male and adult. What was an Ethiopian doing dressed in those strange, slightly dated symbols of Victorian morality? There are no scouts in Ethiopia, only the Red Guard. Did he choose them, or did the others? He turned, stamped his feet in a military parody, and marched away calling, "*Ande-sost, ande-sost.*" One-two, one-two.

As we got down from the truck a man in a white coat came out of a building behind us. He had a serious, handsome face with prominent eyes, curly, almost Italian hair, and a gravelly voice that instead of rising smoothly with the octaves, squeaked and slid over them in excitement. There are few heroes in this book, but he was one. His name was Abebe. He did nothing fantastic, defied nobody, did not end up before a firing squad shouting "Long Live Free Ethiopia!" but just lived in a village with his wife and two small children, worked hard, was kind, and never bullied his patients. His wife was beautiful, his children a delight, his house clean, and his garden full of vegetables.

The man with the square head was called Woldie, a nervous man, who, because he was young and therefore serious, worried even more than Abebe about his job. He was clever, with the sort of cleverness that makes an old man a little devious, a young man an enthusiast.

The thin girl was Leilt. Unlike the others, her English was excellent and had I met her in Addis Ababa I would have been instantly suspicious, but here I was disarmed, possibly by a manner so ingenuous it could not have been staged, and by her obvious fear of our official. Although he had introduced her as the interpreter, he spoke to her exclusively in Amharic, translating my words each time I tried a three-way conversation in English. After a moment he wandered off, leaving us in silence. She asked me if I would like to look around the camp.

Only two of the school buildings were being used by the Red Cross, one for a clinic and one for a store. The feeding and weighing took place in large marquees. The school still functioned, and we walked around to the sound of children chanting their tables. To one side of the tents a field of teff was sprouting, while the health assistant's garden was filled with vegetables. The camp had running water. It spouted out of three iron culverts set in a concrete trough from a deep underground stream that never, Leilt said proudly, even in the severest drought, ran dry. What was not taken by the never-ending line of mothers and children at the taps ran down a cistern to some fields below. It could be drunk unboiled, and later we began to take it back to the hotel for a personal drinking supply. For a long time I assumed it had been tapped by the local farmers' association until one day Woldie told me it was built by an American doctor who worked in the area before the revolution. "But then," he said with the slightly theatrical sigh that I had come to realize announced a double meaning, "the government told us that Americans were stealing all our valuable oil and coffee and he was sent away." He paused. "My brothers, they have both died for the government fighting rebels in Eritrea, but I am still here, and I only see the stream, built by the American."

Janet and Brit resumed the endless task of registering the children. As we spoke, Mole-face approached and they began to giggle. He nodded slightly, and made off in the direction of the stores. Leilt took me to the clinic that Abebe held each day in a small earthen-floored classroom filled with low wooden benches. On the blackboard the last lesson still remained—some lettering in Amharic, a long-division sum and the English word "mankind" written in green chalk. Abebe worked from a small table made out of packing-case wood that was once the schoolmaster's desk. On the benches sat three children, a boy grossly swollen with terminal kidney disease, a baby with pneumonia, and a ten-year-old leaning heavily on a long stick. The usual crones, kept at bay by a small guard, waved long thin arms at him from the door.

As Abebe coaxed the swollen boy over to have an injection he motioned me to have a look at the one with the stick. Slowly and with some pain the child pulled down a pair of khaki shorts. Over his right hip bone was a hole the size of a tenpenny piece, from out of which trickled a thin stream of green-yellow pus. The leg was shorter than the other, held flexed and slightly outward. It was another variety of TB, this time of the hip. As we talked about him in a foreign language the child bowed his head and began to titter in a mixture of hope and embarrassment. If he was not treated he would at the best be crippled, at the worst die.

Abebe was gentle with the child, drawing him closer with reassuring gestures. To some people the practice of medicine is an obsession, kept alive by a wonder at the mystery of growth; others are genuinely compassionate, feeling the pain and fear of their patients. Most doctors are neither, or very little of either. Abebe was one of those rarities who combined both qualities.

We worked through until about two in the afternoon when Amsalu appeared to pick up Brit. Mr. Mole, who I had not seen approach, muttered something in Amharic to Amsalu. The chubby Red Cross man nodded and Mole climbed into the truck. Amsalu said, "We will take him with us as far as Sodo. He has a meeting." At least, I thought, it meant we would be rid of him for the rest of the day. Although it was late he thought they could reach at least Shashemene by curfew. In the morning it would only be two hours to Addis.

Brit came over to say good-bye. In the few days we had been together, I had learned no more about her than on first meeting. She never lost the stillness that I had first noticed, a deep, almost hidden preoccupation that set her apart. She made no special occasion of leaving, embraced each of us, then climbed into the truck alongside the official. Janet asked her how long she would be in Addis. She said there was talk of a German surgical team arriving. If they came she would take them to Wollo province in the north. Amsalu started the engine, she smiled, waved, and turned away. Within a minute they had vanished over the rise.

We ate in a small room wedged between the clinic and store. In it were two beds, each covered in a gray military blanket and on the walls childish histograms in colored pencil, placatory icons to the officials' obsession with statistics. One of them showed a steadily declining death rate, with a peak sometime a month before we arrived. Woldie joined us, then, gaining courage, four others, one of them a tall, thin man I had not met who prefaced all his stock of limited English with the phrase "In your area?" I tried later to persuade him to drop it, but before I got far Mr. Mole sacked him over some obscure lapse. Leilt produced a piece of soap with which, after she had doused our hands with water, we washed.

Ten injera were laid on a table made of two conical baskets, one inverted, one upright, joined by their tips, the base of the inverted cone forming the dish, the base of the upright cone the foot. Freshly cooked maize was laid on the injera and then wat, a bitingly hot curry paste made from beans. A cook, smiling hugely, brought in a chipped enamel bowl of meat in a red sauce. We ate with our right hand, like the Arabs.

The tall, thin man began what was to be a daily litany of questions.

"In your area are there animals?"

I tried to explain about the kangaroo, ending up drawing it. Abebe began to laugh.

"In your area is France close to Australia?"

Most of them had been to either high school or technical college. Leilt had failed somewhere along the line and now was forced to live in her village about two miles away. Woldie had studied engineering for two years, Abebe the three years required to qualify as a health assistant.

The food, although the same type as we were offered in the hotel, was as different as fresh bread from stale. The cook returned with a battered tin, its edges ragged from the can opener and poured coffee into six tiny cups, adding a large pinch of salt to each.

"In your area is this the custom, salt in the coffee?" asked the thin man.

That afternoon we returned to our weighing and measuring. As the lines got shorter a crowd of women and children gathered in the square, each clutching a tiny piece of pink paper. These were the ones too fat to admit to the feeding tents yet not fat enough to send away without a ration. I asked Woldie about his stores. Was there enough to give them rations? His face clouded.

"We are not allowed," he stumbled.

"Not allowed what?" Janet asked.

"Not allowed."

Woldie looked very unhappy, scuffing the new shoes he had

put on for our arrival. I went in search of Abebe and Leilt. Abebe looked embarrassed, and to hide it began fiddling with his sterilizer. Leilt glanced at him quickly and then said, "The officials have told us not to open the stores without their permission."

"When did they tell you that?"

"Last week."

It meant that we would have to go on feeding all the people with pink cards in the tents, although they should be sent home on a ration to come back in a month. At least three-quarters of them could have been dealt with in this way.

The last feeding of the day was coming to a close and Abebe had almost finished his clinic. At the last moment, just as we were loading the car, four figures appeared at the top of the hill carrying a litter between them.

There is something about the way stretcher-bearers walk that tells you if the case is serious. As they got nearer and before a gust of wind brought the sweet smell of gangrene to us, I knew whoever was on that litter had not long to live. They stopped near the truck and set the stretcher gently on the ground. One of the carriers, an old man, came forward on legs so thin it seemed impossible that he could have even lifted the stretcher let alone carried it. He began a long explanation in Wollaitinia. It was his daughter on the stretcher. Ten days ago, because she had not conceived after a year of marriage and her husband was angry, she had gone to the local sorcerer, the *tanquay*, for an injection. After the injection she had become very sick. He stopped speaking, turned, and went back to his corner of the litter. Abebe beckoned them to bring her in.

Inside the clinic Abebe turned her over. The village conjurer's unwashed syringe, probably one he had found in the hospital's refuse, had caused an abscess that had penetrated through to the rectum. Now the entire right buttock was a mass of black soggy flesh, covered in flies. Mercifully she was unconscious, her pulse rapid and thready from shock of the millions of virulent bacteria swarming in her blood.

Abebe said something in Wollaitinia to the old man. He shook his head vigorously. Abebe turned to me. "She should go to the hospital, I have told this old man but he says no. He says she has no papers."

"What papers?"

"If you want to go to the hospital, you must have a paper from the local Farmers' Association, it could take many days."

Leilt asked the old man if he could get them today, but he shook his head, sighed, and squatted resignedly against the wall.

We took her with us anyhow; there was no alternative. Woldie volunteered to come and vanished for a few minutes to reappear in a pair of trousers and red shirt that I suspected he had got from the Red Cross store. He saw me looking at it and smiled, pulling down the collar for me to read the label: BARNEYS NEW YORK.

It was a difficult journey back to Sodo. The Toyota was not specially adapted to carry a stretcher and the woman had to be laid on her face along the narrow bench seat. Every time we hit a bump she gave a delirious moan. Just outside the town, half hidden by the dust from passing trucks, we found Mr. Mole trudging up the steep flinty hill. He had had a flat and the spare tire was missing. Brit and Amsalu had gone off in the other direction hoping to pick up a lift to Addis. We took him with us to the hospital.

As on the first day we visited it, the outpatient ward was deserted. Leaving the porters to maneuver the patient onto the hospital stretcher, I went to cadge a bottle of methylated spirit from the pharmacy for cleaning our instruments.

When I got back, a fat man in a double-breasted suit, who, Woldie told me afterwards, was the administrator, was shouting at both of them and pointing to the stretcher. In pantomime he held out a chubby hand, rubbing finger and thumb together. Noticing me, he shouted in English, "You must take this woman out of here. It is against the regulations!"

"What regulations?" I looked at Mole. He stood there,

silent, and almost immobile, like a lizard on a wall. The woman groaned slightly and shifted position. The wound smelled horribly. "Tell him," I said, "that it is an emergency and we cannot possibly take her back as she is. She will die."

The double-breasted suit shouted, "Why cannot you foreigners respect the regulations of the country you are in. You must obey the law, and the law is that without a certificate she cannot come in."

"We can pay for her, can't we?" Janet said.

We could have, but already it had gone beyond that. Regulations in many tyrannies are like the grass and sticks that conceal the mouth of a staked pit. Sometimes you can go around them, but they will not bear serious weight. "We will leave her here. We have no other choice."

At this, the Mole's small face gave a slight squint of fear.

"If you do," said double-breasted, "she will be put into the street!" But the fat man hesitated, betraying a bluff. We left him gripping one side of the stretcher with a pudgy hand, shouting down the corridor at our backs. Outside some well-dressed boys from the school tried to cadge lifts.

As we bumped out of the yard, our official said suddenly, "This is a very bad country. I was once before the revolution a diplomat." It was such an astounding revelation I nearly drove off the road.

"In Rome, I was an attaché. I traveled all over Europe— Paris, London, Amsterdam—paying the students' fees." He sighed. "I had my own car then. It was so good, riding on those motorways. Such good roads." As though in agreement the car gave a terrific lurch over a pothole. "After the revolution I came home, I was called back . . . some stayed . . . some of them in London." His face, now sad, frowned at the thought of those bedsits, a lifetime of Belling cookers in Kentish town.

"What happened then?"

"I worked for the civil service in Addis Ababa. We had a big plan . . . you know these foolish men now in power. They wanted everybody to have unemployment pay, just like in the

West." He looked over his shoulder, but Woldie, his English exhausted, was staring out of the window. He went on, "But there was no money. Oh, the big speeches, Doctor... the ministers... and the terrible paperwork, each man contradicting the signature of the next." He paused, then added inconsequentially, "I have a wife and two daughters." You could feel the regret around the word "daughters." I suddenly thought of him in a little house in Addis, in carpet slippers, being nagged by a fat wife and two enormous daughters.

He stopped speaking and looked out at the rain which had begun to fall again, mocking the drought. We ploughed down the high street and pulled up at the Dante. The official got out of the truck, collected some papers, and vanished. It was as if I had, for the briefest of periods, been given a glimpse of a whole life, a life given away, and yet preserved in memory, the way a man might show you a prized collection of old stamps in a dusty attic and then throw you into the street, locking the door.

With Brit and Amsalu gone a routine developed, the day starting with fried eggs, stale bread, and the company of five women at the breakfast table. The nurses, experienced and expert in what they were doing, worked hard. The problem was to keep them supplied with food for the camps and to get them there each day. Each morning we sat on the concrete steps of the Dante waiting for the officials to arrive with Captain and the other truck. Each morning a complicated wrangle would start over who was going where. The officials always wanted a truck to remain in town, we wanted both for the camps.

Slowly, but then gathering momentum, a new battle began with the little men in suits. Somebody had told them what the Irish girls had said about feeding the people in their villages. That camps were dangerous places, difficult to keep clean, and while they wasted their time in them, the peasants neglected their land, especially now just after the rains when they should be sowing the autumn crops of teff and maize.

At first they appeared not to understand what we wanted,

and did nothing. One official even gave us some extra food as an experiment. But when they saw how closing the camps would outflank their empire, their opposition was relentless. Double padlocks appeared on the door at Habicha, and Salomon the storekeeper became impossible to find most mornings. The token supplies of food that had been sent to the camp warehouses like decoys now became a trickle, barely sufficient for the day-to-day feeding.

As if to mock us, it was soon after this that the government grain convoys began to arrive. We passed the first of them one morning as we drove to work: twenty Viberti trucks, lining up outside the central government stores in Sodo. They were to arrive every day after that in increasing numbers, traveling with special permits through the curfew hours to come grinding and slipping each morning down the hill outside our hotel. When they had emptied their great piles of sacks into the sheds, one truck would be hoisted on to the back of another and like two monstrous tortoises they would set off back for the capital. In the two months we were there, the convoys never ceased. The grain remained in the government warehouses. What the RRC did with it, how they intended to distribute it, we never were able to find out. Secrecy was a hallmark of all their operations.

The RRC also had a fleet of tankers based in Sodo for the purpose of supplying all the camps who needed it with water. But one morning we woke to find the whole fleet locked up in the car park of the hotel, their crews sent away to Shashemene to take part in the tenth anniversary celebration of the revolution. When we complained to one of the officials, he shook his head. He had heard a rumor that the RRC clerks had forgotten to pay the water-tanker drivers' wages, and they had gone to Shashemene to demand their money. It might be several weeks before the service was started again. This was the sort of thing, he said, which made the task almost impossible.

Only Habicha had water, the other three would have to be

supplied some other way. Every camp originally had three rubber bags looking rather like huge blue lilos that, filled, contained enough water for about three days' cooking. Now only four in all remained: one in the back of my truck, one in Chefisa, one in Bugu, and one in Aro Giorgis. We needed more, but the assistants had repeated the same story that an official had told me about the hyenas. I learned then how easy our life was in the Dante compared with theirs. In each camp they lived in a huge mud-built tucul, a combined dormitory, kitchen, and living room—dark and cool in the day, badly lit and smoky at night. The compounds, though empty at night, still stank of stale food, death, disease, and filthy rags, a smell that brought packs of hyenas and jackals foraging. Later, as the weeks had passed the problem got worse. Hyenas do well during a famine and it was as if a parallel camp of them had established itself around each feeding center: each animal sleeping in a deep hole during the day, scrambling out at night to raid the empty tents and forage in the graveyards.

After dusk the huts were under siege, the compounds filled with the gray hunched shapes, red eyes flickering in the dim light, the smell of their breath like rotting corpses. It took a few days for the assistants to realize that the holes appearing in the rubber bags were due to the hyenas, and by the time the snail-like administration had produced sufficient fencing to protect them half were destroyed.

Pietro had told me that the main monastery in Dolla had a deep well that pumped up water twice a day. It was an uncomfortable, rather paralyzing feeling that a multimillion-dollar organization like the Red Cross was forced, rather like the Ethiopian government, to seek help from the missionaries for almost everything that mattered. Why were we not provided with up-to-date technology? As it stood, the present situation could be compared to using horsedrawn fire engines at a jumbo-jet crash.

Tomorrow was Revolution Day. Most of the Ethiopian assistants would be compelled to attend Party rallies in their *kebelis*, the local cooperatives that foreshadowed Mengistu's plans for massive collective farms. It would mean that most of the feeding stations would be closed. There would be a few deaths. I would try and make up for them by negotiating with the monks for water to supply the camps. But when we got up it was to find that sometime during the night the hotel gates, normally never closed, had been dragged shut, ripping up the grass that had grown along their bases over the years, a new and expensive brass padlock fastened to the lock. The hotel too was shut, metal grilles pulled down over its front and rear entrances. The staff, all the Ethiopian guests, even the cleaners who lived in the small hut in one corner and supplemented their income by prostitution, had gone. The normal roar of Oramo music from two battered speakers in the shop across the road was silenced, and, in its place, howling with feedback, voices harangued a distant crowd in the market square. We were to be imprisoned for the festival, for how long was anybody's guess, perhaps for hours, perhaps days. I sat on the veranda and wondered how much the officials had to do with this, what it was that they had said to the Slave of Jesus.

The others began to emerge, surprised to see us still in the hotel. Tula produced a box of oat cakes, Prudence some tea, and Yushi, vanishing into her room, returned with some foil-covered sticks about nine inches long containing Japanese seaweed. Janet began to boil some water, and Inge produced a large tin of mackerel. The seaweed had the same strange taste as Yushi's sweets, of dust and sugar.

After breakfast we loafed about. Tula read, I struggled with an interim report to headquarters in Geneva. Janet cut Inge's hair, laughing over imaginary lice. Prudence attacked the replies to her large mail. Mainly, she said, from old ladies and previous colleagues in relief work. Yushi sat on the steps, a small notebook in hand and began to fill it with columns of small, exquisitely precise Japanese characters.

Incontinently I attacked the last precious ration of Evelyn Waugh's *Sword of Honour*. After that, all I had was an omnibus edition of Sherlock Holmes and a tattered copy of *Right-Ho,*

Jeeves. An unusual, solitary vulture watched me as I dipped into the world of Guy Crouchback and his descent from idealism to despair.

Abruptly, at noon, somebody began to hammer on the rusty black plates of the gates. There was a movement in the grass and a dwarf cleaner appeared, key in his hand. He must have been crouching there all morning watching us like a Dyak. He unlocked the padlock and swung the gate open to reveal Red Eyes, blinking in the dust. Behind him streams of serious-faced men in rough Sunday suits were heading up the hill away from the market.

The Party had summoned them all to Sodo for the celebration of a revolution that had turned the wheel full instead of half a circle. The throne of Sheba remained, the peasants remained, and, as for centuries past, at Mescal, the holiest of the Coptic Church festivals, the King still summoned the peasants to the public squares to do him homage. They had been told that the new king was not a king, but a man like themselves, yet like the old kings he still took their tithes, their sons, and their taxes, sat down with the foreigners who owned him, and listened to the men with words and papers who had always oppressed them. And the church remained, less powerful now, but still there, its altars half concealed, waiting in the cedar groves.

Red Eyes offered no explanation for our being locked in. In some ways, if he had, it would have been insulting, for we were beginning to become friends. Two nights before he had even refused to evict two of us from our rooms for a Party official from Addis. Both he and the small manager were to keep their new suits of cheap stiff cloth on for the rest of a rather shamefaced day. Giorgis slopped in with eggs and 'tibbs. Gradually the bar filled with officials back from the celebration who looked and sounded as if it were the end of a normal working day. There was, after all, nothing to celebrate.

About two, I took the Landcruiser and set out for the mission. With my Red Cross passport the worst that could happen to me was that I would be stopped and sent back. But within hours the unloved festival had been buried, the crowds, the speeches, and soldiers had vanished. The police waved me through at the barrier and within an hour I was at Bugu.

The mission stood on the top of a hill overlooking a flat valley on the other side of which, twenty miles away, was Sodo. The monastery was built in the style of a Tuscany farmhouse. Opposite it, across a lawn, stood a shed full of Viberti tractors. Next to the farmhouse a flowering blue jacaranda overhung a garden full of vegetables and flowers. Near the entrance to the compound was a long avenue of trees at the end of which stood a windowless clapboard church built on wooden piers. Many of the piers had been eaten away by termites, giving the church an uneven humped appearance like a serpent.

Behind it stood an unfinished stone church, mounted on a concrete plinth, wooden scaffolding and ropes still draped around its walls. I drove up to the old church and stopped, switching off the engine. From inside a Mass, proceeding to the sound of a brass bell, was being sung by an Italian tenor accompanied by an African choir. A slight smell of incense drifted into the cab, mixing with the hot diesel fumes.

I got out and walked around to the south door. In the dark interior the only light was from altar candles and the thin shafts of sunlight that streamed through the cracks in the wooden walls. The nave, stalls, transept, and aisles were crammed with supplicants, all clad in white, shroudlike, cotton chammas, kneeling or crouching on the floor of red earth. It was difficult to see how any more, even if they had wanted to, could have been crammed in. A European priest, arms outstretched, was reading from a missal in Wollaitinia. Above me, in a niche over the door, a wooden Virgin held out a child, the clothes the artist had painted on it peeling off from years of sun and rain. It was a place I could not enter. I was too rich and, as the Arabs say, too far from God.

I walked over to the farmhouse and pulled on the wire bell

handle. The tractors in their shed across the square looked as if they worked, which if they did would make them almost unique in Ethiopia. All tractors had been "inherited" by the state ten years ago at the revolution, and in the years since they had, bit by bit, fallen apart, and could be seen rusting quietly in fields, by the sides of roads, or half buried in collapsing garages.

The light brown shutters above me swung open and a face, half hidden by a pair of Mr. Owl spectacles and a beard as straight and stiff as a yard broom, thrust itself out. "I come," it said in stage-Italian English.

Father Pacificus was about forty-five, wearing jeans and an open-neck shirt. The only concession to his calling was a small crucifix on a silver chain about his neck. He had been in Ethiopia for sixteen years. His glasses, like Sister Prudence's, hugely enlarged his eyes, so that when he took them off to polish them, which he did frequently, his whole expression changed to one of narrow-eyed shrewdness. The Franciscans have a rule of hospitality that must be even harder to observe than that of chastity. Everybody is welcome and made to feel that what he is given is his right in charity. It is ruthlessly disarming and worrying, making you wonder if the extraordinary solicitude you are shown is to make up for what you are missing by not being religious; as though drink, cigarettes, food, and even a bed for the night, are mere consolation prizes for the real thing.

I stepped into an interior smelling of pasta and Italian spices. Pacificus led me up a flight of marble stairs to a sitting room filled with cheap wooden furniture. A bookcase near the window contained rows of motor-racing magazines in Italian.

"You will eat lunch with us, dottore?"

I could smell the lunch—lasagne and spiced chicken. It was painful even to go through the ritual of polite refusal in case he took me at my word. A sixteen-year-old maid brought coffee, a bottle of Ethiopian wine, and a plate of broken biscuits. We talked about Italy, England, and my brother's house in Tuscany, and then about the water supply for the camp. The priest rose and beckoned me to the window. Across the grass square was a tower on the top of which had been hoisted the tank of a Viberti water-carrying truck. Now, painted a deep green, it received water from a bore one hundred feet below the monastery. Pumped up twice a day it was sufficient for the farm, the house, and the building of the new cathedral.

Father Pacificus took me to the kitchen. In one corner was a water purifier. He took out one of the filters. It was absolutely clean. "This filter," he said, "we put in one year ago, we never change him." A lot of Ethiopia, he explained, lay over huge subterranean lakes. Yet in Sodo our water failed almost every other day, and when it did run, smelled of sewage.

The dining room next door began to fill with voices. Pacificus took me to wash my hands at the end of the corridor, told me not to be long, and left me. The toilet was spotless, with an unblocked pan, a clean washbasin, fresh towels, and a scrubbed tiled floor.

There was a barely perceptible pause as I entered the dining room, then the meal resumed over murmured greetings and half-hearted handshakes. I took a chair next to a gaunt-looking man with a day's growth of beard who introduced himself as Father Dominicus. Opposite sat a small, heavyset man of about forty, the Father Superior, Giovanni. At the other end of the table sat a tall man, not a priest, in an open-necked shirt. He wore round horn-rimmed glasses and spoke English with a German-American accent. His name was Klaus.

Giovanni smiled, then continued his conversation with a tall blond woman of about twenty-eight sitting on his right. As she listened to him her long, pale fingers crumbled bread onto the table by the side of a half-filled soup bowl. An expression of defensive arrogance lit up her narrow, sensual features.

Her eyes suddenly fastened on my Red Cross badge.

"God!" she said, "why are you wearing that thing?"

The Superior intervened. "You have met Dottore Françoise, dottore?" He half closed his lids as he spoke, an Italian mannerism that signals embarrassment.

I had not, but I had heard about Dr. Françoise. For the past year she had been in charge of the relief operation in the south, employed under contract to the RRC from a French agency. She had a reputation for toughness and determination. She was not popular with the officials. It was rumored that her predecessor, an East German doctor, was now doing five years in Leipzig prison after the Ethiopian Communist Party had denounced him to East Berlin for trying to escape from Ethiopia to the West.

She tossed her long hair over a narrow shoulder and offered me her hand, grinning slightly at my embarrassment. Giovanni said, with more than a hint of apology in his voice, "Don't let her start arguments with you. She loves arguments."

Chance, or an unconscious irony on the part of the Fathers, had placed her just below a fading photograph on the wall of the order's founder. It showed a man with a narrow ascetic face, eyes ringed by cheap circular glasses, long, thin hands wrung together in front of his soutane. It could have been her father.

Somebody nudged my arm. On my left an Irish-American nun proffered a bowl of chicken. She had a face that you might see shopping in any American small town, except that age and Africa had taken their toll, and the air of optimistic confidence she must have started with had slipped slightly, revealing a tired, sad expression of bewildered disappointment.

She was from Iowa, a place I remembered for flat plains, grain silos, wheat dust, and wooden frame buildings. She was nursing in Bali twenty miles away, deep in the Rift. Directly opposite, an absurdly young-looking woman, very pretty, Hispanic American, and, disappointingly, also a nun, introduced herself as the camp's doctor. Both of them felt that the worst of the famine in Wollaita was over, and, like the Irish girls in Sodo, thought the time had come to distribute a monthly ration to the villages. Conditions, the American said, were just not the same as when they had arrived four months ago when they had found the entire population of the valley starving to death, too weak to climb the eight-thousand-foot road up to the plateau to look for help from the outside world. In the first week they had lost three hundred children. It seemed an inconceivable number, but in a few months, had I known it, such a figure would appear nothing, even a sign that we were succeeding. At the other end of the table a thin Irishman with unhappy blue eyes, his face all angles and wedges, listened to our conversation and nodded. He dandled a small baby, a replica of himself, on his knee, trying to feed it small cuttings of red spaghetti. The American nun explained he was the water engineer. The monks preferred divining for it but made use of him to design the surface installations.

Françoise suddenly said, "You have come too late for this, don't you think, always the same with the Red Cross, big show, the badges, the Red Crosses, but always too late." She began to twist a strand of hair with her long, pale fingers staring at a half-empty Coke bottle in front of her on the table. She went on.

"The problem is that the RRC is responsible for distributing the food to the villages, but they say they have not enough, which is not true, but I cannot get them to change their minds, and commissar refuses to see me."

The chisel-faced Irish boy said, from the shelter of his wife's approval, "For the last week, all I have seen is truck after truck of grain, now will anybody tell me what they are doing with it? Certainly I haven't seen a red cent's worth in the villages." He pronounced worth "wort."

His wife, hugely pregnant, nodded, admiring what were probably her opinions rather than his. I wondered what sort of a woman would risk her life with a pregnancy in Ethiopia, where individuals are worthless coin. Françoise began to twist her hair again.

I toyed with a fork and began to wonder which of us was the police Judas, one of the priests, the maid clearing away the cutlery, somebody just outside the window? The secret police would make it their business to know every word spoken at that meal, for the sunlit room with its long table filled with food stood at the epicenter of a famine. What was being talked about could only bring trouble.

The tall man with round horn-rimmed glasses looked up from a forkful of spaghetti and said, "The peasants are being murdered, just as we did in Poland and Russia." The conversation died instantly.

The Irishman's wife began to fold her napkin with extreme care. Giovanni, filled with Italian embarrassment, said, "Klaus . . . this is really enough, I have told you before not to say such things. . . . We will talk about something else."

He looked round at his fellow priests who had become vacant-faced and self-absorbed, as if they were about to be forced to sit and listen to a filthy story.

Klause smiled slightly at their Italian discomfort.

He looked around. Nobody stirred.

"It is exactly the same as in the Ukraine, forty years ago, a manufactured famine, something artificial. Khruschev, Stalin's henchman, with his fat little piggy face did it, locked twenty-five million peasants out of their granaries in punishment for their opposition to collective farming, five million died."

He went on, speaking with an easy cynical voice, explaining how the government faced severe opposition in the north, some of it armed, to their collectivization plans.

Françoise sniffed. "You can't say the farmers' cooperatives are a bad idea."

"They aren't, but things will not end there."

They began to argue pointlessly.

I toyed with my chicken and thought about the peasants.

The feudal system had left them with traditional tenure, however fragile, and after the fall of the old emperor, the Communists had ratified their rights to what little land each of them had. In doing so they created a kulak class, the seeds of a new bourgeoisie.

But I was sure this was, as in Russia in the 1930s, merely a device to gain time and consolidate their hold upon the country. Deep in their councils the Party dreamed of the collective millennium, and the peasants of Ethiopia, like Stalin's before them, would be the perfect material upon which to experiment. It would make Ethiopia the jewel in her socialist empire, one huge state-controlled enterprise that would be the envy of Africa.

It explained the resistance. To the peasant land is life itself, and government the thief which steals it. To be herded into huge collectives and forced to work for the dreams of Party theorists would be worse than death. That is why there was war in the north. The provinces of Tigre and Eritrea were largely lost to the central government who, like the Americans in Vietnam, controlled the countryside only in daylight. To the east, the Afars, nomads living in the hottest desert in the world, the Danekil, had fought for ten years against Mengistu, ambushed his convoys with ancient rifles, killing his tax gatherers and sneaking into the provincial towns that ring the desert to rob his banks.

I wondered about the huge grain stockpiles in Sodo. Was Addis preparing for a future famine, was it sheer miscalculation, a bureaucratic overrun, or were they deliberately moving grain to the south? With it the government could force the rebellious peasants in the north to accept resettlement on the collective farms in the south. If not they could die. It would put an end to the resistance movements which, so far, despite the bombing of their settlements, the dynamiting of their wells and the execution of their leaders, still threatened not only the regime in Addis but the Soviet bases along the Red Sea Coast. If the rebels could be starved out of the north,

Moscow would get the depopulated zone around its bases paid for almost entirely by Western food aid.

"Some wine, dottore?" Giovanni pushed a bottle toward me, interrupting my thoughts.

I chose some Coke, and three Ethiopian girls came in to clear away the plates. Giovanni said something to them in Amharic. Although he was laughing, his face was taut. The Irishman began to say something about the famine but this time Giovanni stopped him in his tracks. "This is enough. On this subject I hear no more. . . ." Françoise smiled slightly at her Coke bottle. "And nothing from you, Françoise, either."

"Then we talk about God, Father."

"No, you tell me you don't believe Him, so we will not talk of that." Instead he began to talk about his first months in Ethiopia, how he had arrived on a Saturday a confused young man just out of a seminary in Tuscany. His superior met him at the bus station. As they drove through the frightening poverty of Sodo, a place that was to be his life, and where he would in all probability be buried, he was told that he would be expected to preach the sermon in Amharic at the next day's benediction and, when he had found his feet, which should take only a couple of weeks, at the high Mass. The superior added that he would also be expected within three months to have a working knowledge of Wollaitinia. Father Giovanni smiled at us and shrugged his shoulders. It could only be compared, he said, to a cyclist being asked to take the wheel of a Maserati. He caressed the word Maserati as if he was stroking a woman's arm. Because of his accent, the congregation had not been able to make out a word during his sermon. But after a while he became aware of odd disturbances in the sea of faces, of movements at the back, then sudden, isolated shouts of laughter. A man just in front of him left his seat hurriedly and almost ran, crouching with laughter, for the door. Amharic is a language of double meanings, of insults thickly disguised as compliments, where even a word for a table can have three interpretations, two of them nasty. He never found out what it was that he had said, but his parishioners still laughed at the memory of that sermon.

The tension in the room broke leaving only Françoise picking slightly at one of her teeth. She shrugged.

Giovanni carefully put his napkin in its silver ring, smiled slightly and said, "I think at this time we should have some coffee next door." We rose. Through the scraping of chairs I heard Françoise say to one of the nuns, "I am arranging a meeting of all the nongovernmental agencies in two weeks in Sodo. You will come, please."

Outside the door a tall, anxious-looking Ethiopian of about thirty stood waiting. He was not a peasant; his hard Arabic features were too blunted by good food, his skin softened by a life spent in offices rather than in fields.

As Françoise came out he started forward, saying something to her in Amharic. "No!" she said in English. "I will not."

He followed her into the room with the motorcycle magazines where coffee was laid, leaning slightly forward to repeat himself.

She flung herself into a seat, picked up a cup of coffee, and ignored him. The man stood there looking down at her and said in English, "But I have no money!" It seemed an act of desperation to confront her here, but his eyes flickered sideways at intervals, searching for effect. "I will not borrow you money!" Françoise said. She turned and said something in Spanish to the nun doctor. The man stood irresolute, then turned and walked out. Pacificus's face had hardened. "He is not a good boy, that Petrus, not a good boy. You know, Françoise, you should not provoke such people, they have much power. Even I think he was listening to our conversation outside the door."

"It is the second time he has tried to have money in advance on his salary."

The nun doctor asked if he worked for her.

"Forced on me by the RRC, a sort of half policeman." She picked up her coffee, shook her hair slightly, and lifted the cup to drink. Her hand was absolutely steady.

The man called Klaus had vanished.

I looked at my watch, feeling guilty at leaving the others at work. Seeing the gesture, Pacificus rose and offered to take me across to the pump house.

We arranged that I could take water twice a day, bringing the Landcruiser at times when the monastery was quiet, the priests at prayer, and their need for water on the farms and housing at a minimum. If I did not come the Captain would.

On my way back to the camp I thought at lot about Françoise. Her lack of tact and her singlemindedness were admirable qualities to me, but anathema in Aidgame. She had passed the stage of cultural cringing, a sort of panic aquiescence to even the most extreme inversion of values, providing it came from an "authentic" Third World source. Everybody becomes a victim of cultural cringe in Africa, but a few manage to cure themselves, learning to see the reality rather than a world peopled almost entirely by characters from a Tom Wolfe lampoon.

I saw her only twice more, at a meeting in Sodo and once briefly on the road, bumping past me in her green station wagon with the black fir tree on the doors. We stopped and talked a few moments, away from the stage atmosphere of the mission, about neutral easy things: the road, the car, the rains. After a year working against such tremendous odds her face was drawn. But the closed bitterness that I had seen on her face at the mission had vanished in the open air.

Later I heard bits and pieces of her story, but most of them I recognized as the charitable constructions of the nuns, seeking to put an innocent face on her outspokenness. It was said that her father was titled, a count, and that Françoise's youthful idealism found this intolerable.

What reasons brought her to Ethiopia could only be guessed at. She had originally asked the League of the Red Cross to take her on, but they had refused, probably not for any personal reason. Contrary to a popular idea, they recruit few European doctors for their overseas teams. Instead she joined a French aid organization who sent her to Ethiopia at the request of the RRC. They could find no Ethiopian doctor willing to undertake the arduous field work involved.

She arrived to find the local RRC officials too terrified to even discuss the rumors of a famine in the middle of one of the government's showpiece agricultural areas. There was enough land, there could be enough food, but fear and doctrine leaned against the granary doors. Françoise forced their hand, hounding them with threats of publicity in the West, figures of mounting death rates, and just her intimidating presence. In the end they became more frightened of her than their political masters. It must have been a frustrating time for her, and one that she must have quickly realized would only make her hated by the officials. She had spent weeks in the bush, sleeping in the back of her wagon, setting up camps, organizing the local communes, nagging the RRC into supplying water and grain to the starving peasants. Much as they disliked her, the Ethiopians had chosen well when they chose Françoise. She had that quality of toughness that brought success to the early explorers of Africa, an enduring wandlike resilience of both body and spirit.

9

ZEALOT

WHEN I GOT BACK TO THE HOTEL that evening, it was to find we had visitors. Svensen, two Japanese newspapermen, and Reinhardt, a young German boy of twenty.

The newspapermen were in their rooms, recovering from an accident with the car near Shashemene. Their driver, approaching a crossroads down a hill and seeing another car edging out from a side road accelerated at it, lost control, rolled over three times, and landed the right way up in a heap of gravel. I did not have to be told that everybody climbed out of the wreck unhurt. Punishment for stupidity and carelessness is reserved for the innocent in Africa.

Reinhardt was in Ethiopia with the youth volunteer program, a scheme that attempted to bring the young people of rich countries into contact with the those of poor ones. The idea was to link them together on projects: adult literacy classes, teaching mothercraft to teenagers, simple English lessons, basic mechanics, small rural development such as clearing wells, planting trees, growing bees. Perhaps, because they had the highest rates of social security pay and therefore could afford six months off work, the volunteers were nearly always from Northern Europe.

151

In one of the most expensive restaurants in Addis I had listened to a volunteer, a tall blonde with bad acne, explaining women's oppression in Sweden to an Ethiopian student. It takes a long time to get such ideas over to somebody living in a genuine dictatorship, but it can be done. The Ethiopian sat there, listening, hands cupped under his chin, fascinated by the sight of her expensive American cigarettes and the half bottle of German lager she was drinking.

It was obvious as we shook hands that Reinhardt regarded us as if we were low relatives who had gate-crashed a party full of celebrities. He said to me in badly fractured English, "I think I must spend as much time as possible with the local people."

And so it was. None of us was to see much of him for the next week. At breakfast time he would avoid us, sitting at another table among the truck drivers as they shoveled down great grunting mouthfuls of stale injera and rancid meat. After a while, embarrassed by his presence, they stopped coming, so that our only companion was a police spy in a neat suit who sat spinning out his bread and coffee on the far table.

Reinhardt saw us as villains. But Africa's villains are no longer exclusively white, male, or rich, nor its heroes invariably poor and black. They lay beyond such a division, in a dreadful world full of mistakes, uncertainty, and death. Reinhardt would not have long to wait before he was to discover this for himself.

Svensen spent most of that first evening closeted with two of the officials trying, I assumed, to translate into modern Swedish liberal idiom the duplicitous language of fourteenth-century Europe. He came from a world rich enough to afford a degree of truth and justice. In Ethiopia either virtue can prove fatal. Such a misunderstanding is a common feature of the Aidgame, whose players seek affection from people who often see them only as prey.

The two Japanese newspapermen made their first appearance at breakfast the next morning, both wearing expressions of carefully assumed sadness like rented suits at a funeral. One was fat, had a bad skin, greasy uncombed hair, and an air of sleepy resentment as if everything, including the effort of taking his seat, was forced on him by circumstances. While his companion, about half his size with an alert apprehensive face, a neat safari suit, and a large camera, jerked into his place with a single nervous twitch.

Once seated the fat one leaned across the table, offering me a handful of clumsy fingers. The agile one sprung to his feet, stepped back four paces, and to the whine of his camera motor took ten pictures. I picked up my fork. There was another flash. Somewhere in a Tokyo newspaper archives are about a hundred photographs of me eating an omelette.

In the far corner, watched by an apprehensive cook peering through the serving hatch, two more Orientals were burying their heads in bowls of saffron-colored rice. They were slightly different from the two on our table, their clothes poorer, faces more skull-like, and their hair, unlike the two in front of me, stuck out as if they had been victims of a failed electrocution.

Inge muttered to me out of the corner of her mouth that, worn out by the constant photography, Yushi had locked herself in her room. The fat man looked up sharply and a slight atmosphere descended on the table. I asked him about the other two Japanese in the corner: were they cameramen? Ladling a mouthful of egg into a fat mouth, he shrugged. They were Koreans, nothing to do with them. It could have been a coincidence, or it could be the nearest thing to Japanese speakers the police could find. The police spy got up and left, dodging out through the back door so as not to be seen deserting his post by the officials who from their vantage point in the café across the road could see all comings and goings.

Svensen joined us a few minutes later. The journalists began to ask him about a car to take them about the camps. He gave a slight laugh and said there might be difficulties. There was a pause. Then the fat Japanese journalist rose slowly from his chair and began to shout. His paper, he yelled, had donated ten thousand U.S. dollars to the Red Cross. It was not good; they would take the money elsewhere. His companion took a couple of photos as if to emphasize the point.

Svensen explained that because the Mercedes they had come down in was a write-off, they were short of cars. There was another blue flash. Ten thousand dollars, repeated the Japanese with a menacing hiss. Another flash. The two Koreans looked up sharply at the mention of dollars, then bent to their saffron piles again. Svensen remained calm, explaining that if they had no cars they had no cars, but that they could be squeezed into one of the ambulances instead.

The fat man stopped shouting, wiped his forehead with a large handkerchief and began to hiss slightly. The little man cracked open his camera and laid a roll of film on the table like a chicken laying an egg. The thin one said something in Japanese, the two rose, bowed, and left the restaurant.

Svensen turned to me. Perhaps, he apologized, it was the shock, the effect of the accident yesterday that made the fat one so rude. Suddenly he said to me, "You know, this is one of the reasons why you should have a driver."

For a moment I was speechless, first with rage, then with admiration. It was the most stunning inversion of reality that I had ever heard. A man who had stepped out of a near-fatal accident was now urging his subordinate to hire a driver so as to increase the risk to himself. It seemed barely credible. But as I looked across the table at the smiling, slightly nervous face, I knew he was serious. In a way I didn't want to ask him his reasons, they could only spoil it.

It was, he said, grasping at a straw, the insurance. The officials were worried about the insurance and, he dropped his voice a register, my driving. It seemed that already I had almost wrecked the engine, so it would be better if I had a driver. I tried to explain into his patient face that they only wanted the car so that they would have complete control of my comings and goings and thus control the program. But it was impossible.

I changed the subject, asking him about the food distribution. He became very uneasy.

I wondered if he grasped it at first. His face wore a vague agreeable smile, but his eyes were unfocused, his thoughts elsewhere. Now and again some word, some gesture, would momentarily catch his attention before he sank again in his own private thoughts. I began to feel like some distant, badly tuned radio station broadcasting strident fractured messages in a half-understood language. The bland smile accused me of at the best a silly enthusiasm, at the worst a dangerous monomania.

At the end he suggested another meeting, ludicrous in a country of so many useless meetings. Besides, the hidden agenda of restricting the food to the villagers was by now obvious. I left him there in front of a small cup of coffee and went off to work.

Despite the arrangements for water with the monastery, there were still problems. Chefisa, the farthest camp, suffered most. Somehow the medical assistants could never bring themselves to organize a water crocodile if the Captain did not turn up with one of the big, blue water bags. They had seen Mr. Mole's defeat over the cans and perhaps they feared his revenge. Then a crowd would mill about the entrance shouting and arguing with the sabanyas who smacked at them with thin bamboo wands in reply. One morning I saw as I drove in two small heaps covered in flour sacks in the corner next to the registration desk. From each a pair of small feet protruded.

A few days after our arrival a boy of about nine leaped onto the runningboard of the car and said, "Pump water." He had a handsome, intelligent face, a large head, and a vocabulary of about one hundred English words. His name, Amiot, meant "Revolution." He had attached himself to Prudence as an unofficial interpreter to the children.

Prudence had delegated to him the organization of the water crocodile. Each morning he would gather about one hundred children together and wait for a specific order from her. Then he would lead the crocodile through the high grass to an old windmill two hundred yards away and, standing on the crumbling brick pump house, supervise the filling of the cans by two hundred excited, slightly trembling small hands.

One morning about midday villagers brought in a boy of about seven in extremis; twitching and mumbling, eyes gray and sunken from a combination of fever, dehydration, and delirium, signs that suggested typhoid. The health assistant at Gununu, a gray-haired old man with gentle manners and a sad thin smile translated a story of several other people in the same village dying with a similar sickness. If the patient survived the afternoon he could not be left, or the curfew and the hyenas would put paid to him. Amiot was left to watch the drip we had put up. Late in the afternoon, as the last feeding was taking place, the child's father returned with a sheet of an old school exercise book. It was stamped at the bottom with the local commissar's seal. Above it the thin-faced assistant filled in the details of the case in Amharic and gave it to me to take to the hospital.

We left at about four. There were six of us in the truck, along with Abraha, the driver: Prudence, Yushi, the boy, his father, me, and Amiot, who claimed he knew somebody in Sodo and wanted to visit him. He spoke of the town as if it were fabled, like Manhattan or Paris.

We had to go slowly, not only for the boy, who muttered and groaned over each bump, but because of the sliding red mud under our wheels. The father, a short thickset peasant, crouched by the side of his son who lay propped up along the narrow vinyl-covered bench, Prudence supporting his head, Yushi steadying his legs. Amiot sat, excited beyond measure, in front, clutching a small transparent plastic bag in which were two pencils and a broken ruler. We reached Bugu at five to find an anxious Tula waiting under the African chestnut.

The child, semiconscious, was desperately in need of more fluids. But his drip would not work in the car, and we had not enough time to take it out, put up an infusion, and still reach Sodo by dusk. I decided to risk feeding him by mouth. Abraha was sent off for some water. We waited. He returned, climbed back into the truck with a plastic cup and spoon and leaned over the boy. I went back to the driver's seat. The father groaned slightly. Outside the sky darkened with a promise of more rain. After five minutes, something, some noise or slight moment made me turn. Water mixed with froth was dribbling down the side of the boy's face, there was a movement of the jaw, halfway between a yawn and a bite, then the face relaxed. The father, half weeping, half chuckling with fear, leaned forward and began to plead with the inert face, cupping it in his hands, smoothing the eyes closed, and holding up the chin, but the only movement after that was water running through his fingers onto the floor.

It began to rain.

The six of us must have sat there for at least three minutes, listening to the sound of each other's breathing and the patter of the rain on the roof. Prudence, who had moved to the front with me, to make room for Tula, sat staring straight ahead, tears in her eyes. The father put both arms around his dead son's neck and began to whimper. Abraha opened the door, went over to the tucul, and brought back a length of bandage. The old man tied up the jaw, and when he had finished, abandoned himself on the floor, weeping. Above him the body lay still half propped-up, dead eyes staring directly at some Japanese lettering on a fire extinguisher fixed to the roof. Tula was crying softly in the back.

Making a mistake in medicine takes you through the same emotions as a murderer but without the fear of retribution. Horror, wild rationalization, futile attempts to put the blame, if only in your own mind, on others. Then, as the days go past, a sort of blunting takes place, sleep returns, and soon, unless some particular incident reminds you, the matter fades from immediate memory. The mistake becomes instead another tombstone in a small private graveyard of the mind, seldom visited but never quite forgotten. Time blurs the details on each headstone but never quite obliterates them.

"We should try and take him back to Chefisa," Prudence said.

The problem was the curfew. If we drove quickly, which was next to impossible, we might reach Chefisa in time for us to get back to Sodo before nightfall. And it was not only the curfew. It was dangerous to drive cross-country in the dark. Not only because of police if they found us out after curfew, but also because of guerrillas operating in small groups from across the Kenyan border. But we felt compelled to try, unwilling to abandon the old man and his son eight hours' walk from their village.

But the engine was not inclined to show us any compassion. Every fifteen minutes it smoked and banged angrily, then stopped. By six we reached halfway, stalled in a small clearing. On one side was a village school, its windows shuttered with packing-case lids, on the other three tuculs. A bed of marigolds grew at the door.

Abraha said, "We must not stop here. It can be very bad trouble with the police."

Some villagers approached, two men in white chammas and a woman carrying a child. Abraha got out and began talking to them. One of the men went away and came back with a key. The man could stay for the night in the empty schoolhouse with his son; in the morning they could send a message to his village for a stretcher party. The peasant, weeping, climbed down on thick legs from the back of the truck. Abraha and Yushi eased the body over the back. I had comforted myself up to now that the man probably had many children, so that the others would in time make up for the loss of this one. But in a few moments even that rationalization was ripped away.

As I caught the boy's feet, the old man pointed a stubby finger directly at the sky, gave a yell, holding his face up to the sky, shouted something at it in Wollaitinia.

Abraha translated. "He says, this was my only child. My wife is old! Why!" I knew the answer to that, or a bit of it.

We carried the body into a classroom that was already almost pitch-black and laid the body on a long table. Through the gloom some twenty desks, dimly made out, seemed to wait as if filled with ghosts expecting a lesson to begin. The old man squatted in the red dust by the table. He would wait there for twelve hours with the ruins of his son above him, cut off by the curfew and the hyenas from the other villagers. In Africa to have no male child is a tragedy, to have no children at all a catastrophe, for it is a life condemned to the knowledge of the extinction of your line. During the night the old peasant would know all this.

We left him there, climbed into our truck and began the slow jerking journey back to Sodo.

The following morning Svensen held a meeting. We sat around the long breakfast table, spooning Bulgarian jam onto slabs of dry bread and listened to him. It was not a meeting about the dead child—deaths lay outside his prerogative (besides what was one more among so many?)—but about cooperation.

It was not a brief meeting, but among all the verbiage it was possible to separate several strands, all of them incompatible. Svensen had been told to cooperate with the local administration and to make sure that we did. But for us that meant cooperating with the very people who had brought about the disaster in the first place, people whose sole aim appeared to be the preservation of the throne at the expense of the people. An aim they pursued without compassion, sentiment, or guilt. No state in Africa seemed free of this legacy of the Middle Ages. Yet Geneva still clung to the pious hope that education, investment, and example would improve the attitude of the rulers toward the ruled, even though the history of the whole continent's steady decline provided evidence quite to the contrary. It was not even a matter of a few steps backwards, a few steps forwards, providing a net gain. It was a relentless and purposeful descent into chaos. We were, although we did not know it at the time, on the edge of that chaos. But before we were plunged into it we were being treated to a ringside seat at its causation. Traveling in Ethiopia at the time was like examining a patient with the symptoms of a sinister disease that somehow came in an unfamiliar sequence. It was going to be some weeks before I realized exactly how fatal a prognosis the peasant farmers had. Yet all the clues were there.

The smallest unit in the district was the *kebeli*, loosely based on a village and its surrounding land and functioning as a farmers' association, a type of cooperative. Under it the peasants still had a modicum of land tenure, but gradually it was being eroded in favor of large farms with "mass" labor. Slowly but surely the simplest decisions would edge their way upwards, propelled by a craven fear of misinterpreting the Party line. In the end everything, even the number of chickens per household, would be decided by a central planning committee of Communist bourgeoisie in Addis. And this explained the fertile fields and the lack of food. There had been a drought for one year, but a year's drought is within the capacity of the peasant to survive. The paralysis came from another cause. A whole complex peasant economy developed over the centuries had been deliberately destroyed to make way for central planning. Everything was paralyzed. There was nothing to sell, nothing to buy, and nobody dared decide when to plant or when to reap. The only currency now was the grudging permissions issued on school exercise-book paper by the local subcommissar.

I stumbled on confirmation of this secret tragedy a week or two before I left Sodo. We visited a small village near Habicha. Unused green land lay all about it, yet starving children queued for West German flour and French biscuits. In mime I asked the villagers why they did not plant crops. Three of them looked pointedly at a Party poster in crude red and purple fading upon the worm-eaten door of what once was a village church. One of them began to laugh, then somebody said something in Wollaitinia, and the laughter spread. They were still laughing when we left.

The country was in the grip of a dogma that insisted on collectivization as an article of faith. To abandon it would be to surrender, and to surrender meant a reckoning. Not only with ferocious neighbors who, although in a similar or worse plight themselves, were quite willing, even longing, to go to war—but also with the relatives and friends of all those the regime had murdered, imprisoned, and enslaved over the last horrible ten years. Numbers that run into tens of thousands.

Eight years earlier Mengistu had begun to fear for his throne. Demands were being made for popular elections, a bicameral legislature along British lines, and an elected president. Abandoned by or abandoning his American allies he turned for help to a political doctor whose prescription has never varied, the Soviet Union. For the Moscow cure, the patient must become a convert to Communism, swallow a Soviet base or two, and accept obligatory military aid. The military aid is never the latest, always expensive, and quite often does not work. But in Ethiopia's case, excited perhaps by the prospect of controlling the entrance to the Red Sea and therefore putting a hand on the West's windpipe, the Suez Canal, they made one exception. They sent him a small unit of the East German Volkspolzei.

Unlike their military aid there was nothing secondhand or useless about the Volkspolizei. What the Russians were giving Mengistu was a secret-police force with one of the finest pedigrees in suppression in the world, with roots going back to the great imperialist Bismarck and reaching forward into the twentieth century to an apogee under Hitler. At the time of the Ethiopian terror in 1964, many senior Volkspolizei officers had in fact been serving members of the Gestapo. For, at the end of World War II, the capitulation of half of the Third Reich to the Russians had meant little more for them than adjusting a detail of uniform, swapping a swastika for a red star, before it was business as usual.

The inheritors of the tradition of Kristallnacht and the Final Solution advised Mengistu to hold a classic set piece terror that would kill off all those suspected of opposition and even those who could, if they wished, oppose the regime in the future.

Equally importantly, they told him to kill a leavening of completely innocent people, so that a yeast of fear would spread through the country. For as Stalin said, "If we only arrested the guilty, what would the innocent fear?"

But it was not just a matter of persecuting the innocent. The Volkspolizei explained to Mengistu that every terror must be tailored to suit its victims, otherwise the memory of it would too quickly pass. Not only individuals, but nations, always held something particularly sacred or dear, and if he wanted to be remembered he must add some special, uniquely Ethiopian, flavor to it.

So Mengistu searched his heart for the most terrible thing he could do to bring his people through fear to the truth of Marxism-Leninism, and he thought of burial. Ethiopians hold burial to be one of the most important rites in life. To lie unburied, to be forgotten in death, is so awful that even today, those who whisper to you their memories of the Terror, can hardly bring themselves to speak of this part of it. Before Mengistu only the cruelest of chances would let a man die alone, and even among strangers the dead were always accorded proper burial. Even in the north during the great hunger, every one who died was carefully laid out, washed, shrouded, and buried, even when those in the burial party could hardly stand for lack of food. So the little army major added his own twist. He ordered that the bodies of the slain should lie unburied like Creon's nephew and his generals on the plain of Thebes, and that anyone who attempted to defy his edict would themselves be slaughtered. One morning the people of Addis woke to streets filled with corpses and a sky dark with vultures. The Red Terror had started.

And he was remembered, and not only by Ethiopians. Five years later, on the other side of the world, I heard an Egyptian doctor who had lived in Addis during the Terror describe a nightmare journey to a United Nations cocktail party in the city. There were hardly any street lights then, and throughout the five miles their Mercedes weaved past the dark shapes of bodies lying in the broken rutted roads. But worse was to come. As they approached the center they saw that the lamp-posts were strung with corpses, not of men, but of young schoolboys who had tried and failed to rescue their fathers' and brothers' bodies for burial. And so it was a terror both peculiarly German and yet Ethiopian, a whole city turned into a tropical Lidice. Behind the little Negro with an expression of perpetual surprise on his face, stood the ghost of Heinrich Himmler.

When it was over, of the five thousand students at the University and Colleges of Addis Ababa, only fifteen hundred were still alive.

Mengistu did all this in the name of the collective. Now we sat in a hotel in Sodo and tried to reverse one small part of it. An elderly Swedish colonel, a nun, an English nurse, a girl from Denmark, a Finn, and a middle-aged doctor.

Not surprisingly the meeting achieved nothing, except a series of secret resolutions by each of us to go his own way. As one of the officials listened to us talking about the death of the child yesterday I saw his eyes narrow at our distress. To people from poor countries Europeans are surprisingly sentimental.

Svensen left soon after, in a new Volvo sent down from Addis with a driver. He shook hands with each of us in the yard next to a couple of aged goats waiting to be slaughtered for our evening meal and got into the driving seat, somehow forgetting his own advice about having a local driver.

The next day the RRC water trucks had vanished from in front of the hotel. Unbelievingly the drivers must have come back from Shashemene during curfew and driven them away. It smacked of Party authorization. It was rumored that they would return in a week. Nobody believed it, not even the men in suits. Now our only contact with the capital was the occasional telephone call, the line terrible and likely to be cut off. But in the official's office next door to the commissar's the telephones never stopped ringing. Brit called once late at night from Bati, in the north. Things there, she said, were very bad, with twenty or thirty people dying every day. But she thought it would improve. She promised to come down and see us sometime in the next six weeks.

I got in one evening to find Françoise in the restaurant, sitting with the nurses and making jokes about the Red Cross spending their time drinking. Tula hated it, and after a few moments got up, muttered something rude in rasping English, and vanished. Françoise watched her go with a malicious smile. I asked her what she was doing in Sodo. She had come in to see the commissar Slave of Jesus about a meeting of the nongovernmental organizations. She thought maybe in a week there would be some prospect of holding it, but she was not yet sure. But she refused to be drawn any further and changed the subject abruptly.

She had to spend the last month of her contract in Addis. Brit Ulman, she had heard, had a small flat in the suburbs which she kept going even when she was out of the capital. As Brit was going to be away from Addis for the next six weeks she wanted to find out if she could borrow the flat. The talk drifted to housing, flats that rented in Addis for over two thousand dollars a month, hotel rooms that cost over one hundred dollars a day. Françoise laughed. At the moment she was staying in something much more expensive just outside Sodo. Not that it cost her anything, but each house must have cost a fortune to build. She was going out that night, but if we had nothing better to do, we should take a look. Curious, the three of us drove over after dusk, past the warehouse then down a narrow unmade road that ran by the side of a small factory. Immediately behind it a country lane branched to the right.

Along the right hedge at intervals of a hundred meters were driveways, at the end of which stood a large well-built house. Ten in all, they were like the ordinary houses in Sodo in shape, a conical tucul as the central feature, with an occasional rectangular shed to one side. But there the similarity ended. These houses would not have looked out of place in the pages of a glossy architectural magazine.

Prudence knew some nuns in the last house. That evening over coffee, one of them told us the story of how the houses came to be built.

In 1976 the World Bank had financed a United Nations agricultural mission to Wollaita. The idea was to study the local patterns of the agriculture and then to recommend to the peasants through the kebelis some alternative crops that might improve their chronic poverty. It was a major effort. Teams flew in from New York, Lagos, and the Middle East, a block of offices was built in the town and the sign WADU, WALLAITA AGRICULTURAL DEVELOPMENT UNIT appeared everywhere. Soon building commenced outside the town. It took time, but after a year ten houses had gone up.

The houses, including the one we were sitting in, were large, made of stone or brick, and manufactured to Western European standards. The central feature was a circular thatched roof, something similar to a tucul. But the layout was much larger, and the simple practical lines of a native hut put up with only shelter in mind had given way to a romantic, almost Dadaist recall of a more primitive agricultural era. The unintended irony of the undertaking was that the primi tive past was not past at all, but alive and all around us from the desperate ruined crops in the fields and thin ragged children begging in the lanes, to the crowded unsanitary shacks in Sodo, most without windows, proper doors, or furniture worth the name. But if such a view was only a prejudice against an overflamboyant design, it was when the nun told us the price that any doubts I had had about this being an authentic United Nations project vanished. Each house cost over forty thousand U.S. dollars, the combined annual income of five thousand peasants.

Strangely, once the houses were built, the initial enthusiasm flagged. It was, the nun said, as if the agricultural mission had come face to face with the absolute limit of what they were prepared to do, a limit beyond which lay the unthinkable: actually working in the fields. And so, frightened by finding themselves right at the frontiers of an empire that centered in the smart cafés of the East Side near the United Nations building, and ended here overlooking fields full of medieval peasants, the Aidgamers lost heart, intrigued briefly, then left. The offices were converted into storage rooms for the papers they left behind, the huge workshop was locked and shuttered, its farm machinery left to rust quietly in the sun, and the street of ten houses, shunned by the peasants, began gradually to decay. Two years later the nuns, like bees finding a hollow tree, moved into one of them.

There was, however, a legacy, and it was the peasants who were the unfortunate inheritors. Before the bureaucrats flew out to Rome, London, New York, or Moscow, they stopped briefly in Addis. There they prepared their recommendations. The province of Wallaita, they decreed, should abandon its traditional dependence on bananas and sorghum, and instead plant false bananas, a type of root crop. There it would have ended, like most United Nations reports—once written, instantly forgotten.

But it did not end there. The report, instead of being quietly buried in some forgotten filing cabinet in Addis, was resurrected and insisted upon by the Party. They saw in it an endorsement, however slight, of the notion of collectivizing the province's peasant holdings.

The nun finished her explanation and smiled. Prudence looked uncomfortable. Attacks on the government made her uneasy, not out of any sympathy toward them but out of an innate sense of propriety. We were, after all, their guests.

"I have been told the houses are going to be used by the Yugoslavian electricity workers. Why shouldn't workers have decent homes?" she asked defensively. Janet looked glum. At this point Françoise walked in and the conversation switched abruptly. My wife asked her about her work. With only a few weeks left on her contract, Françoise wanted the various nongovernmental agencies, until now working in complete isolation from one another, if not in outright competition, to meet. All of them must know by now that while there was famine in Wollaita it was among green fields. The answer must be to close the camps and get the peasants back on their land again. She felt she could bring sufficient pressure to bear on the Slave of Jesus. We should in the meantime prepare our figures for it.

Françoise hoped to hold the meeting in a week but until the officials provided us with sufficient food to make a large-scale distribution, we would be unable to discharge anybody on a monthly ration. We all knew that once the truly starving had been dealt with, the camps would soon lose their original purpose and become free restaurants, attracting peasants and their children from miles around. Already the nurses had begun to make spot checks on cheaters who crawled under the tent sides, or mothers who withheld breast milk from their infants so that they could remain. There were also tricks such as the manufacture of false ration cards (some of them, considering the education and means of the forgers, highly professional), and pleaders had appeared at the side of the road, holding out pieces of paper written by bazaar writers asking for extra rations.

One man, with a squint and the agonized expression of a saint on the griddle, stood each day half kneeling by his staff on the road just above Habicha Bantu. Janet said the health assistants knew him and had told her he had good land and five cattle not far away. But after passing him each day for a week curiosity overcame me. We stopped. The old face looked craftily at me for a second through the window. Then he salaamed and, rising, offered me a small wallet made of newspaper. Inside was a folded piece of paper similar to a child's Christmas card.

It is a curious thing—I have it in front of me as I write. Although written in English the letters waver in the cursive style of Amharic. A central prayer lists the virtues of the Red Cross, the number of children of the supplicant, how many had died, and a small history of the famine. All of these are encircled with lettering that says, "Marxism Leninism is our only Guide. Long live Marx Engels and Lenin!"

It was irresistible. Woldie giggled. I looked out of the van window at the old man's bright crafty eyes. Life had not been entirely beaten out of the peasants. I gave him two kilos of flour.

It was a good sign, marking recovery. Severe famine numbs the mind and robs the victims of all thought except food. Letter writing, pleading, robbing, and cheating cease, to be replaced by hunger, silence, and a dreadful stillness. Despite these favorable signs, we felt frustrated, unable to take the next essential step, rehabilitating the victims in their villages. And in the back of our minds was the question: Why were we sent here at the end of a famine?

Two events, following one upon another, changed all this. Two days after our coffee with Françoise a large Mercedes truck appeared in the Dante car park. It had been detached from the relief operation in the north and came complete with a driver. There was also a passenger, a thin-faced young Ethiopian of about twenty sent to collaborate with Reinhardt over the youth projects. He wore a smart two-piece suit decorated with a tiny red and white badge in the lapel. For a moment I thought it was one of those given to blood donors, or a holy medal of the Sacred Heart. But as he shook my hand, fixed me with the ruthless stare of a fanatic, and said, "Serve the People" I saw the badge was a bust of Lenin. This was a member of the Party Faithful, a real believer. He knew Reinhardt well, greeting him with more than the usual three hugs. At the sight of Reinhardt and the truck the officials' faces became sad and preoccupied. It had been sent to move food (at Brit's instigation, I guessed), something they wished to prevent. But they would be hard-put to find a plausible excuse not to use it.

For the first four days they claimed the driver was "resting." Then the truck had to have its brakes attended to and at last, when no more excuses could be reasonably put forward, it set out to Sheyla with a promised load of wheat flour. The camp prepared for its arrival. Five hundred people lined up good-naturedly in the sun, supervised by the mad boy scout. Janet and Leilt set up some scales.

The idea was to give each of them five kilos of flour and some assorted seeds that we had discovered in the back of the warehouse. At about noon it ground down the hill, engine screaming on the steep slope, Red Cross flags fluttering on its wings. The rat-faced official followed in a Toyota, his face pensive.

Both vehicles stopped by the store and the thin official got out. A long altercation began between him and Woldie. Abebe looked slightly disgusted and retired to his clinic. Leilt went back to the feeding tents. After about ten minutes the official came over to me, smiled slightly, and apologized for having to go back to Sodo for a meeting. Within two minutes his car was a plume of dust on top of the hill.

The driver of the truck removed the pins of the tailgate and let it fall. Inside was a bale of empty sacks.

I asked him what had happened to the flour. He shrugged. His job was to collect a hundred empty butter tins.

Fifty yards away, the crowd, shuffling and murmuring, lined up in a corridor between two sheds where they had been funneled that morning to await the distribution. A low wall prevented those at the front of the queue from seeing the official's gift of a pile of empty sacks. Once they did, there would be a riot.

Woldie suggested that we distribute all that we had left in the camp's store as slowly as possible, and tell those who got none today to come in the morning. Peasants were at ease with delays and administrative mess. They would suspect nothing if we temporarily complicated the paperwork to slow everything down.

But tomorrow, if we had no food with us, we would not be able to come. That night we took all the staff back with us into Sodo. They could not be left to face the mob.

I was too late for eggs at breakfast next morning—the only alternative being Bulgarian jam on dried bread, 'tibbs, or fatty beef in hot curry. I sat spooning the saccharine taste of the jam into my mouth and watched Prudence's face. Now the game had progressed to a point where only the major pieces remained on the board, the men in suits had offered their first serious threat of checkmate.

I ate my jam and waited. Through the dirty restaurant window I could see Woldie standing by the truck, uncertain and defiant, waiting for us to start back to Habicha. Leilt and the others lurked in the shelter of the hotel sentry box at the gate, two of them squeezed into it, giggling. Uncharacteristically, only the officials were absent. I went to look for them. But when I entered the musty Red Cross office they were already in full retreat. One of them, the one we thought the most senior, had hoped to make a stand behind the termite-eaten desk, but he was outflanked. Sitting on an upturned oil drum, a copy of *The Collected Works of Yuri Andropov* open on his knees, was the keen young Ethiopian Communist with the ascetic face who had come with the truck the day before. The officials had acquired their own jailer.

Until today they had held all the cards. Complete power over the staff—they could even arrange for their indefinite detention without trial—the keys to the warehouse, access to the commissar's office which renewed our permits to remain in Sodo. There was almost no limit to what they could do. Except that, like all the officials in Ethiopia, they stood in mortal fear of the Party. Not its physical embodiments, the police, the army, the massed peasants who were at this moment practicing to march past the Emperor in Addis the next week, but what the Catholics call the church invisible, its mysteries. And here in his own office was a priest of the mysteries, sitting opposite on a rotting packing case marked GIFT OF THE UNITED STATES OF AMERICA. FRAGILE. HANDLE WITH CARE.

There is a saying in Ethiopia: "You never know what will come out of a friendship with a foreigner." If I were to start complaining in front of this priest, the Party would demand a reckoning. The Party, it was true, was thought to want the food kept in the storehouses. But who could speak for it?

Who knew what was in the Party's heart? The officials knew that to make trouble with a ferengi in front of this zealot could only end in the fortresslike building in Shashemene where other foreigners would break their fingers and attach electric wires to their genitals.

So they gave in, and, once the truck took its first load out of the warehouse, it became unstoppable, going back each morning for more. The Party had defeated itself in an effort to seek redemption in the eyes of the young man.

After that, as if to reassure themselves of their power, they fired "In Your Area" and immersed themselves in a new intrigue. We were now close to a great feast of the Ethiopian Coptic Church, the feast of Mescal, the celebration of the finding of the True Cross. It was a feast that the officials, priests of a new secular order, abhorred. They planned to use it to demonstrate, beyond a doubt, their loyalty to the teachings of the God Lenin.

10

MESCAL

THE TRUE CROSS, the Coptic Church teaches, was not discovered in a Roman cistern by the wife of the Emperor Constantine, but descended in a hail of fire and light on a mountaintop in Wollo, a province in northern Ethiopia. Each year huge numbers of pilgrims converge on a spring high in the mountains, below which, it is said, the Cross is buried. On that day the spring acquires miraculous properties. Throughout the rest of the country the miracle is celebrated with a week of feasting. Tens of thousands of oxen are slaughtered and their meat eaten raw with limes, peppers, and spices. Now a week before Mescal, in preparation for slaughter, the cattle were being moved from village to village, not in herds but singly, each one accompanied by its owner and four or five excited boys. They were spending their capital, but who could think more than a year ahead? It was better to rely on tradition than on hope.

Mescal fell just after a feast that was of equal importance to its rival religion, Marxism—the Tenth Anniversary of the Ethiopian Socialist Revolution. It was just about Mescal ten years earlier that the last emperor, Ras Tafari, the Lion of Judah, King of Kings, who claimed descent from the Queen

172

of Sheba, was driven away from his palace in a green Volkswagen between two NCOs of the revolutionary army. He was never seen again. The new order swept away the monarchy, abolished titles, and disinherited the feudal landlords. Instead, the state took over ownership of the land, and the commissars inherited the mantle of the feudal chiefs. But two thousand years of custom are not abolished by merely changing titles, and the first to succumb was Mengistu.

Maybe Ras Tafari's tiny ghost came whispering to him at night in the stucco palace in Addis guarded by the stone lions at the gate. Slowly at first, but then more quickly, he began to adopt the mantle of the old man he had deposed. Repression, feudalism, and the terrible banquets that Ras Tafari used to hold were revived. Gatherings of terrified officials mouthing their soup under the scrutiny of the new socialist Emperor. A false word, an insolent gleam in the eye, could lead straight to the squat-walled prison near the railway station. Soon, nobody, as in the time of King, dared leave the capital for long. All power, like a huge river diverted from its natural course, began to flow back to the Lion Throne, on which it was rumored, the little Major had begun to sit. Mengistu, like Haile Selassie before him, was besotted by pageantry, so this year to celebrate his accession to the throne of Judah, a week of celebrations had been proclaimed. It brought the new religion even closer to the heart of Mescal.

There had been a huge parade in the capital. Columns of tanks with their long barrels pointing downwards in respect, battalions of peasants, picks and spades on their shoulders, soldiers, airmen, and sailors, feet swinging the goosestep, all had marched or trundled past the rostrum on which Mengistu and his ministers had stood. Jets, consuming vast quantities of fuel, had screamed overhead, and there had been speeches, long speeches, extolling the achievements of ten years of revolution. Land reform that had brought more famine, a foreign policy that had brought war, an internal order that repressed instead of governed.

And there had been feasts. The feasts in our camps had

been attended by the near-skeletal remnants of Mengistu's peasantry clad in sacking and waited on by flies. But in Ras Tafari's old Imperial Place in Addis Ababa there had been a different kind of feast. Some of the brightest names in the struggle against colonialism, racism, and fascism had. sat down to tables loaded with food and wine to be served by tuxedoed flunkies. Nyere of Tanzania, Kaunda of Zambia, Obote of Uganda, Mugabe of Zimbabwe, Doe of Liberia. More speeches had been made. The enemy—Western countries with their insolent democracies, their racist aid programs, their constant scheming to undermine the correct control of the peasants—had been vilified. South Africa had been held up to obloquy, and international banks condemned. Now the fleets of Mercedes had left, the personal jets departed from the crumbling airport.

All that remained in the capital were the huge plywood arches, already swelling and splitting in the late rains. And in the villages small rostrums from which, a few days before, unelected bullies had harangued a despondent starving peasantry for its ingratitude.

The country settled uneasily to await the religious feast.

Mengistu had dreamed that his celebrations would eclipse Mescal. That the size of this year's celebrations would mark the beginning of the end of the old feast so that in years to come it would wither away, and people would celebrate the anniversary of the People's Victory rather than that of a foolish religious fable. To ease the religious festival's death the Party decreed that the customary week's holiday after Mescal would be abolished; everybody would work.

For the officials it would be a test of faith. The medical assistants in the camps might celebrate the feast, that could not be prevented, but there would be no holiday afterwards. Mescal was to be killed off.

But the medical assistants were not the only ones for whom the coming of the young zealot changed things. Suddenly Reinhardt, the German youth volunteer, dropped his preoccupation with our whiteness and began to join us at breakfast, first with the zealot, then, after a few days, on his own. One morning, while we discussed the problems of getting gasoline permits, he announced he could get as many as he wanted from the head of the security police. An awful silence fell. Tula began an elaborate examination of her egg as if suspecting it were bad. Two small spots of color appeared on Prudence's cheeks. Inge lit a self-forbidden cigarette, Janet gave a small, stifled gasp. Reinhardt smiled, pleased at the effect of his news and asked if he could spend some time working in Sheyla camp.

It was clear that the German was no more than astonishingly naive, and the zealot a political romantic who saw us as representatives of some sinister organization. If we attributed deeper motives to him or subtlety to the zealot it would only serve to drag us down into the same morass in which he and all the Party officials in Sodo floundered. None of us doubted that Reinhardt had been asked to report on our harmless chatter. If what he reported came charged with double meaning to his hearers, we could do nothing about it. We took the gasoline and let him come with us.

Meanwhile, the heavy Mercedes truck set off around six each morning for the camps, loaded to the roof with sacks. It seemed an unqualified victory until one day, standing watching the porters unload the white sacks marked GIFT OF THE FEDERAL REPUBLIC OF GERMANY, Woldie said gloomily, "My people, they want me home for Mescal, it is an important festival for us."

Janet suggested he make up a roster, and those who could not go on the day could have some time off later. He shook his head. The officials had forbidden all leave for Mescal.

It promised to destroy all morale. Most of the health assistants had not seen their families for months, and after Mescal there would not be another opportunity. Travel permits were never that easy to get, and if they did not get permission to go home now, they might have to wait a year.

The officials were tireless, driving sometimes all day from camp to camp to conduct interviews, reinterviews, and appeals over the ruling on leave. But the sentence never varied. For the celebration of the revolution, there had been as much leave to give out as anybody wanted, for Mescal none.

We stayed at home for Mescal. Those in the camps who still needed daily feeding were small in number, and the rest of the peasants would be too busy gorging themselves on raw meat in their villages to want to come to the feeding centers.

After breakfast we sat about, sunbathing, dozing, reading. A thin spiral of Geez chant from the distant Coptic Church fading in the wind. Janet searched her jeans for lice, running a fingernail down the inverted seams. She said, "You know it's strange but yesterday I walked to a village near the camp. I wanted to show them how to use sweet potato tops, you can use it like spinach. But you know they wouldn't." I asked how it had managed to grow in the drought. Tula, still ill from an attack of dysentery, went slightly pale, got up, and disappeared into her room.

Inge suddenly turned over on her blanket and said, "There is no point in staying here, I came to work, not for a holiday." Janet said, "I think we are being made fools of."

Five vultures, perched on a bare tree in the center of the courtyard, strained their necks as if trying to overhear.

Without opening her eyes Prudence suggested that two of us should make a survey among the Nomads of the Gamo-Gofa desert one hundred miles farther south. She had worked there in 1974 and she would like to see it again. If we had had food shortages here they should be far worse off there.

Suddenly I realized that everything depended on Françoise and her meeting. But at it there would be tremendous opposition by the commissar to a general distribution of food. Somehow he would rig things so as to continue with the present useless status quo, tying up several agencies in a famine that was virtually burned out. I outlined what I thought might happen. There was an uneasy silence. Prudence's face tightened. "In relief work I don't think you should engage in politics. Besides with you and the officials it is a matter of personalities."

She used the phrase "relief work" as if it had quotes around it, verbal gates to shut out the uninitiated.

But the daily intrigues to outmaneuver the men in suits were not the result of differences in personality. We were there to distribute food to the starving, not ration it according to Leninist theory. I was certain that somewhere in Addis was a secret protocol on Western Aid agencies shaped to meet the ends of the Party that the officials were here to see carried out. Because there was no accommodation with them that would offer our victims an advantage, there was bound to be a struggle.

Yet Prudence's position was not a conscious endorsement of the officials. She was being diplomatic, her own views held far in reserve. Her natural respect for authority, her vows of obedience, made a view of a world dominated by anarchy and malice difficult to accept. In Geneva the same attitude was reflected in the "clinical" examination of hunger and death in the Third World, an examination that took no account of evil intentions. The causes of suffering were held to be economic, environmental, or historical, not the conscious work of man. Thus governments of the poor were to be placated like so many noisy children while we, the more culturally advanced, set about remedying causes they were too socially immature to understand. It is the most dangerous of all our delusions, that somehow evil is half-witted and can be outflanked. The officials, sitting among their broken packing cases, were perfectly aware of our blindness. Our myopic view of them they exploited in their councils. They knew that a knowledge of a moral order, even if they were on the wrong side of it, dealt the possessor an invincible hand.

But in the end it was a position that meant the work itself could not succeed because any success on our part must destroy our relationship with the officials. It was an unconscious process, a tortuous channel leading back on itself, buoyed with good intentions.

Yet maybe in the long run we were both wrong. The peasants whom we were supposed to help were too far removed, too alien, too medieval, to be understood. At best we stood in danger of romanticizing them. At worst using them as counters in a game of moral blackmail. Only the peasants understood the peasants.

It would be worth waiting for the meeting, but if they did not let us start closing the camps and distributing in the villages I would ask for all the team to be withdrawn. To continue the charade of the camps would be to perpetuate the misery of the peasants. And if we were allowed into the villages it would need no more than two of us to run the distribution program. The rest should be moved. In the meantime Prudence and Inge could go to Gamo-Gofa.

Tula, back from her room, glanced up, gripped her knees tightly, and stuck her head back into her book. Inge sat silent, shoulders hunched. The relative inaction and uncertainty were sapping morale. I wondered about the north of Ethiopia and how Brit was getting on. Obtaining permits for a war zone would be unimaginably difficult.

The next morning I was surprised to find the officials welcomed the idea of losing two of us, but it took a day of calling Addis and Shashemene before we were sent the travel permits. Prudence and Inge left soon after for the desert.

The rest of us returned to work to find many of the health assistants off with fever. Examining them it seemed to be the effect of too much raw meat. In the afternoon Abebe took me to see his six-month-old son who had had high fever, shivering, and drowsiness since the day after the feast. I gave him chloroquine and told Abebe to keep his fluid intake up during the night. There seemed no reason to think he would not be fine in the morning. But although the child's mother was there, I did not look closely enough at her face. If I had I would have seen the terror on it.

The next day, the child was dying, covered in a gray blanket on his parents' bed, head to one side, eyes fixed in one corner of his skull. Every few minutes a wave of seizures, starting in his face, spread down his body like ripples in a pool. On the wall above him was a montage of pictures from magazines, models with cruel faces staring over bottles of Chanel perfume, low black racing cars advertising cigarettes, a picture of a cruise liner, and one of New York taken from above the Pan Am helicopter pad.

I was aware of Reinhardt coming into the room as I bent over the child, and as I turned to pick up a syringe, I saw him in the corner trying to comfort Abebe's wife. Janet and I were both professionals, and hardened ones at that, but even so the peculiar ironies of this particular disaster were remarkable and difficult to bear. Abebe, the kindest of men, who worked so hard for his patients, might well lose his son. I wondered what effect this horror would have on the young German.

There are many causes of fever and fits, but without laboratories the diagnosis was at best a guess. Cerebral malaria was the most likely; the only other thing which came to mind was relapsing fever, a variant of typhus transmitted by body lice. Its treatment, while dangerous, is effective and dramatic. Abebe thought the drugs for it might be available at the government pharmacy in Sodo. Instinct begs you not to leave a dying patient, but it seemed worth a try, and I was the only one who could drive the truck.

It took an hour and a half to make the round trip, and as I got closer to the camp on the return journey I had already persuaded myself that the answer was in the blue Unicef bag lying below the gear stick. I imagined Abebe's face as the seizures stopped and the child recovered. Abebe and his wife were models of Western behavior, who had, despite pressure from relatives, limited their family to two children. If everybody in Ethiopia did the same, there would be no famine. In them resided our hopes for the theory that if you can provide African parents with a guarantee that their children will survive, they will not have so many. It was an Aidgame trap, a subconscious search for willing imitators. I increased the speed of the truck, crashing and bumping over the deep ruts.

But only Janet was there to meet me when I arrived, walking toward the cab and shaking her head. The child had died an hour after I left.

They buried him that afternoon. Reinhardt, Janet, and I stood in the small clinic and watched the procession pass the window. The child's corpse was carried in a square cardboard box. Along the side, just peeping from under a child's blue blanket used as a pall, were the words TIDE WASHES WHITER WASHES BEST.

There were only men in the procession. They passed close enough and in such silence that we could hear the pounding of their bare feet on the grass and their breathing. Within half a minute the file had vanished through a gate that led to the cemetery.

They left a blank, green square after they had passed, a square framed by the window and filled with green fields, blue sky, and a childishly shaped mountain in the distance with a white cloud about its summit. Nobody spoke, nobody moved. I knew then that we were in the process of something unutterably evil. Not evil in the sense of bad, or tragic, unjust or wrong, but an active intentional evil that now lay exulting over that valley. It was the evil of foreknowledge, hubris, the destruction of innocence.

Through the window lay Africa, lying in the bright endless sun, a continent unchanged since the first breath of creation, its beasts once fabulous, its wastes under the eye of God. A place in which there is no room for the gray subtleties of Europe, the threat of winter that huddles men in corners to think. In Africa there is only the light, sudden colors, the vastness of sky and plain, the sun, and sudden, invisible, swift death—unpredictable, unavoidable, frequent. Men do not dwell on it here as they do in Europe, or raise memorials to it, huddle crosses in wet fields to it, worship it, or plan how to avoid it. In Africa it is unchallenged. To challenge it would be to challenge the Gods.

But Abebe was different. In him I had witnessed a reenactment of the Fall. He had eaten the tainted apple and glimpsed inside the Pandora's Box of medicine. But why it should be him I could not understand. Perhaps it was his innocence.

He knew that the old world of Ethiopia with its menacing religious taboos, feudal lords, and remote emperors had died. That what was left, the Party and Marx, were without life, the old order dead but propped up to keep the peasants at bay. After it vanished there would be science. Abebe had entered the world of Victorian scientific optimism, becoming a kind of Abyssinian H. G. Wells. But he still lived in the village and the villagers were watching him, half envious of his white coat, stethoscope, and familiarity with the ferengi, half hoping he might fall. The death of his son came to them as a sort of relief. It confirmed the old wisdoms. But Abebe was too far from them now and could not return even though his new God had failed. He was in the vanguard of a massive regiment of puzzled, bewildered people stranded without culture among our machines. The medicines in their bright containers, labeled Roche, Bayer, Unilever; the needles, the fat packs of intravenous fluids, the trucks the feeding tents, our books, all were building sure walls about this paradise and when complete would lock out the inhabitants forever.

Going back to our hotel we sat close to one another in the Landcruiser, silent. I turned once to find Janet in tears, and I felt an emptiness as if it were my own child. The death of Abebe's child is something that since then we have skirted around. We too lost a child in Africa, and there are parallels that are too hard to think about.

"I never wanted to come back to Africa," Janet said. "It is a bad place."

We returned to Habicha the next day for the wake. Tradition demands that the bereaved keep to their house for seven days, and we found Abebe sitting on the floor wrapped in a gray blanket, his face miserable and bored, his wife sitting next to him, the thin beauty of her Arabic face distorted by a night's weeping.

He said, "It is an evil world, and he is well out of it." But the words, put into his mouth by others who scarcely shared his grief, meant nothing, like the widow who says, "It was a merciful release."

A small boy brought us two low, three-legged wooden stools, their seats adzed into the shape of thick saucers. Abebe offered some beans and traditional funeral foods, watched by a line of mourners sitting against the wall. Abebe turned and said something in Wollaitini to Leilt, the eighteen-year-old village girl who acted as a general helper and interpreter. There was a slight movement and all heads turned toward him. Leilt, who had snuggled up to Abebe's wife, said with an apologetic smile, "He says he would like to come back to work. There is no point in this sitting around." Abebe intercepted my glance, shrugged, and repeated it himself. Leilt said, "I will come back too."

The others lowered their eyes, puzzled. For them this breaking of the funerary rights was without meaning. Tradition demanded that seven days should be spent in the house. To go out, to work, meant lack of respect, disbelief. There was a long murmuring, somebody reached forward for a handful of beans, Leilt's sister offered coffee spiced with salt. When I looked again their faces were blank. Whatever they felt, I was not going to see it, and for Abebe I saw there was no place in this garden. To them he was already part ferengi.

We closed the clinic and went back to the hotel. There a message was waiting for us from Amsalu, the Red Cross administrator. He was coming through Sodo and could give Janet and me a lift to Lake Langano for the few days' leave we were due. I was surprised; Amsalu was not an unkind man, but his character did not lend itself easily to such gestures. I wondered if his solicitude had anything to do with the Red Cross team visiting the country from Geneva that he had mentioned when I last spoke to him. They would be due in Langano about this time.

The next day Abebe was back in his clinic, silent, working down the lines of patients with a syringe or listening to their chests with the black and silver Unicef stethoscope that had given him so much pleasure before, and to which he now seemed to cling as if it was some kind of talisman.

The last but one patient that afternoon was a child of four, its symptoms exactly the same as that of Abebe's son. High fever, some vomiting, a slight stiffness of the neck. A clear spinal tap confirmed the likelihood of it being cerebral malaria.

Abebe tried to avoid looking at the child, busying himself over the drip when he came closer, and then retreating among the patients on the benches. It would be hard on him to leave the child here, far better in the circumstances to take it to the hospital. There really wasn't a choice, except that the mother, sitting on a bench, began to jerk her head angrily at the mention of the word hospital. Its chances of survival were slim, so slim that even the difficult journey would not shorten the odds against it much more. But by five, the mother relented. The child was treated as far as it could be, and loaded into the back of the truck. The young patient needed more than medicine, and if it was the same illness that had killed Abebe's son, by taking it to town I was at least sparing Abebe a night-long vigil and a painful reenactment.

The twenty or so peasants who crowded about the truck to say good-bye represented nearly all the mother's village, a small place five miles further on from Sheyla. Long, thin Ethiopian hands thrust small brass and silver coins, all they had, and worth almost nothing, through the driver's window at her tearful frightened face.

An hour later, accompanied by the old chief with his long staff, she carried the child through the doors of the hospital. Being under five it required no papers. It was too much to contemplate what would have happened had it been older.

I returned the next day expecting news of its death. But, instead, I found that the villagers had sent a young man of about twenty with an anxious face and a smattering of school English to see me. After we had left the hospital there had been a fight, with whom he did not know, and the child, not having the right papers, had been sent away. The mother wanted me to come to the village.

With the help of Leilt I asked him how they had got home. He shrugged.

"They had walked."

"How long did it take?"

"Many hours, until the sun rose."

"Did the mother say how the baby was during the journey?"

"Yes. It had made strange movements all the way, but at dawn had become quiet."

It was a fourteen-mile walk from the hospital to the village. The old man with his gray hair and staff and the young mother with her dying child had set out about midnight from Sodo and walked for five hours through the night. Jackals and hyenas must have followed them, eyes burning like devils from the eucalyptus groves on either side of the track. The child had probably had several major convulsions. I thought of the few coins pressed on her by the villagers, and the slamming of the hospital door.

By now the child would be dead. The only point in going to the village was to confirm the boy's story and perhaps to make a complaint to the Slave of Jesus. Somehow the bad news seemed to offer some slight relief to Abebe, easing his guilt, the calling card that death always leaves with survivors. He had been fighting with his wife, who, becoming hysterical, had left him the night before to return to her own village.

The beehive huts of the village lay quiet in the morning sun as we arrived, a few children darting and ducking in the shadows of some large eucalyptus trees. Leilt knew the place well and led us straight across the flat, closely cropped grass to a large tucul in front of which a goat was tethered.

Although we had left the car some half a mile away, so nobody in the hut had heard us coming, there was no surprise at our arrival. The mother sat with the child on her lap in the semidarkness, an ox and a donkey staring at it through the bars of their stall. Accustoming my eyes to the darkness, I bent over the child, expecting it to be dead or almost dead. It lay there quietly tugging at its mother's breast. Its fever had vanished and the stiff neck of yesterday had gone. As I stared at it in disbelief, it kicked one leg in contentment.

An old man brought me a three-legged stool and offered me a large pawpaw, then turned and said something to Leilt who giggled slightly, "The man says this child has always been bad in the head."

"What does he mean, bad in the head?"

"Since he was born, he cannot walk, or sit up, or speak."

She went on with the depressing litany. "He wets himself, dirties himself, and the mother is not sure if he can see."

Out of every four robust, well-fed children who contract cerebral malaria, on average only three will survive. In the malnourished, almost none. Yet this skeptical shape, brain-damaged at birth, belly swollen with months of hunger, its gut full of worms, its chest probably alive with tubercle bacilli, only partly treated, had survived, even exposed to a fourteen-mile trek in the middle of the night with the delicate coverings of its brain swarming with parasites. Three days ago, the same disease had taken off a healthy, well-nourished baby, the pride and joy of my health assistant. The sense of evil that oppressed me in the camp as the Tide box passed returned.

The mother raised a happy face at me, saying something to Leilt. She translated. "Could you give it some medicine to make it speak, now that it was better?"

I tried to explain that the child's brain was damaged, probably at birth, but my words had no effect on the trusting, hope-filled smile. The old man brought salted, hot coffee in tiny clay cups, poured from a rusty tin, then, after a few polite words, we rose and left.

"In Your Area" met us at the edge of the village, offering to walk back with us to Sheyla. At first he talked about his sacking by the officials, but his English failed to do justice to the complexity of it, and he reverted to the usual litany of questions preceded by his strange formula. Then just before Habicha, frightened of meeting any of the suited men, he left us.

As we descended the steep path into the camp, I told Abebe of my plan to take three days off. He turned, glancing at me sharply. How were we going to travel without permits from the commissar? I explained that ours, unlike permits for local people that were only valid for one journey, were valid for a month. But the look he gave me was wary. He feared we were going to leave for good.

Suddenly I became tired of it all. Something, the fatigue, the heat, the fact that I had had nothing except a few tea-spoonfuls of salted coffee since breakfast, made me long to get away, to break out of the close relationships demanded by peasant life, to become anonymous. Whether Abebe saw my impatience or not he made no sign, neither then or when, as usual, they saw us off that evening from the compound.

We packed everything that night and went to bed early. Amsalu was expected at seven, and with luck we would reach Lake Langano by lunchtime the following day, giving us three full days away from Sodo.

11

THE EMPEROR'S SUMMER PALACE

IN THE LATE AFTERNOON Amsalu finally arrived from Gamo-Gofa. Reinhardt, who since the death of Abebe's son had become morose and withdrawn, asked if he could return with us to Addis Ababa. I caught him looking uncertainly at me, as if he wanted approval. The plan now was to stop halfway, just outside Shashemene, bathe in one of the lakes, and stay overnight at the old summer palace of the emperor's daughter, the Princess Ras Tafari, now a government hotel. The princess, who by now was a very old lady, was rumored to be still alive in a prison somewhere in the north. She had started life in the Imperial Palace, had been educated at an English Ladies' Public School, followed by three years at Oxford, spent the '30s in emergent Ethiopia, gone into exile in London with Haile Selassie during World War II, and returned to Ethiopia to be imprisoned in the '60s.

Nobody seemed interested in us at any of the six road barriers on the eighty-mile journey. Amsalu had his driver with him, a round-faced man of thirty called Yohannes with a puzzled witless expression. His driving was horrific.

Yohannes's imaginary world contained no pedestrians, and their reality, particularly in towns, drove him mad. As soon as we passed the barrier at the entrance he would abandon the crown of the road from which in the country, only the largest of trucks could dislodge him, and take to the gutter, racing down the village street like some frenzied mechanical street sweeper, horn blaring, intent on forcing every walker off the road forever. Once clear of the town, he would relax back into his dawdle. Yahannes's driving technique seemed universal. Witness to it lay in the numerous wrecked trucks on either side of the road.

We reached the foothills leading to the emperor's summer palace at five, turned off the main road by the new telephone exchange and began to climb a narrow track with high overgrown banks similar to an English lane. Halfway up Amsalu gave an order. Yohannes swung the Mercedes up a small track that led off to the right, drove along it for about five minutes and stopped. A waterfall weaved two ropes of water over a cliff to our left before disappearing among thick foliage in a cloud of steam.

"Swimming," said Amsalu.

We got out of the truck and crossed a crude plank bridge guarded by a small wooden paybooth. A bowed old man in a bus conductor's hat sold us a ticket, a bar of cheap, highly scented soap, and a rough towel. Beyond the bridge the waterfall ended in a culvert leading to a stone tank. Here twenty years ago the Lion of Judah had bathed, watched perhaps by the ancestors of the two sad-faced lemurs with long black and white tails who clung to the branches of a tree two hundred feet above us. The water was hot and full of green slime. Yohannes sat in a corner of the pool and watched us, his face a blank of furtive puzzlement at Janet's bikini. A few hundred yards away, half hidden by cedars and fir, was the summer palace.

I do not know what I had been expecting, perhaps some medieval fortress converted to a simple hotel, or tuculs with doors and Western amenities. Instead, it was something that Wodehouse's Bertie Wooster would have recognized, a 1920s bungalow, full of the tasteless furniture of suburban Oxford.

Its original owner, the princess, would be nothing more than a crone now, withered and bent by ten years in a cell with only a cracked chamber pot for company. Slightly to the right, a smaller building housed the staff, some guest rooms, and a restaurant. There was a small circular lawn, a fountain with a bronze pan, and neat flowerbeds of marigolds and daisies. Two thousand feet below in the valley three lakes with swampy uneven edges shone dully in the gray evening light.

It was a place of ghosts. Served by two young waitresses in black uniforms and pinafores we ate 'tibbs on the veranda, while Amsalu grilled me on the cost of hi-fi equipment in London. The sun vanished behind a mountain and the hyenas began to bark, singly at first, answered only by dogs, then joined by more and more of their own kind. A wind trickled about the tall plane trees, increased in strength, then died. Some frogs began a loud chorus from the pond. Amsalu said suddenly, "The emperor spent much time in this place. He came here in a Rolls-Royce each month from Addis."

The scarlet imperial Rolls must have followed the narrow road we had come, its huge 1920s headlamps picking out the shapes of peasants bowing in the dust. The small figure in the back barely glimpsed through the thick tinted glass. The inheritor of the Throne of Judah and the Kingdom of Prester John, lost in the preoccupations of medieval power.

Lights began to twinkle in Shashemene, not the brilliant lights of the nighttime West but the uncertain flickering yellow produced by ancient generators. Somewhere among them was the Rastafarian community that Haile Selassie had allowed to settle here. At the start there had been two hundred, all of them from Jamaica, but even though they were considered too mad for political persecution by the revolutionaries, only a handful now remained, dreadlocked, working a small carpenter's shop, and waiting for the resurrection of the man who had given them their land.

We had planned to stay at the hotel, but I made an excuse over the state of the toilets. I had no wish to spend a night with such terrible ghosts as the dead emperor and his court. Amsalu looked puzzled, but if I had told him the truth he would have laughed. For what power had the figures from half-forgotten pages of school history lessons over the living? He lived exclusively for suits, smart shoes, and shiny aluminum-cased Japanese transistors. The dead were nothing.

The hotels in Shashemene were nearly all full. Janet counted three Mercedeses in the courtyard of the Ethiopia, the most expensive hotel, and it took an hour to find rooms in a small brown-painted hotel whose courtyard was filled with ancient Fiat and Viberti trucks.

It was a bad night, the beds filthy, the floors sticky from liquid wax poured on unswept dust. From at least four rooms —including Amsalu's—came the crackling of the BBC World Service. I dozed, uneasy at the sound of hectic worrying voices interleaved with bursts of urgent music. One by one they fell silent and I slept.

Just before six a siren blew, signaling the end of the curfew. Footsteps began to pass our window. Amsalu turned on the World Service, a Surrey voice announcing riots in Khartoum. Outside, the drivers were making their way to an open ditch at the back of the hotel which served as a toilet. The Vibertis started up, coughing and choking over cheap Russian fuel, their exhaust fumes filling the rooms. I went in search of a better toilet, but the only other one was in Reinhardt's room. Its bowl was decapitated halfway up from its base, and the surrounding floor was awash in the wet feces of the previous occupant. The bed was only ten feet from it.

Yohannes appeared and within ten minutes everybody was dressed and waiting at the car.

It took under an hour to reach the lake resort, which lies in a valley eighty miles south of Addis. It was the only place in the country foreigners were allowed to visit on just a tourist permit. To go anywhere else meant getting at least three other special passes and being accompanied by an Ethiopian guide or official.

On the road to Langano Amsalu urged Yohannes to even

greater heights of recklessness. He had been shortlisted for a visit to London and Geneva with the Red Cross and in consequence had become obsessive about the Swiss team. It explained his interest in London the night before. But when we arrived there was a message recalling him to Addis. Inevitably the delegation had been held up in the capital by permit difficulties. Amsalu was to bring them down to us in two days.

Lake Langano, named by the Italians, is about twenty miles long and ten wide, the hotel complex a series of three-room bungalows built on a gently sloping beach, each house shaded by thorn trees and bougainvillea. The bungalows had one overwhelming attraction, clean toilets and functioning showers. We showered, slept, and in the afternoon lay on the veranda in the cool African winter sun reading. Janet went to the office for a towel and came back excited. It was possible to phone overseas from the manager's office. It took us an hour of shouting and frantic winding of the ancient cranked telephone to get through to the operator in Addis. Janet spoke first, yelling against the static, then briefly at an enormous distance I heard her twin sister's voice in her kitchen in London. There was a television on in the background and I could hear my two nephews arguing. The line went dead, I cursed —a donkey across the road raised its head in seeming reproach.

As the day wore on limousines with the bright orange diplomatic plates began to whisper into the compound, parking under the thorn trees. Doors slammed, and half asleep I listened to French, German, and Russian mixing with the gutturals of Swahili, Sotho, and Yoruba. A truck belonging to the International Committee of the Red Cross parked outside a bungalow at the end of the beach, a young couple got out and, holding hands, vanished into their hut.

Weaver birds, attracted by the water, chattered in the large thorn trees, darting in and out of their complicated nests which, undisturbed behind the wire fence of the hotel, had grown into complicated colonies completely engulfing the trees. Just before dusk several water snakes, their bodies humped like miniature versions of the Loch Ness Monster, swam close inshore. Inge had told me that hippos bathed in the lake, surfacing during the day in the middle and coming in at night to deposit huge turds and footprints on the sand. The sun set at six and a new moon rose over the lake, the water magnifying the stars.

Supper, in a circular restaurant built over the water's edge, was at seven. The food, served by elderly waiters in red jackets and black dress trousers, lacked all imagination. There were three main dishes based on Italian recipes but heavily influenced by the marked stodginess of Soviet cooking. It would be bearable for two or three days, but for longer, 'tibbs at the Dante seemed infinitely preferable. Fifteen people leaned over bowls of lukewarm Russian tomato soup, took a collective sip, then glanced up at their fellow diners, eyebrows raised. A Swiss diplomat wore his napkin tucked between a large red jowl and a tight green shirt. His small wife, nestling in his shade, picked at a dry roll with short nervous movements. The French began to laugh at the food, and a Canadian complained about the price of the Hilton in Addis, mispronouncing the word *birrh* as "beer." The couple with the International Red Cross truck kissed and gazed into each other's eyes, her hand on his leg. Behind me an upper-class English voice started browbeating his companion over something they had or had not done in Kenya. Through the windows the lights in the villages around the lake shore went out. Ours would be left on until midnight.

Afterwards in the bar the man with the English public-school accent introduced himself. He looked absurdly young, hardly more than twenty with a fleshy, slightly overindulged face. His companion, who looked remarkably like a very young version of the Duke of Edinburgh, was Dutch. For the past two years they had been running a fifty-hectare farm in Kenya, growing flowers. The flowers were picked, packed into cardboard boxes, and trucked to Nairobi where they were loaded onto one of the many ancient cargo planes that ply the night skies of Africa. By morning they were being auctioned to American flower buyers in Amsterdam and the following morning were on sale in the streets of Manhattan. Flowers are light, hardy, and cheap to grow, and the project had become so successful the owners in Amsterdam found themselves owing 60 percent in taxes to the Kenyan government on a half-million U.S. dollar profit they had made in the second year.

The United Nations had taken up the idea and asked them to start a similar scheme in Ethiopia. Their firm had agreed and sent them to Langano for six weeks. This time the profits were to be split fifty-fifty, half going to them, the other half to the government. Apart from the profits, it promised employment to over five hundred otherwise starving peasants.

But it was not that simple. In a country awash with informers, nobody, they discovered, took any decisions worth the name, passing them instead up the line until they reached the politbureau. It was a system that applied even to farming. The first day they arrived they found that all the secateurs for cutting the flowers were locked up in the stores and requests for them met with apologies and shrugs. Addis would have to be consulted. All collective farms in Ethiopia were managed from the capital, and nothing could be done, not even the smallest thing, without permission from there. They applied and waited, but the weeks passed and nothing happened. After a month with no production they decided to go to Addis and see the manager themselves. After a week of evasions, denials, and whole days spent in dusty rooms with only the cheap yellow paper of the *Ethiopian Gazette* to look at, they finally tracked him down in an office just off Revolution Square. After a shaky start the meeting began to turn in their favor; slowly, over a whole morning, they managed to persuade him of the importance of flexibility when selling into a competitive market.

Convinced, the manager offered them carte blanche, signed papers giving them complete authority over the operation and promised to waive the paperwork so that the company aircraft could turn around at the airport in an hour instead of two days. They seemed set to repeat their success in Kenya. The papers were sent for stamping and the meeting relaxed, the manager picking up the phone to order coffee. They sat around chatting. There was a knock on the door and the manager rose to let the waiter in. It was not a waiter who stood outside, but two policemen, who handcuffed him and led him away. Collective farms, it seemed, were state secrets and revealing state secrets to ferengis, treason. The two boys, chastened and slightly apprehensive, returned to Langano.

Since then they spent much of their time by the lake, reading, swimming, or listening to the BBC, unable, because of the censorship, to write to their head office about what had happened. All they could hope for was that lack of production would stimulate their recall.

The next day I sat on the terrace in the early morning sun, reading. It was pleasant there with a cool wind blowing gently off the lake surface. The Swiss Red Cross man, the one I had seen with his girl the night before, asked if he could join me. He spoke English with the same lilt that he spoke German, acquired from a childhood spent in some village high in the mountains. He had a thin, humorless face with the broad shoulders and thick arms of a Swiss peasant farmer, which was what he had been until he took up training to be a vet six years ago. After qualifying, feeling the need to do something different, he volunteered to work for the Swiss Red Cross.

He had been in Ethiopia for three months, working in Wollo, when he had caught amebic dysentery and had been sent here to recuperate. The girl was his fiancée, who had come over from Geneva for a couple of weeks. But I sensed that it was something much more than severe dysentery that had brought him here. A preoccupation on the thin, drawn face spoke of a mind imprisoned in a labyrinth of unpleasant memories. For an outsider to share them was like a visitor to a prison asking to be shown the worst and most violent of its inmates.

I waited. Just below us on the beach three French children

whispered excitedly about the fish that darted hungrily about in shallow rock pools waiting for scraps to be thrown over the wall.

"You gone da," said the vet suddenly.

I glanced at the beach wondering why he should ask, but it was not a question but the word "Uganda." His face had become self-absorbed, like somebody watching a film. Before he came to Ethiopia he had been sent to Uganda for six months from Geneva to work in the Luwero triangle, once one of the richest and most colorful provinces in the country, but now a silent, abject zone of terror, most of the peasants either dead or in refugee camps across the border in Kenya. He had organized an emergency feeding program for the few people who had chosen to remain, a task constantly interrupted by drunken soldiers intent on robbery, murder, and rape. His Swiss face puzzled over the illogicality of what he had seen. He told me of mass executions, of a day when he drove a man for three hours with a bullet in his head to Kampala only to realize that the hospital, once one of the medical showpieces of Africa, was now no more than an insanitary first aid station.

He said suddenly, "In many ways what is happening here in Ethiopia is worse."

He took a sip of coffee, his hand was trembling quite badly. "You see in Uganda you can understand it, it is a war, and the troops, they have no leaders, it is very bad. In former times in Europe it was the same. But here"—he shrugged—"here it is very nasty. My job is to feed people. In the morning I take out a truck full of flour, go to a village and give it out. Sometimes there is maybe a queue of five, six hundred persons for this flour. Sometimes during the day, some fifty of them will die while they are waiting for it. Now they are telling us that we should only give food for those the Party makes papers for. I tell them I am not doing that. We are the Swiss Red Cross, I tell them."

He paused, then said, "Do you know how many people are dying in Wollo? Maybe one thousand every day. Some days it is so bad the people, they try and block the road by holding hands together. There are many bodies on the roads, many."

I thought of Sodo and the few graves, some fifty per village over a period of six months. Why had we been sent to the one area where we were of the least use? When the people from Geneva came I would ask for us to be transferred.

Late in the afternoon of the next day the delegation arrived in three Mercedes jeeps.

There were four of them: the Joanna Lumley lookalike who had briefed us in Geneva, the representative of an Italian charity—a short square-set woman of about forty called Emma, an older German man with a bald head, soft features and gold-rimmed spectacles, and a young American press officer called Peter. None of them was Swiss. All of them wore nervous, uncertain looks, as if they had been asked to impersonate the real thing and were now, faced with the reality, unsure of their lines. Amsalu, Yohannes, and Bjorn Svensen stood in a loose triangle about them, like nervous sheep dogs with an over docile flock.

We left for Sodo half an hour later, sharing a jeep with Joanna Lumley's double and the Italian. Lumley was an agreeable companion. Her real name was Sonia and her slightly fractured upper-class English accent seemed at home among the stiff-jointed gutturals of Amharic. Since we had met in Geneva she had been promoted. But she had been ill with diarrhea from almost the moment she had stepped off the plane, and had acquired the slight gray tinge of the accomplished diarrhearist. We had to stop three times during the journey for her to dash behind the bushes.

The Italian tried to talk politics, ritually denouncing South Africa before turning to the independence movements in Northern Ethiopia, strings of initials coming easily to her: TPLF, ELF, MLFE, like a teenager might talk about a current pop band. They were names I had only vaguely heard of although I knew that one, the Tigrean Peoples Liberation Front, was so left wing it considered even the Albanians to be dupes of the Capitalist West. Listening to the Italian I wondered why the Red Cross had failed to brief us on the war, or on the history of modern Ethiopia. Later I learned that one of the most secret illusions of Aidgame is that there is an "objective" or "scientific" reality that transcends the mere human folly of politics in the Third World. Like all such unprovable and therefore religious notions, such an idea confers on its believers a feeling of invincibility; in the case of Aidgamers, an illusion of being clothed in an armor of rationality that makes them proof against the day-to-day deceptions of corrupt and tyrannous regimes. It wasn't the first time people had been sold ideas like this. I thought of the Mad Mahdi's followers before Kitchener's guns at Omdurman, armed only with the word of the Prophet, or ten-year-old Iranian boys clutching plastic keys to Paradise as they ran onto Iraqi mines.

We met the next day at breakfast. There were only four of us; Inge and Prudence were still away in the desert. The delegation was going back that night to Addis so they split up. Svensen took the press officer to Chefisa. The bald-headed German with the gold-rimmed spectacles went with Inge to Chefisa; Lumley who, after a night of rehydration fluid, was much better, said she would come with me to Habicha Bantu. Emma, her mouth full of egg, instantly volunteered to come as well.

I wanted to talk to Lumley about moving the team to the north, but it was something that had to be done in private. If Emma was to inadvertently mention what she had heard to anybody in Addis it could easily reach the ears of the Party. In the hope of putting her off spending a day with me, I drove to the street of WADU houses, reciting from the nun's script the story of how they were built. But she had the stock repertoire to shield her from my attempts to sap her beliefs, phrases such as Inappropriate Development, Lack of Coordinated Planning (can there be such a thing as uncoordinated planning?), Needs, and Relevance.

Lumley talked about the countryside, the Coptic churches, the small farms. I tried to find out how a degree in history from Edinburgh would lead you to Ethiopia. She was vague on the subject. Most of us were.

We got to Habicha in the midmorning heat. Abebe came to meet us, surprised and touchingly delighted that his fears of our leaving had proved groundless. I introduced my guests, telling him they came from Geneva, but the information seemed to mean nothing to him.

We walked around the camp. The evil that three days ago seemed to hang like a leaden fog over the valley had evaporated, although wisps of it were left; in a look, a place, or behind the hedge of juniper trees that hid the graveyard, visited most nights now by the jackals.

I had told both Lumley and the Italian about the tragedy before we got to Habicha, and once or twice I caught the latter watching me, as if about to ask something, but as the morning wore on she became quieter, more withdrawn, and then, complaining of feeling sick, retired to the truck to lie down.

I talked to Lumley about Françoise's meeting, then asked her about the north. Were the stories that I had heard in Langano true? The great difficulty, she explained, was that the Ethiopian government wanted Red Cross money but no supervision.

She looked briefly around for Amsalu, but he was a hundred yards away talking to Woldie, so she continued. Very few permits were being given to go north: Médecins Sans Frontières, World Vision, and Save the Children had all met with obstruction. The maximum number of us they could send was four, two would have to remain in Sodo.

We took Emma back to the town and left her in Tula's room with a bottle of rehydration fluid.

It was over lunch that day that I first heard the phrase "Resettlement Area." The government, Lumley told me, had a plan to shift tens of thousands, some said hundreds of thousands, of starving peasants from the north to the south. Even then it seemed an insane plan. The people in the north spoke different languages and were often Muslims instead of Christians. Lumley had learned of a resettlement area near Chefisa at Bale. She would like to see it. But that afternoon her dysentery returned and I had to go alone.

The valley lay eight thousand feet below the Sodo plateau, was about thirty miles long, and varied in width from ten to twenty miles. The road came on it suddenly down a narrow track turning a hairpin at the edge of some trees. From the top the fields and houses looked blue in the distance. It took me two hours to reach the floor, bumping over huge rocks the size of footballs, washed down in the torrential rains.

Bale was a scheduled resettlement area from the 1974 drought. Then, ten thousand peasants had been forcibly evacuated here from Tigre to join a small traditional community of Oramo, different in language, customs, and religion as the Irish are from the Greeks. Amidst the deep hostility of the enforced hosts, collective farms were started. But after the paperwork was done, a promise to connect an underground stream two miles from the settlement evaporated, the stone-filled wells in the town were never cleared, seeds were not delivered, and scanty rains, alienation, and despair did the rest. The land, barely enough for the original population, had given out. Last summer over five hundred children had died.

Accompanied by the local commissar, a burly man with a pistol in his belt, I walked around the impoverished plots, trying to avoid the panic-filled eyes of the farmers. This year there would be no food. A young man with eight children kicked at a dead maize stalk and shouted something to the commissar in Oramo. The burly official's hand made a reflex move toward the holster of his pistol, then looking at us, he checked himself and said with a forced smile: "He is bitter because the West have not sent more food." But we heard later that there had been several killings of Party men in Bale.

I drove back out of the valley. Just as I left, one of the priests from the Franciscan mission arrived in an ancient jeep to talk with the commissar and deliver some food to the village. I had not seen him before. He was a young man with an unruly, black beard and a sad, plump face. He had spent many months in the valley, a resort of typhoid, malaria, and relapsing fever, running a small feeding center and trying to get the officials to let his mission connect the water. I left him there in the oppressive heat of the Rift arguing, cajoling the commissar and two village leaders.

The delegation met up that night pleased with what they had seen. But the theology of my approach still worried Svensen. I had not taken an official with me to Bale, that was very worrying. The conference of NGOs was another source of worry. The officials, Mr. Mole and Mr. Rat among them, had asked him to order me not to reveal our mortality statistics tomorrow: they had described them as "sensitive." We discussed the Bale valley, but he refused to make any promises. Headquarters would have to be consulted and again it was wrong of us to go there without proper local authority. The bald-headed German beamed through the strictures, "Everybody haf worked hard, very good." Before they left early the following morning, Yushi took a photograph of all of us on the smeared steps of the Dante.

That evening Prudence, Inge, and Françoise appeared together accompanied by Wolde Mekonnen, the Red Cross delegate from Gamo-Gofa, a young man with a round face, a dark-brown suit, and a woolen tie. Prudence seemed to have made friends with him. Françoise's truck had broken down at Arba Minch, and she had caught a ride with them back to Sodo. Françoise announced that the meeting of all the nongovernmental organizations involved in the relief work would definitely go ahead in the morning.

At the time I wondered why the Slave of Jesus had allowed the meeting. However difficult it might have been to refuse Françoise, it could not have outweighed the danger of holding a public meeting of Western aid officials, none of whom were likely to support the Party line. In Marxist Ethiopia thoughtful gestures toward foreigners in matters of politics could lead to jail.

Mr. Mole, who had told me about his European tour, appeared, ostensibly to meet the Red Cross man. With a nervous duck of the head in the doctor's direction he sat down and said to her in French, "I hear you are having your meeting tomorrow." Françoise nodded. Inge looked extremely tired and slightly ill. She had lost weight, and was irritable. After ten minutes she excused herself and went to bed. The two officials remained, sitting opposite each other at the end of the table, Prudence between them. Suddenly they seemed almost interchangeable. The same suit, the same modest face, the quiet insinuating manner. Prudence asked Mekonnen if he would like a second beer, pressing his arm with a thin, tired hand. The little man glanced at his companion, refused, and rose, excusing himself. The official did the same.

Prudence forced a bright smile onto her face and arranged to meet Wolde Mekonnen in the morning to discuss the field report she would routinely have to send to Addis. When he had gone, I asked her how she had got on with him. Her face closed with tiredness, "It will all be in my report."

Françoise began to grin, sensing the tensions between us. Prudence sniffed, got up, and left the room.

Françoise's meeting to force the issue of closing the camps and distributing to the villages started at ten the following morning. We assembled in the Farmers' Association Hall at the top of the hill by the police barrier. Mr. Rat stopped me on the way, repeating Svensen's message to me about the statistics. "Under no circumstances are they to be made public." Inside the hall his superior, a small weasel-faced man from regional headquarters in Shashemene repeated the same thing.

The room was long, low, and paneled in cheap boot-polished brown wood, its plasterboard ceiling stained from a leaking roof. In one corner stood a small speaker's rostrum — behind it, over a small stage, a large photo of Emperor Mengistu.

The room was packed. Apart from the familiar faces of Sister Frances, the girls of Irish Concern, and the fathers there were many I had never seen before. Middle-aged crew-cut Americans, slight-faced Canadian French, twenty or twenty-five nuns, some Germans and a tall man with a shiny bald head and fleshy features. Amsalu, Mekonnen, and the regional director of the RRC sat directly behind me, slightly forward on their chairs. I began to write some notes. An official behind me drew a sharp breath.

Slave of Jesus, followed by the hand-waving regional director of the RRC and a thin, fox-faced man appeared at the stroke of ten, taking their seats along a table on the rostrum. The noise in the room subsided. Fox-face whispered to the commissar. His square peasant face clouded slightly, then he stood up and walked to the rostrum.

He spoke for three minutes in Amharic and badly in English for two. Wollaita, he said, owed the relief organizations a debt of gratitude. He read out the names of the organizations: Oxfam, the Red Cross, Irish Concern, more than twenty names in all. Then he paused and looked directly at his audience. "In Democratic Ethiopia policy is formulated by the Party, which is the will of the People. This meeting, which will be the last of its kind, will not formulate policy." The commissar stopped speaking, stared at each row of faces in turn, collected his papers, and took his seat. There was a short silence, then the cadres at the back of the hall began to clap, some of the nuns joining in out of politeness. The Americans sat with their hands folded.

The hand-waving director from the RRC rose and tiptoed to the rostrum as if he feared to stop the clapping. But it quickly petered out.

He said nothing that I had not heard a thousand times before, a dreary litany of clichés about Third World debt, industrial exploitation by multinationals, planning, what rich nations owe the poor. He could have been a deacon reading the blessing after the bishop's savage sermon. His voice faded from my thoughts. I watched the Slave of Jesus. There was a consistency about him that in some ways made one respect him. The square face believed implicitly in order and will. The same as had once been preached by Hitler, the doctrine of *Eiserne Willensnatur,* "The Iron Will." Nothing changes. National Socialism, Communism, both stood on a firm bedrock of evil, consistent and predictable, denying all choice to those they purported to serve. I saw now where the officials fitted, a gray screen of faceless men like a shoal of pilot fish probing, listening, nudging us along a path marked out secretly by the Party.

Fox-face followed the RRC director.

Quickly disposing of the details of the famine, he turned to why the meeting was called. Françoise, he said, was not the easiest of people to get on with. He smiled tolerantly all the same and went on. What Slave of Jesus had said he not only supported but so did the broad mass of farmers, intellectuals, and workers. Policy was an expression of the Will of the People. The cadres clapped enthusiastically.

"Fucking bastard," an American voice whispered behind me. I turned, a fattish priest of about fifty smiled benignly at the speaker. Only Mr. Mole and Mekonnen shared the bench.

There was a pause. I began to see now why the Slave had agreed to hold the meeting. Françoise stood up and the commissar looked, almost uncertaintly, at her as if doubting her ability to speak. She walked to the rostrum, no notes in her hand, and, without hesitation, began.

It was a brilliant ex tempore performance. She started with a word completely forbidden in Aidgame, an alogos, like the Jewish Yaweh, or the Mohammeden hundredth name of the God. "Peasants." She used it again and again, driving home the difference between the people in that room and the gray ragged figures crawling about in the mud outside. The statistics showed inescapably that the camps must be closed. Not only did they attract scroungers, keep the peasants off their land, and tie up huge administrative resources—she turned toward the rostrum—they tempted governments to use them as a magnet for aid, storing the food for other reasons. When the donors understood this, the aid would stop. If governments thought that the famine was transient, or at least something that might not occur again for two or three years, they were wrong.

Therefore, if they wanted any further assistance in combating malnutrition, the government must agree to allow the foreign health teams into the villages every month to weigh the children and select those who needed special feeding. The monthly infant disease and death rates, the morbidity and mortality figures, would be an index of the district's agricultural output. If they rose suddenly the authorities would have ample warning of an incipient famine.

The Slave of Jesus' brow furrowed, his eyes becoming fixed in midair about ten inches from his nose. There was an uneasy stirring in the hall. To propose auditing the effectiveness of collective farming was outrageous. Mass labor and the ownership of the land by the state were articles of faith. Even to imply that they might fail was an appalling heresy.

Françoise paused, smiled slightly and said, "I propose that all those who agree with closing the camps and surveying the villages raise their hands."

She raised her own with a smile. In complete agreement all the representatives of the nongovernmental organizations raised their hands. Slave of Jesus, his jaw set in a horrendous line, rose, stared at Mr. Mole, and walked out, slamming the cheap frame door behind him.

Orders came the following morning for four of us to leave Sodo for Addis, preparatory to going to the north where the famine had worsened. That evening we sat around the table to decide who would stay. Tula dug herself in behind a tearful face that brooked no argument. She was going.

As one of the most experienced members of the team, Inge knew that she could not be left behind. Neither would I leave Janet behind. But as long as the others bowed to Tula's determined glare there was no choice. And bow to it they did, but not before engaging in a ritual exchange of self-sacrifice that no one around the table believed. Janet made no move, relying on the tacit assumption that she would go with me. Inge, desperate to go, volunteered to stay. I, for good measure, knowing Addis would not deprive the team of its doctor, offered to join her. Yushi, struggling with the unfamiliar tones of our tense angry English, searched our faces for a clue, gave up, and volunteered to stay. The trick was to get your bid in first. Prudence defeated a desire to keep her options open to the very end and made her bid last. It was a fatal mistake. She could not take advantage of the other bids and offer to go, nor could she just quietly offer to stay—it would appear too obvious a ploy. She was forced to prepare the most vehement case for staying in Sodo, and it was accepted. Prudence and Yushi would remain.

For appearances, the discussion went on for another hour, fueled by the emotional effect of our farewells in the camps during the day. Tula had tried to leave Bugu quietly, but two orphans she befriended had chased the ambulance down the road in tears until they were just small gesticulating dots half hidden by a cloud of dust. Abebe had refused to believe Janet and I were going until the time of the evening ritual of shaking hands. He took my hand, hesitated, then embraced both of us five times, the number demanded of friends going into a far country never to return. I last saw them as I had the first time, a line of figures standing outside the mud clinic. The old woman at the gate, a lone and toothless Greek chorus, waved in farewell. We drove over the stone ridge at the top of the hill and the figures disappeared. They live on in my mind, always waving, half hopeful, half despairing, knowing they have been left to the evil mercies of monsters and bullies. It was too painful even to weep.

Janet was apprehensive about going north, for it would mean putting our trust in Ethiopian officials in a place close to the war. If there had been a real choice she would have preferred to stay on where we were, maybe for six months. All the nurses, but especially Janet and Tula, had become very close to their Ethiopian teams, whatever they felt about the web of Party intrigue that hampered our work. As if to underline the finality of our parting, a tearful Leilt appeared at the hotel just before supper to bid Janet a second good-bye.

I lay in my sleeping bag that night and tried to read Sherlock Holmes by the light of two candles stuck in a saucer. As Holmes pursued the mystery of the Speckled Band, my thoughts kept floating from the master's precise English to the events of the past week. We had saved some lives, but for how long it was impossible to judge. If we had contributed to the closing of the camps, so much the better. (Much later, in fact, I would learn that the camps never closed.) The people were better off in their villages than being the victims of an aid program. The obscure lies of the officials meant nothing to me. In the end the peasants would destroy them.

The answer, I knew, lay in the north and I wanted desperately to get there. How could a country render 50 percent of its land totally infertile? Why did they not ask for help before? Apologists in the West, riddled with guilt, say that they did. But Ethiopian officialdom filled me with little confidence in its ability to tell the truth. I wondered if perhaps Africa would get on its feet only when all the aid ceased. Then the people would be forced to overthrow their rulers or perish themselves. I fell asleep and dreamed I was in London. I had borrowed a book from a library and nobody would let me return it. I awoke during the night with the Conan Doyle still in my hand.

The next day the officials had vanished, their office barred and shut. I saw none in the café across the road, none came to the hotel. It was as if the formula of our departure had exorcised them. Then the following afternoon, minutes before we were due to leave, the small face of Mr. Mole appeared in the driver's window, bidding us good-bye. Behind me, perched on a pile of tents and stoves, Tula made a slight raspberry noise. Inge peered at him from behind a huge pile of equipment filling the space between her and Tula and gave a grunt. The prospect of our departure, which even now at this late hour he only half believed, had changed him into a small man calmly contemplating months, even years, of quiet bungling, serving masters who he knew would not have the bad manners to check on what he did. In the Kingdom of Bureaucratic Abyssinia the debased coinage of a man's word was challenged only by fools and ferengis, neither of whom would ever know the real language of clan, tribe, or party. But it seemed that as the familiar deceptions reasserted themselves, his uncertain features betrayed a slight hint of nostalgia for the stressful days that were about to vanish, like the face of an alcoholic back in his bar after a prolonged period of abstinence.

We shook hands, the nurses called out unintelligible good wishes, he smiled and vanished back to his room.

At the top of the hill the guard who normally ignored us saluted, opened the boom, and stood to attention as we passed. I sometimes wonder if it was on the orders of the Slave of Jesus, who, behind that grim fanatical mask may have appreciated the irony of our attempts to outmaneuver him in a kingdom where he was absolute despot.

12

AIDGAME

THE FOLLOWING AFTERNOON on the outskirts of Addis we crossed the narrow-gauge railway that the French had built for the Emperor Menelik, and began to climb the long, concrete military road into the city. Our crippled engine had been nursed this far, but the last five miles to Red Cross headquarters in Addis involved a climb of more than four thousand feet. In the thin air the weakened compression banged and slapped the cylinders, forcing a halt at every hairpin. Trucks brayed at us with huge klaxons, then pulled out to swirl past in a cloud of blinding acrid dust. Tula, eyes unfocused with anxiety, stared straight ahead, waiting for one of them to pound us in the rear or, with a flick of a giant fender, send us tumbling into a ravine. Inge slept, her thin face still held in a frown. Janet had her head buried in a tattered copy of *Anna Karenina*, oblivious of the noise and staggering engine.

The strain of the journey had already distanced the four of us from Prudence and Yushi. Leaving them had upset the others and made me, who had masterminded the false democracy of their choice, realize how much the sinister methods of the Party had begun a subtle rape of my morals.

In two months there had been no rain in Addis. A thick, yellow fog hung over the city, trapped by layers of cold air drifting from the mountains that encircled it. In the center the huge portraits of the Emperor Mengistu still gazed innocently over Revolution Square, denying all knowledge of the ten thousand people who must have perished from famine in the north since his troops goosestepped past the presidential rostrum, or of the four men whose eyeballs had been shattered in the electric chair soon after at the central prison. But after Sodo, the city looked clean, almost modern. Only the larger number of shuttered shops, the weaving beggars, and the long irritated bread lines snaking out of tiny doors at the sides of government warehouses hinted at the reality.

A cleaner, disconsolately pushing a brush across the yard of Red Cross headquarters, greeted us with an indifferent stare. The office windows were blank, the main doors closed, the car park —except for Amsalu's Mercedes jeep—empty. We pulled up with a final bang of the exhaust, and the engine quit.

Amsalu's face meant trouble. Maybe one of the officials had been on the phone to the Central Investigation Center just off Adua Square. People knew it as Sostegna, or "The Third Police Station." A hint, a warning from there would effectively isolate us as securely as if we were on Mars. For "The Third" was where they kept files on everybody they suspected, especially Ethiopians with foreign contacts. And it was there those suspected of disloyalty to the Emperor Mengistu were taken, some never to be seen again. A few lucky ones, those who totally cooperated with their tormentors, get sent on from the Third to Alem Bekagne, the drab concrete block opposite the headquarters of the Organization of African Unity. Alem Bekagne means "The End of the World." Nobody came out of it.

The same two commissionaires were at the Ghion Hotel, the same porters in yellow jackets rushed to pick up our filthy bags, but inside things had changed. Where there had been torpor and solitude, there was now frantic shouting, movement, and crowds. The musty quiet of the old hotel had gone, and the lobby was filled with international bureaucrats from the large agencies, the noise of money, empty promises, and unfulfilled expectations. They were all there: men in authoritative suits, women in stern casuals, United Nations men, World Bank officials, FAO agronomists, moneylenders from the IMF, and a sprinkling of technical aid directors, all stamped with the same concerned passionate faces, the carefully casual clothes tailored to each emergency, the eyes tired by long flights. Each mind a library of compromises and deceits, ruled by the iron law of the well-paid short contract renewed only on condition of total acquiescence.

The floor in front of the checking-in desk was strewn with expensive, importantly labeled luggage, cameras, and large aluminum tins of TV film. The tables, and what empty chairs there were, littered with battered copies of the major international newspapers—*The Wall Street Journal*, London *Times*, *Figaro* and *La Stampa*, *Time* and *Newsweek*. In the evening the cleaners would eagerly gather them up. In a week black marketeers would risk six months in jail to sell them at five dollars a copy.

We checked in, went to our rooms, showered, deloused, showered again, and put on clothes left behind in the luggage depository. At six we met in the restaurant, a bowing black Jeeves of a waiter ushering us to our seats.

A voice behind me said above the hubub, "Je vous assure, mon cher collègue, le paiment est bien assuré."

At the next table a small black man, features smoothed by years of dining in the best restaurants, sat posed in a four-hundred-dollar suit in front of a filet mignon. Opposite a tall chinless man of about fifty, a few strands of reddish-blond hair bound across a skull dotted with red freckles, goggled at him like a fish confronted with a hook.

The thin man's Adam apple bobbed uncertainly, hands gripped the thick linen tablecloth. He leaned forward and announced in a somber Norwegian singsong, "My fishpaste is highly nutritious. We can supply ten tons per day, but we must have transport. The U.N., your department, promised it ten months ago."

Across the aisle waiters carrying white napkins began pulling out chairs. Four Americans walked in. One was an enormously fat man of about thirty, so fat he walked tilted back like a woman at the point of confinement. The party took their seats. The fat American leaned forward and said something in atrocious French to the waiter, stuffed a napkin under a chin which lay folded three times over a bursting collar, and bent to his spaghetti, eating it in one continuous reverse vomit from plate to mouth. He finished, wiped his lips, then reached forward, caressed a pile of bread rolls with pudgy fingers. He seized two and stuffed them rapidly into his mouth.

The four of us sat silent and rigid, imploring each other not to look. Tula gave a slight snuffle, Inge smiled with embarrassment into her soup, Janet twisted her head from side to side as if trying to shake off a cobweb. I felt my sides begin to heave.

We snuffled and choked behind our pretentious menus, pretended to bend down to tie shoelaces, laughed at imitation jokes, pinched arms until they bruised, pulled our faces straight until teeth began to ache. But the fat man offered no relief. He ordered a plate of soup, spooned some of it into his mouth, then lifted the plate and drank the residue. The waiter wheeled in a serving dish of turkey. The fat man watched the others being served, eyes narrowed. When his turn came he seized the waiter's fork and doubled his portion. Half an hour later he finished his meal with a peach melba and three eclairs. We watched, the last two months drifting away in our muffled hysteria—the gray officials, Abebe's son, the boy who died of typhoid. In one corner a small wind and string ensemble swung into a Victor Sylvester foxtrot, waves of chatter from the gathering crowd of diners obscuring the bleating lines of "Blue Moon."

The telephone woke me at seven next morning. It was Brit, her voice distant then near as the power fluctuated.

The slight breaks in her usual tone of flat optimism spoke of a terrifying catastrophe. Over five hundred people, increasing by five hundred a day, had gathered outside the old medieval market town of Bati in a last desperate hope of food. Once thriving, the town had been reduced to an impoverished collection of shacks set on a river infested with amoeba and schistosomiasis. Her tale was a catalogue of disaster. Each morning they found at least fifty dead, a Swiss International Red Cross man had been killed in a road accident, the hospital water supply had long been disconnected, and even if it had not been, it was undrinkable. There were no drugs.

Then there was the politicking over "feeding rights." By now the major agencies were awash with money and living in fear of their donors. Everybody in the West knew about the famine, and those who had given money would want to know what was being done. Under the eyes of the Western press the agencies had to be seen to be doing something. Large camps were visible, compassionate, and caring. Permission to open such centers, permission to feed the starving—even if it meant submitting to the humiliating intrigues of the government officials—was now eagerly sought. One day the officials favored the Red Cross, the next Médecins San Frontières, then a regrettable show of impatience by one of the delegates, a risqué political joke, might swing the odds in favor of an outsider such as Irish Concern. Maybe tomorrow it would be the turn of the Israelis, who, somewhere in the desert, were rumored to be moving toward Bati. The same sort of thing was going on all over the north. Suddenly the RRC, once despised, became, as the sole representative of government policy on the famine, the key to winning a major round of Aidgame. It was rather as if a bankrupt, attending the auction of his squandered estate, had been suddenly invited to be the auctioneer.

But the greatest danger, Brit continued, came from the local Party officials' attitude toward the refugees. They were becoming dangerously frightened of the growing mob which, camped like a gray cloud of locusts on the hills around the town, threatened to engulf them. She didn't elaborate but began to read out a list of supplies that were needed immediately. It took twenty minutes. When the phone went dead I looked at the sheets of scrawled paper. What Brit had asked for would fill three eight-ton trucks and tomorrow was a public holiday. It might be a week before we could fill such an order.

We drifted over to Red Cross headquarters in a pessimistic mood after a poor breakfast of eggs soaked in garlic. There were few staff about, dust filled the corridors, and the single flush toilet next to Amsalu's office stank. Our Toyota had been removed, Amsalu had locked his door, and it was only with difficulty that Inge found our letters. Stranded, we sat about on the dirty stairs, smoking, reading stale news from home and speculating about filling Brit's list.

Inge went to the toilet and returned with news of a new assistant chief delegate to Svensen, a Swede called Lundqvist. She had worked with him in Somalia and spoke highly of him, but in Aidgame as in show business praise is so lavishly poured on everybody it can mean everything or nothing.

Svensen himself appeared at ten, his thin erect figure slightly bent as he climbed the stairs toward us. After greeting the others he took my arm and led me back outside into the center of the yard, paused, stared at me with watery blue eyes for a moment, then said to me, "You know, the Ethiopians are, as you say in English, on to you."

I stared at him in surprise, wondering if he really knew what he had just said. Scandinavians often neglect the subtle idioms of English in favor of an almost clinical mastery of its technicalities. Had he really been told by the Ethiopians that I was not what I seemed (a favorite method of theirs to denigrate somebody)? Or did he mean they had united against me over Sodo and wanted me out? He watched me closely, a jokey, almost fatherly, expression on his pale face. The significance of holding the conversation in the yard suddenly struck me. The Swedish colonel was not such a fool as to talk about such things inside a building that was almost certainly bugged. It meant he believed some extraordinary fabrication he had been told by one of the staff, possibly Amsalu.

He stood there uncertainly, hoping for an answer, a decent man who believed what people told him. How they must have suspected him at Security Police headquarters!

But we had done exactly what we had been instructed to do by Geneva: emptied the camps of all except the very ill and returned the rest of the people to their villages.

Such a success would have found little favor with the Ethiopians. Suddenly, almost but not entirely unexpectedly, they had been washed into the center of a disaster worse than World War I, with daily casualty rates exceeding those of Paschendale or Verdun. Confused and frightened, their only remedy, huge feeding programs, seemed the only rock to cling to. Then we came along and tried to close down their camps. Closing down their operations implied their failure, and, as in most aid programs, threatened bureaucratic livelihood. Famine camps meant foreign aid, foreign aid meant jobs. And then there was the Party. The Party wanted the camps in the south to remain open. Nobody disobeyed the Party.

Svensen thought for a moment, his innocent kindly face squinting against the bright winter sunlight. It was not the actual work—that, he agreed, had been well done. Everybody said so. It was the development of good relationships with the Ethiopians he was worried about, and in that I scored no marks at all. "You see," he said, "you come on very strong for the Ethiopians."

I offered to resign. Resigning delegates, especially if they are experienced, are taken very seriously by Geneva, and to threaten Svensen with such a weapon was underhanded, mean, and by his lights, dishonorable.

He looked shocked, then refused, and we stood there slightly ashamed, each feeling he had been ill mannered. He began to speak at once of the famine in the north, and still talking, we left the bright sunlit yard and walked upstairs to meet his new assistant.

Lundqvist sat behind a huge desk, smoking a cigarette, its end wet and fragmenting. He was about fifty, his eyes dominated by a pair of half-frame glasses fitted with immensely thick plastic lenses. His movements and voice were slow to the point of torpidity, his English too perfect. Geneva had sent him to advise Svensen, but Svensen excused himself and left the office sideways, his eyes never leaving Lundqvist's face.

Lundqvist stubbed out his cigarette with theatrical precision, made some vaguely flattering remarks about the Sodo operation, and asked me to give him more details. It soon became obvious that talking to him was a one-way gate, deliveries going in, but no payments coming out. His inability or unwillingness to answer questions he blamed on his advisory position, the lack of time he had had to learn what he called the "operational setup." Secretaries came and went with bulky files. He offered me some coffee. I asked him about Bati. Lighting his fifth cigarette, he said, "Already the disaster has begun. It started with the arrival of the first foreign aid."

If it was an attempt at lateral thinking, I was too tired to rise to it, or to think of its implications. Maybe Lundqvist was right—none of us should be here. But you could accept that premise only if you saw the success of our own societies, our ability to feed ourselves and have a surplus to give away, as destructive to others. We parted inconclusively.

In the streets that afternoon people read for the first time about the famine. The country's only paper, the *Ethiopian Herald*, printed on cheap stained paper like a parish magazine, showed blurred pictures of hills and people that the editorial claimed were starving. But nobody seriously believed a paper that so crudely rearranged group photos of Mengistu among world figures so that he was always standing next to the most important one, forgers so contemptuous of the reader that they often left the scissor line showing between the figures. In the city's main hospital, a ramshackle skyscraper without working elevators, that smelt of berber spice and sweat, the doctors were shown a video of the BBC's famous documentary about the famine in Wollo behind doors locked and guarded by the secret police. Afterwards they asked for volunteers. To our inquiries about permits and supplies, Amsalu replied that there were no trucks, and the pharmacist was away on a course on drugs to promote fertility and he himself was ill.

The chanting from the Coptic cathedral across the square started at two on Sunday morning. All night it floated in and out of the room pawing at my sleep. At six, fully awake, I lay there listening, my mind half on the problems of getting supplies, half on the idea of going to Mass. The Mass won.

The church was modern, perhaps built twenty years ago and raised on a plinth of steps that met every wall. On them a crowd of beggars, old women, hawkers, and elderly men slowly circled the walls, for some reason unwilling to enter the darkened chantry. Others stood in surrounding gardens, praying, talking, or begging. At the entrance were two half-open cast-iron metal gates. A dozen crones in white head shawls clung desperately to the closed gate as if forbidden to enter.

I took off my shoes and entered the lantern-shaped church. The sound of the chanting seemed to recede, then intensify, then recede again. Icons of sloe-eyed saints peered through the incense and candlelight over the humped forms of chamma-clad worshipers prostrate on the cold stone floor. A choir patrolled through them, holding T-shaped crosses and singing from tattered leather hymnals. The Mass itself was invisible, held behind the icons that completely shut the altar from view.

An hour later as I wriggled my feet back into my shoes, a hand touched my shoulder. I turned to see Brihanu, the man who had first met us at the airport, a chamma rucked around his neck over a neat blue suit, smiling quietly at me, a Party cadre who went to Mass. It seemed months ago since he got us our driving licenses and fixed our permits to go to Sodo. He still drove the broken-backed Peugeot. He took my arm and led me through the gates and across the road to where a twice life-size bronze statue of Lenin gazed with an inane grin over a small stone parapet at the city. Below its nose was a filthy, rubbish-strewn river.

Brihanu pointed to him with a soft grin. "We call that Lenin walking to the airport without his suitcase." It seemed a trick, something to make me launch into a polemic about the Party. Seeing my anxiety, he smiled, taking my shoulder.

"This afternoon I want to take you somewhere special, a present. Meet me at two with the rest of the team."

He arrived exactly at two in a white VW with a huge Red Cross painted on the roof against air attack. Inge, Tula, Janet, and I squeezed into its torn seats, and Brihanu drove us south toward the outskirts. After three miles he turned suddenly down a concealed, badly rutted side road that led to a car park guarded by four armed sentries. Along one side was a green corrugated fence overlooked by a watch tower. Brihanu got out, paid one of the urchins crowding about him some small cash to look after the car, and led us to a gate. An old man sold him five tickets at a birr each and we passed through the wicket.

The green corrugated fence with its dog-tooth paling did not, as I had first suspected, conceal a prison. Instead, we found ourselves on a steeply sloping hill leading down to the same muddy river that I had stood by with Brihanu in the morning. In front of us was an enormous ornamental garden, filled with plants, exotic trees, laurel-crowned Roman heads on marble plinths, gazebos, and, halfway down to the river, an Italianate villa, its arches entwined with flowered creepers and surrounded by Mediterranean palms. We walked slowly down the hill, passing a wedding party in Western evening dress coming the other way. "Here," said Brihanu, "is the place of weddings."

The villa smelt of damp earth, wet plaster, and stagnant pools. It was full of plants that otherwise would die in the cool night air of Addis. "It belonged to an Italian capitalist, but after the revolution he gave his house and gardens to the people and stayed on to look after it as a keeper. He is dead now, he was old."

Inge prowled about looking at the plants, back hunched, hands clasped behind her. Janet, a passionate gardener, called out the names of the plants excitedly. But the memory of the orphans running after our truck at Bugu still haunted Tula, making her tearful and withdrawn. After ten minutes Brihanu led us out of the villa, down the hill to a flat space at the river's edge. On the grass a marriage party sat quietly, in its center a bride in a formal silk wedding dress. A man holding a single-stringed violin with a box-shaped case got up from behind the groom, greeted Brihanu, and pointed to an open-sided hut with four or five chairs. We went in. The man bowed and snapped his fingers behind his back. A woman of about thirty rose and walked toward us. She had a pinched face in which were set two sad, preoccupied eyes. She had no teeth.

The violinist flourished his bow and adjusted a small neat tie. Outside the wedding party remained silent, their impassive faces waiting for his return, the groom and groomsmen stiff and posed in their unfamiliar evening dress like a Victorian photograph.

Brihanu said, "They will play for you a song about Gondar, the ancient capital where once the tribes came in their thousands to do homage in the dust of the Negus, the king; then one of love, then one of the death of friends." Inge crouched tense and uneasy in a corner.

The man drew a thick-stringed bow across the fragile gut of his instrument. The woman wound thin brown fingers tightly around her knees, set her head back and waited, eyes half closed. He began to play.

Ethiopian music is almost unbearably sad, thin, dying laments woven in a tapestry of conflicting tones, Western in form, Arabic in style. The beat, a slow tapping on the leather case of the masenko, mingles with the shifting notes of its single string. The woman began to sing, a wild lament that seemed to have no limit, rising and falling, spreading and retreating to the sad advice of the violin which, faithfully taking each phrase, added or subtracted to it before surrendering it to her for the next passage. When it was over he put five birr into the singer's hand and kissed her on both cheeks. Her lack of teeth made her seem like an old woman.

Brihanu said, "We Abyssinians"—Ethiopians always use the term "Abyssinian" when they wanted to apologize for something they think discreditable or weak—"we Abyssinians are a sentimental people. Even the slightest of sad songs moves us. What else would you expect of a people who talk in parables?" His face was set in a deep frown. He looked along the path in front of us. "If you pay these singers they will put the names of your friends or loved ones in the song, or tell your favorite stories. The clever ones find out by talking cunningly to you before they play where you come from, who you are, like a teller of fortunes, then they sing as if they know all about you. It is good manners to please a stranger."

"Even if it is not the truth you tell him?"

"In all people's hearts there are many truths, and in the Abyssinian heart ten times ten truths."

I looked to see if he were smiling, but his face was impassive.

Suddenly, he stopped, moved off the path onto the grass and turned his back on a short, stocky man walking toward us. Footsteps passed.

"That was my brother, an evil man, a thief. I have not spoken to him since the revolution." The man did not even glance back.

That night I lay under the thick East German blankets of my bed in the Ghion and thought about Brihanu and the Italian garden. Had he been trying to stage a crude political allegory? Some sort of warning? Ethiopians are masters of intrigue and it seemed unlikely that he of all people would be guilty of such a solecism. The only explanation was that he had made it deliberately crude. Ethiopians set almost no store by Western sophistication in matters of politics, merely regarding us as clever toymasters, wanting in sense.

But it hardly mattered, all I had to do was hide behind the rules of a contract that forbade all discussion of politics. I fell asleep to the whine of Antonov prop jets taking off and landing at the airport.

A visiting representative of the British Red Cross joined us the next morning for breakfast—a large, noisy, perspiring man of about thirty-five whose fat skin looked slightly sticky even in the morning cool of Addis. He talked with great speed, narrow eyes focused either on the tablecloth or on a spot about four inches above the top of his listener's head. An elderly waiter in a dinner jacket so old it was turning slightly green brought him a message on a metal tray. A BBC reporter had phoned ten minutes earlier from the Hilton, asking to speak to him. The absorbed face changed to one of attentive calculation. Muttering excuses, he rose, took a frantic swig at his orange juice, and left. The waiter proferred the tray at Tula for a tip.

Whatever his business with the BBC, it did not take long. When we arrived at headquarters the gnomelike figure of Ato Mariam, a senior official of the Ethiopian Red Cross, long cigarette holder clamped between his stained teeth, stood waiting at the top of the steps with him. Mariam shepherded us into his office, sat down, flicked some ash off his holder, and treated us all to a mischievous grin. He asked about Sodo, eyes narrowing with pleasure seconds before any of us spoke. When we had finished he shot his cuffs and turned to the British Red Cross man.

The BBC and British Independent Television were on their way to Bati and would arrive early tomorrow, before we even left Addis. The secretary general looked amused and screwed another yellow cigarette into his holder, examining my face as if this piece of news meant something. There was a knock on the door and Svensen entered, face respectful, holding a telex. More TV teams were on their way. Would we, asked the secretary general, be able to leave immediately? A vision of arriving empty-handed in Bati to face not only the dying thousands but the hostile questioning of the TV reporters did not appeal. Perhaps if I could have the drugs and equipment that Brit had asked for? The little man raised his hand reassuringly, they would be dispatched within two days. Meanwhile, we would be given a check to purchase the supplies we needed from the government medical stores, and we would be given a truck for those we needed immediately but would not have room for in our Toyota. The rest would come later. Brihanu had been told to get our permits ready first thing tomorrow.

The carte blanche was unprecedented. All we had to do was to present a certified check to the government stores to get whatever we wanted. News of this astonishing sidetracking of the bureaucracy spread rapidly. By midday the chief pharmacist came hurrying from his conference on fertility to try and put a stop to it. Each item, he said, must be taken to the Red Cross warehouse, unloaded, properly invoiced and shelved, then reallocated to us after we had obtained the necessary papers from headquarters. He would see that the whole matter would take no more than a fortnight. Fortunately he was too late to put his plan into action. The seven-tonners, loaded with blankets, tents, and cooking equipment were already somewhere on the road to Bati. The Toyota was crammed with medical supplies and locked. I had no intention of letting him have the keys. He became quite angry, but there was nothing he could do except content himself with shouting and raging at the loading clerks. After a while he walked off muttering, got into his car and drove off.

At about three a new telex arrived at headquarters. The TV teams were delayed and might not be arriving for a week. The smiles and assurances that we had left at headquarters in the morning were now gone. There was muttering about insensitivity and needless haste. There were complaints that our truck was blocking two spaces in the car park. We returned to our hotel knowing that unless Brihanu came up with the permits we could be left in the city for weeks.

We packed our best clothes in their plastic wrappers, added mothballs and deposited them in the hotel luggage repository, sorted out our luggage and went to bed early. We would know in the morning.

We assembled at six in the hall, paid our bills and stumbled out, the siren marking the end of curfew still sounding, to wait for Brihanu's VW. He arrived at seven with four packages wrapped in cheap white paper. One contained twenty cartons of milk, one the same number of small buns, the third some loose cigarettes, the fourth sandwiches. He produced a Michelin map of northern Ethiopia and handed it to me.

"I have all the permits, but the Ethiopian Red Cross will not provide you with an Ethiopian guide. It is against the law for ferengis to travel without one, but I will phone a friend in traffic control at Dese. You will not be troubled.

"Give the milk to the poor if they try to stand in your road, the matches and the cigarettes to the soldiers. The sandwiches are for you. If you follow me I will take you to the outskirts of the city." He started his engine and waved at us to follow.

Already trains of trucks were heading like huge earwigs toward the city barriers. Most, when they left the city, would move east toward the port of Assab along the safe lower road crossing the Danakil. Our route would take us almost due north for two hundred and fifty miles, then due east for the last fifty down a pass into the Danakil desert.

Nobody stopped us at the barrier, the boom was down lying halfway across the road as if dropped from a truck. The solitary soldier barely waved his hand to tell us to pass. Beyond was a stone bridge and a grove of fir trees. Brihanu waved at us to pull off.

As he walked back to us I began to wonder about him again. He seemed to have an endless supply of good suits. The one he was wearing now was a silver herringbone with neat-patterned Italian shoes. To this day I have never understood how Brihanu could have been so different from other officials. While most Ethiopians were panic-stricken by foreigners, Brihanu was extraordinarily at ease with us.

Coming up to the window of the jeep he looked carefully at each of us, smiling slightly. "I will come as soon as I can, and bring more food. Melons perhaps. God will be with you."

He embraced each of us four times—a casual friend merits one embrace, your closest relative ten—got into his car, waved, and with a clatter of noisy exhaust swayed back toward the haze of pollution that shrouded the city.

We drove across the bridge out into the country.

13

SPECTERS

MINUTES BEFORE we had been in the midst of a noisy, roaring city, now, apart from some solitary donkeys, a couple of sheep and a small flocks of goats, we saw nothing. What trees there were began to thin out, giving way to a desolate prairie broken here and there by long, brown, stone walls and the occasional hut. No cars passed, we saw no people. It was as if we were running off the edge of the world. This was the dead zone between the famine and Mengistu's capital. Eighty miles away in Debre Birhan there would be roadblocks and soldiers preventing refugees from reaching the capital. A Russian helicopter chattered overhead, swinging slightly to look at us, then swung away to the west.

It was along this stretch of crumbling, weed-filled concrete that the Italian armies who defeated the last emperor, Haile Selassie, had come. Now another army was waiting beyond Debre Birhan, an army of starving ghostlike men with burning famine eyes, more dangerous to Mengistu than white men in halftracks and tanks.

After two hours the prairie gave way to a rolling escarpment covered in short yellow grass. The road twisted and turned through it, passing deserted houses and tumbled stone. A huge wind blew and it began to rain, a slight gray drizzle that turned the windshield into a soup of mud and crushed insects. We struggled into warm coats. Inge passed around some coffee. Twenty miles away on the crest of an escarpment some small black rectangles announced the outskirts of a town. We passed through its barrier half an hour later, to be immediately among throngs of traders, beggars, farmers, and townspeople. The division between life and sterility on either side of the barrier was absolute.

Inge suddenly shouted, "Look!"

We were aware rather than saw the ghostlike, gray, ragged figures everywhere, flitting in and out of groups of traders, holding thin, wasted hands up to men on horseback, crouching over uncontrollable diarrhea in corners, over ditches, even in the road. In the center of the market square an old man and a young woman circled a water pump, distractedly begging for alms among an indifferent unseeing crowd. Next to the pump on a pile of gray rags, a skeletal two-year-old child with a skull-like face held its hands out through a cloud of flies and screamed with pain. Two more lay prostrate in the mud, their feet almost touching a pile of oranges over which a turbaned man shouted a price. A peasant led his donkey in front of them and the tiny tragedy was swallowed in the crowd. Within two minutes we were outside the town and descending a long pass.

There it was the same; at the sound of the engine, starving figures began to emerge from the thin cover of dry grass and black bushes along the side of the road, sticklike arms extended, palms upwards. Gray figures warned on the horizon, and on the surrounding hillsides small groups were gathered under trees, standing, sitting, or lying, faces turned toward our truck. Some lay in absolute stillness under a dense cloud of flies. Soldiers at the barrier farther down shouted something. Two detached themselves and began to run down the hill on heavily shod army boots. A group of ghosts heading toward us flitted back into the grass.

After Debre Birhan the road climbed steeply, skirting the

deepest part of the Rift so that our Toyota seemed like a fly edging up to the rim of a gigantic bowl. It took four hours to reach the summit set in a landscape empty of people with only the cry of moor birds and a bitter east wind. A hundred yards farther on the road vanished into a tunnel. It was only here in a place too cold and bleak for the specters to exist or have the strength to climb up to that we could eat. Tula brought out the sandwiches that Brihanu had bought, pressed ham and cheese that must have cost him a substantial portion of a week's salary. Survival in catastrophe depends on detachment, but the packets of milk and bread mocked us from a ledge above the driver's seat.

The tunnel was half a mile of unlit track filled with a deep layer of loose gravel so that the truck swayed and slid like a small boat in a swell. Midway two dead donkeys lay side by side in the half light, their swollen bodies shaped to the smoothness of stranded whales. The gravel was deepest there, slowing us near the stench. In the sunlight just beyond the exit two young soldiers laughed inside a guard post of rough breeze blocks surrounded by a concertina of barbed wire. Armed sentries patrolled the narrow ledges and paths immediately above. If a starving man climbed the eight thousand feet from the valley below he would be turned back here. There was no other way across the pass. The ghosts of Debre Birhan must have come from the west where there was supposed to be fertile land and good rains. A little farther on, over the edge of the precipice, the road zigzagged down eight miles of hairpins, slashed through a village, fell toward some oddly colored green-yellow vegetation, then headed north up a wide valley. Around the hairpins three Red Cross Mercedes trucks were coming at tremendous speed, exhaust stacks belching, klaxons hooting. To the right, both in the distance and immediately above us, mountain pinnacles shaped like filed teeth marked the old limits of the Kingdom of Solomon.

In half an hour we passed from high, cold moorland to desert. At the foot of the pass a decaying town leaned against the mountain, killed by beggars, overwhelmed by them until the inhabitants had either joined their ranks or fled. They swarmed everywhere, ants in a piece of decaying timber, camping out among its wrecked buildings, crawling about the road, or just lying inert in the ditches and drains. The stronger bartered rags and sticks in what was left of a market, while here and there whole families gathered in corners waiting for the end. We handed out all of Brihanu's milk through the windows, and drove quickly away.

The road surface changed from concrete to tar, wet in the afternoon glare. Small hills of gray stone led down to fields of cinders. A green police Toyota raced past, followed by a long file of open trucks filled with sharp brutalized faces among a forest of rifle barrels. A mile farther on the convoy swerved off the road and headed into the desert in front of a huge plume of dust.

Unlike the town that had died at the foot of the pass, the towns farther north had instituted a kind of apartheid between the fed and the starving. Life continued normally for the fed. Shops opened, cafés were filled, people wore suits, chatted, read the yellow pages of the *Ethiopian Herald*, while between them, unseen as the ghosts of Debre Birhan, walked, crawled, or lay, hundreds of gray, ragged skeletons. How did they become the ghosts? Suddenly? Overnight? Were they only landless peasants or were there destitute traders among them? There was no rubbish in these towns, the ghosts ate or burned everything that was thrown away.

We made our last stop for gas at dusk in Kembolcha, then turned right toward Bati and the desert. The examination of our papers at the town barrier was thorough and repeated by a police patrol a mile farther on. The road began to descend again through a narrow pass, spinning about on itself, crossing dried-out wadis, passing through short tunnels adorned with curved Roman arches. With each descending curve it got hotter. A moon rose, revealing the fringes of a great desert.

The Danakil is said to be, outside the Gibson in Australia and the Empty Quarter in Arabia, one of the hottest places in the world. It stretches some two hundred miles from the foothills of the Ethiopian Plateau to the Red Sea. Temperatures often reach one hundred and forty degrees Fahrenheit and its nomads, the Afars, apart from an unsavory habit of taking testicles from enemies for bride price, wear several layers of clothing to keep in what cool air they can in the paralyzing heat. Until the middle of the last century the Danakil cut off most of the Coptic Kingdom from the outside world. Bati, which lies on its edge two thousand feet above sea level, was one of the few gateways to it. Songs written in the Middle Ages still circulate about the beauty of its women.

The gray light lit mirror-flat stretches of sand interspersed with bluish-black mountains, salt pans, and long furrows of exposed basalt rock. It was a threatening, hellish place that seemed alive yet in which there was no living thing. Along the road, dark, ruined villages loomed up, here and there a flicker of red fire in one of the houses caught the shadows of an impoverished interior. After two hours, the satellite repeating station Brihanu had told us to look for appeared high on a ridge against the sky. Around a corner an electric light blazed behind a set of blue pillars. A notice on the side of the road with an arrow said KURSA HOTEL.

Brit came down the steps to greet us, wearing exactly the same clothes as when we had parted: long gray frock, old-fashioned silk blouse, and red scarf. With her was a fat, impeccably dressed man speaking perfect English and constantly patting his hair into place. He introduced himself as the manager, Teferi Dessie. Brit later told us he was in exile from Addis for the next two years. In a room at the back of the hotel he kept a beautiful wife of eighteen. He was over forty.

Like at least three-quarters of the roads, the railways, the bridges, the offices, and the hotels, the Kursa had been built by the Italians. Its veranda roof was supported by blue-painted Doric columns, its walls yellow, the floors red tile. Inside was a large, bare room with a small bar in one corner. A cheap colored devotional of Lenin's arrival at the Finland

Station hung on the end wall, at the other a prewar map of
Ethiopia much stained with grease. The rooms lay at the back
in a separate building. Those nearest the toilets were barely
habitable. Teferi would give me a key before we went to bed
"for the private bathrooms" around the back. Otherwise, he
said, we would have to share with the truck drivers.

A high wire fence surrounded the sleeping quarters to keep
out both thieves and the packs of wild dogs that were already
howling in the surrounding scrub. Two badly torn cats played
with their kittens outside a kitchen almost entirely filled with
a wood-burning stove. Bougainvillea grew everywhere.

We sat down that evening to cold 'tibbs, hard bread, and
bottled mineral water. Brit told us the death rate had risen to
over seventy a day and was getting rapidly worse. There were
now over thirty thousand people in the camp with five
hundred more arriving each day. They were being supplied
with some food, but the problem was registering them, finding out who really needed food, and then making sure that
they, not the healthy, got it. In addition the food had to be
trucked up from the Red Cross stores in Addis. As we stood
talking, convoys of grain trucks passed the hotel from the
ports heading north to the highlands. Bati was not the only
camp. The highlands were in the grip of famine, and in the
north was war. Whole cities there were dying, and in the
mountains isolated villages waited silently for the end.

Two of the trucks pulled up outside, doors slammed, and
the drivers, laughing and shouting, climbed the long flight of
steps up to the restaurant. They wore machine pistols over
their shoulders.

To get to Bati they had climbed four thousand feet out of
the ferocious heat of the Red Sea plain leaving behind them
the salt pans and gray wadis of the Danakil desert. It was
there that the Afars, the world's toughest nomads, lived. The
road from the port of Assab to Bati was dangerous, and the
Afar guerrillas were crack shots and mad with hatred of the
government. They took no prisoners. Yet we were to see their
caravans and camel herds each day in Bati, their riders armed

with Kalashnikovs or ancient Mausers. The few police and government soldiers in the town gave them a wide berth. Nor were the tribesmen affected very much by the famine, adept at survival and self-disciplined, they managed to find all the food they needed. Their children were healthy, their women extraordinarily beautiful. Dangerous as they were, they would never harm us.

And there were others who had fought the government. In the long borderlands between the desert and the highlands lived semisettled and settled farmers. But they lacked the tight discipline of the Afars in the face of catastrophe and the famine brought them to heel. We were to find many of them in our camps, apathetic, their children dying.

Beyond the hill tribes and the Afars lay the Red Sea, and the Russians. They had established themselves along its coast, poised at a moment's notice to close the waterway leading to Suez. The more empty land that lay between them and the Afars the better, so the Ethiopian government, obedient to its Russian masters, continued with its policy of sealing off the tribesmen's waterholes and driving off their cattle.

We left the drivers there, bent hungrily over their fatty 'tibbs after the tension of the desert crossing. I went to bed, undressed, lay on top of my sleeping bag and plunged myself into the adventure of Holmes and the Red Headed League. It was best to put out of mind the next two months. They would come. At eleven the distant humming of a generator ceased and the compound was plunged into darkness.

14

BATI

TWO MONTHS LATER I lay in the warm darkness and thought of the day's unchanged sequences, trying to etch them on my mind. It was eleven at night. A dog howled somewhere out in the desert. A cat squealed. Something slithered under the dry, dead leaves outside my door. There was a dull, grunting report. The light of a distant fire flickered against the window. Three miles away thirty thousand people lay dying for want of food and water, while farther out in the desert their kinsmen, armed with ancient rifles, crouched in foxholes prepared to take on a modern army. Janet, sick with amebiasis, stirred feverishly beside me. Tomorrow I was taking her to Addis for some blood tests.

It was eleven at night, the end of two months in Bati. Why had we come? Adventure and pay? A pursuit of scenes that never will be painted, photographed, or filmed for television, over which no memorial will be raised. Not the great dramas of shuffling, dying peasants, the mounds of corpses, the fly-infested children. But the look in the eyes of a commissar as he ordered the seizure of a peasant's ration card. The sound of a young boy crying by a wall. "What is the matter?" "I am hungry." The terror of an eight-year-old child's hand pulling you to a tent where her mother, the last of her family, stares motionless at the sky.

Everywhere there were the cameras, the newsmen, the urgent microphones thrust before the lips of the dying, all groping for the salacious, the thrill of death, like a crowd around a gallows gasping at the drop. But I was looking for something beyond that, for what Prudence had looked for among those butchered remains in a Palestinian camp, the "Heart of Darkness," the unwritten laws of animal survival that destroy our humanity. These small scenes that I pursued were skirmishes on its outer fringes, patrols making first contact with the unalterable demands of nature. Demands that laugh at laws, morals, love. Man, says *The Heart of Darkness*, is an actor forced to take part in a play whose lethal lines he must eventually say and die. I wanted to know it was untrue.

The absurd politics had come to mean less and less as the days passed. By the time we arrived in Bati it was far too late to do anything—even if we had had the power—about the ravages of incompetent agricultural policies, brutal Party hacks, the desert war, simple indolence, or even plain greed. Once again the peasants had been abandoned to the judgment of nature. We could only temper its merciless revenge.

Prisoners say their days pass with frightening speed, one indistinguishable from the next, while the weeks and months crawl by. So it was with us. Each day was unchanging, set against a fixed landscape devoid of color. A world of gray dust, black rocks, and dry, fissured watercourses looked down on by bare hills. Life became a relentless competition between exhaustion and depression, its pain avoided by always thinking of the future: getting home to Europe, the first meal in Geneva, a visit to a large shop, winter clothes, a clean lavatory. Petty illness plagued us and a tired numbness hung to each leg so that the endless walking through the dust ate at the nerves. In the valley the air never moved. Only at night did a slight cooling bring relief.

The day had as always begun and ended in the graveyard with the muezzin's cry: "There is only one God but God, and

Muhammad his prophet . . ." In the morning as the voice, coughing slightly now from weakness and a chest infection, trailed away on the loudspeaker, the gravediggers set out from the camp toward the five low hills to the north. They carried long crowbars, a few shovels, and many picks, for the desert here is iron hard. As they passed across the square in front of the hospital, people fell back in front of them, as from a procession of priests or magicians, set aside, marginals of society. For everyone who watched them knew the hands carrying those picks and bars might well carry their corpses tomorrow, even this evening, easing them onto the circular shelves they dug ten feet below the ground. Only the ferengi knew they would never be touched by these men, even in death.

The diggers were building a new city on the five iron hills above the camp, five hundred circular towers of carefully stacked stone topped with sloping roofs of earth, a city of the dead. Each house in the city was made by digging a circular hole, then cutting a shelf around its wall——on the shelf they would lay the bodies. Usually by ten a.m. three such holes had been made. Then the men rested, often in the waiting graves, eating small chappatis made from wheat flour, smoking vilely smelling cigarettes or chewing chat, a stimulant that wipes out sleep.

After they had rested, their leader would go to a tent at the head of the hill where the clerk, by now half crazy with the same drug, would have prepared a list of the night's dead, carried by relatives up the hill toward a square tent of black plastic. Adults were carried here, the aged, and above all children, borne in the arms of their fathers, heads flung back, small feet swinging. In the black tent they were numbered, their names recorded, each given a shroud made from a flour sack, then laid in rows to wait.

Their people would come to bury them in the afternoon, gathering around the pits to shuffle and weep while the gravediggers laid each body head to toe on the circular shelves. When there was no more room, the pit was filled with stones. By five the small houses, each containing perhaps twenty inmates, would be shut forever. The survivors, usually four, sometimes only one, and sometimes that one a sole surviving child, would make their way back to the camp. From the town the muezzin would cry out again from the tall mosque, among lengthening shadows. Jackals, hyenas, and a strange catlike animal not unlike a sphinx, that remained clearly visible in the day just outside of accurate focus, would stir themselves for the night's work.

Each morning we ate breakfast on the hotel veranda looking across the road to a range of low scrub-covered hills patterned with empty dried-out terraces. A herd of camels about one hundred strong made its way down a defile, their young scurrying about at the rear, fed back into the pack by small boys with long poles like fishing rods. We heard the muezzin's dawn cry as an army truck in Russian camouflage backed up to the guard post of the satellite station and disgorged the morning watch. Deep in the base of the valley an old man walked, half bent, in a flourishing garden at the side of a narrow flowing river, his plants the only living things to be seen aside from camels, humans, and kites. We drank our first glass of the Kursa's fresh orange juice. The food would falter, at times run out, but the orange juice supplied from the garden below us was always available.

At eight we left for the camp, taking the road through Bati.

The town was three kilometers away, clinging to the side of a brown, treeless hill. It had not changed since our arrival two months ago. Long, struggling terraces of corrugated-iron shapes, a mosque, a potholed, dust-filled street surging with an aimless crowd of peasants, beggars, Party officials, camels, donkeys, and soldiers in green fatigues. The terraces led down to a river that cut a deep trench in a stretch of gray sand, its black greasy water slipping slowly from rock pool to rock pool before vanishing around the corner of the hill toward the desert.

When we had first arrived the camp was hardly noticeable. Something that, driving through the town, the casual traveler would have hardly noticed, although close up it was unforgettable. The entire floor of the valley had been covered in a mass of gray, ragged shapes which, indistinguishable at a distance from the mud-gray sand, became a sea of skeletons draped in gray sacking, hideous caricatures so bereft of flesh they seemed mere collections of triangles shrouded in cloth. Unwittingly or instinctively, they had formed themselves into groups of about two hundred, separated by narrow paths to carry out the dead, admit more in their place, or allow the stronger to wander scavenging for food, shelter, or scraps of bush to light a fire at night. The lucky ones had built small wigwams of cloth and paper, inside which the sickest member of the family lay or sat, their filthy rags flapping like Tibetan prayer flags. Around the families a steady procession of weakened, staggering women and children headed back and forth from the river, carrying certain death in the jars on their shoulders, for with schistosomiasis the water brought other more sudden plagues such as bacillary dysentery, typhoid, and hepatitis.

Now, two months later, there were lines of white and khaki tents stretching to the low ochre hills a kilometer away. We pulled up in a hollow square of corrugated buildings, its entrance guarded by two men with Red Cross armbands and thin wands of bamboo. A pump chattered to itself inside a tin shed fifty yards away. The square was almost empty save for a few latecomers pulled along by ragged mothers toward a building in the far corner. From it came the roar of five thousand children. Under the supervision of Tula and Inge the first feeding of the day was in progress.

Mikael, the Red Cross supplies officer, a middle-aged man with close cropped hair and a permanent smile, stood in the yard watching stripped eucalyptus poles being unloaded from a ten-ton truck. He had built this strange, corrugated laager against the famine. We talked about the various problems. Two trucks of flour had vanished near Dese, the blankets supplies were now adequate, thanks to a consignment from the London *Daily Mirror*. Two of the cooks were in prison for fighting. The German stoves were hopeless and the cooks were going back to wood-fired cooking.

The refugees were fortunate in Mikael and another Ethiopian called Gabre Mariam, the Red Cross's chief delegate to the district. Neither spared himself. Within weeks, working with a vast army of local carpenters, peasants, electricians, and clerks they had transformed the valley from a deathtrap into a partial haven. The nightmare of the officials faded.

The chief nurse Deresa, a man of about twenty-three in a long doctor's coat with a half belt at its back, joined us. His face was badly scarred by acne and he had a high-pitched, squeaky voice that added an urgency to everything he said. He was our second head nurse. The first one, Hailu, had been arrested by the commissar of Bati, charged with too close an association with foreigners and imprisoned in Kembolcha prison. Deresa, like Hailu, came from the rebel-held province of Tigre which both had been forced to leave because of the fighting.

We usually assembled at about eight in the clinic, a corrugated-iron shed put up by Mikael soon after we arrived. A Kawasaki motorcycle with a bright yellow gas tank leaned on its stand outside. Behind an upturned tea chest, Marcos, a long-faced, serious man in tortoiseshell spectacles, was dispensing medicines to a queue of peasants. He rose to shake hands, his narrow face overcome with shyness. Although a nurse, he had recently begun medical studies at Addis University, but family problems and lack of money had forced him to quit temporarily. He had been taken on by the Red Cross for a few months. Deresa called the nurses together.

Most of them were, like him, refugees from the north. The local health department, not knowing what to do with them, had ordered them to Bati. They were all men and except for one, all under twenty-five. They watched me anxiously, straining at my English while Deresa translated. Six of them were called Ali, one Wolde, and a thin, vacant-looking youth with a silly grin, Kirobel. There was an old man, Desta, long and thin with a set somber face. He came from Mekele and had worked for a German missionary hospital in the town until they were forced out five years ago by a government anxious to demonstrate its revolutionary fervor. Since then he had lived in retirement. Deresa began to read out a list of duties from a ledger, pulling with his free hand at the belt of the white coat he had inherited from Hailu.

Hailu's arrest was still a mystery to me. He had been there to greet me when I first came. A big, chubby-faced man with tightly cropped hair. The first day he had insisted on coming with us to the hotel for lunch but when the moment came he lost his nerve and sat apart at another table. His courage, even if it had failed slightly, set a seal on our friendship. Lunching with the ferengi was for vetted Party men, and I suspected he had tried to break a secret rule.

We had worked hard that first month, although we had almost nothing, just a truckful of medicines and a small frame tent from which to dispense them. Each morning we would set out to visit thirty thousand tribesmen. Organizing them in rows, calling up the stretcher bearers to carry away the sick, arguing with the local officials, getting workmen to put up more and more tents. At night Hailu was always there, groping among the rows of dying people in the tent we used as a hospital, holding a tiny kerosene lamp to the pinched faces, searching for the dying, putting up drips, distributing blankets. He taught the untrained assistants how to feed the children, kept the tent sweepers to their jobs, made the mothers bring water and food from the kitchens for the children they had despaired for.

He began to teach me Amharic. His school English improved by leaps and bounds. He was always asking questions about England. What was it like? Did everybody have a car? He warned me about spies. Did I know that the Party had told him to report on me? Everybody, he said, had to present written accounts of conversations they had had with the foreign aid workers to the police. I must be very careful.

But things are never what they seem in Abyssinia and if you are wise such remarks put you instantly on guard. The old emperors maintained a tradition of agents provocateurs that the new regime has continued. Agents in restaurants, taverns, even in the street, approach strangers with seditious remarks—agreement produces handcuffs. I remained silent, and now he worried me slightly, much as I liked him.

Then the trouble had come.

We had difficulty in getting measles vaccine essential to prevent a lethal epidemic. Hailu had spent days arguing with government officials about it. There were eight thousand children awaiting vaccine and every passing day increased the risk of an epidemic in which hundreds would die. Eventually he had a terrible row with a health official in the small shed that served as an autopsy room. It was a mistake. The official had the drinking ear of the powerful commissar of Bati. Five days later Hailu was arrested, charged with "Too close an association with foreign elements," and breaking a government gate at the entrance to the camp. He was taken away to security headquarters in Kembolcha. It seemed a horrible blow, designed I was sure, to weaken my authority. Always strike at those around your opponent, in that way you will isolate him.

But Giorgis, the tall, thin nurse with the glasses came back from Kembolcha with the news that he had visited Hailu in jail and my ex-head nurse was going to serve only a few weeks. Then he said something very strange. "Hailu saw you driving past a café he was in the other day, when his guards were taking him to the jail. He waved, but you did not see him." For a moment I wondered if his arrest had been a charade. People going to prison rarely stop for coffee with their guards. Could the Party have planted him in the camp for their own reasons? Or maybe the guards themselves were so outraged by what the commissar had done that they had decided to show their prisoner some kindness. I favored the latter. But whatever political pressures he was under, he was an excellent nurse and a brave enthusiast in a very gray world.

Hailu's arrest brought the vaccine in the end. The scandal it caused, even if only whispered in corners, focused attention on its importance. Three days later seven thousand doses arrived from Dese. We vaccinated five thousand children in five days.

Deresa asked the night nurse Muhammad to make his report, pulling me back to the present. The thin, spare figure rose slowly and began to speak, Deresa translating. Ten patients, six of them children, had died of the usual things: kwashiokor, hypothermia, or pneumonia. We had run out of charcoal for the heaters, and there was no kerosene for the lamps. Toiba, the night watchman, had not turned up. Somebody said his eldest child had died the day before.

We talked about putting up another big tent, and about a small outbreak of jaundice in one section of the camp. There was an announcement that we could now get tea around eleven in a small hut behind the clinic. Marcos leaned over and whispered something to him. He turned, grave-faced to me.

"Nurse Ali died, Doctor . . . in Dese two days ago."

There was a pause. Outside one of the guards shouted at an importuning Afar and cracked his switch in the air. I could not believe it. Ali was nineteen. Short and rather fat, he had hated Bati, hated the tent he was forced to sleep in and only wanted to return to Dese. Five days ago he had come pleading for leave, saying he was ill. I let him go.

Marcos said, "In Dese they say he had cerebral malaria. Maybe he did not take his chloroquine." It was possible. Bati lay in a malarious area. Ali came from the mountains and would have had no resistance. I heard myself say, "Terrible, terrible." It was beyond words. Death, so many deaths, had exhausted sorrow of meaning.

Deresa pursed his lips, got to his feet, and read out the list of which tent each of the nurses would be in charge of for the week. I told them I was going to Addis with Janet tomorrow. Deresa said, "Don't forget to come back." I smiled. There was nothing I would have liked better than to go home, but if I did, I would have felt I had failed.

Deresa and I headed for the House of the Dead.

It was a large, circular building right in the center of the camp. Maybe it had been intended for a sports store, a grain silo, or even a café. Now and forever it would be shunned, as would be the ground on which it stood. Its thatched, circular roof sat on walls of semiopen palisades. We entered to the bowing of a small man in an embroidered skullcap holding an Arabic rosary. Inside, the gaps in the walls let in a slight breeze while slivers of light crossed and recrossed the pummeled earthen floor. Two men in skullcaps squatted by a man-sized wooden trough. There were holes in the floor of the trough. Below it a narrow channel full of soapy water led under the walls to the outside. One of the squatting men had a sponge in his hand. In the far corner two assistants were lifting a body out of its covering of gray rags. Carefully, backs bent under the weight, they eased it over the other bundles and laid it in the trough. The man with the sponge began to wash the dreadful, wasted belly. To either side were more corpses, mainly children, small legs and hands poking from below shrouds. In one corner two brothers of about five and six lay curled up on their sides. They looked asleep, as if after a day's exhausting play.

Deresa asked a question that included the word *mot*, "dead" in Amharic. The man with the rosary snapped his fingers; a younger man with a clipboard rose from a corner and walked towards us, opening the pages of a double-entry cash ledger.

All three consulted the close-written lists. The day hung apprehensively on this moment. In the first month the death rate, like some terrible thermometer, had risen each day without stopping, reaching, after a month, sixty a day. Then, one morning, Hailu discovered a recurrent mistake in the addition and we realized the death rate was double what we had thought. I had felt faint and went outside to walk about a little.

Now Deresa said, "Thirty-two."

"Good."

The man with the embroidered hat said something to Deresa and tapped his stomach with the flat of his hand. The corpse washers began work again, their eyes watching. "This man say he is hungry, the work is heavy, he has many children, can he have food?" Deresa looked slightly embarrassed, caught between his countryman and a ferengi. I made vague noises in the back of my throat, turned, and left.

We began to walk away, the destitution becoming worse the farther we moved from the camp center. The latest arrivals did not even have the luxury of a few sheltering branches with which to protect their sick, but contented themselves with scooping shallow pans out of the ground about ten feet in diameter. During the night these provided some protection from the wind and intense cold which sought out and killed those so starved they could not fuel their own body heat.

Small pits scooped in the earth were used for cooking, but there was a drastic shortage of firewood and, as the camp increased in size, so the women had to travel farther and farther away to find any. Even then it was wretched stuff, the last rakings from a stripped landscape.

A small, frantic crowd of men and women began to gather behind us holding out their children, begging for medicines. Old women beat their breasts with withered hands then held them outstretched and beckoning, heads to one side, edentulous gums working. Most of them were about forty or fifty, but twenty-five years of continuous childbearing in the desert made them look seventy. Here and there we would stumble on a small bundle lying in the dirt on his own, legs drawn up in an agony of cramps from a mixture of diarrhea and hunger, no longer capable of crawling back to his tent. Haile Mariam whistled and the old men with the shit-stained stretchers came trotting, loaded the bundle onto the canvas and set off for the tent hospital.

Figures dotted a slight rise to the north. Deresa laughed and pointed. "The Afars are back." They were nomads who had twice been driven out of the camp by government troops. This would make their third return. We went to meet them.

Their camp was on a small hill, compact and set aside from

the rest of the refugees. It had a determined, cheerful air about it, children playing around each small family group, pots boiling, men cleaning their teeth with short, white, sharpened sticks, younger women preparing thick pancakes of flour, older women gossiping or soothsaying. The few sick they had with them were not starving. Even in old age the women were handsome—spare and dignified with intense black skins and large eyes. Opportunism had brought them back, not starvation. They hoped to obtain some of the free grain, maybe some of the powerful ferengi medicine, and their chief wanted military information about the hated Party. A man with an old Lee-Enfield cradled in his arms rose from a sand pit to greet us. Behind him an old woman rose as well and patted her stomach for food. A hand reached up and pulled her down.

The United Nations was keen on abolishing nomads in the Subsahel, a policy that found enthusiastic support among the Ethiopian Dergue. The Afars paid no taxes, refused to obey the Party, and had fiercely resisted the idea of working in collectives. Their life was the desert. To change their minds the Party set about systematically blowing up their wells, driving them off their traditional grazing grounds, and impounding their camels. It was unwise. Within a few weeks dead government officials were found in many district outposts around the Danakil. Punitive expeditions were sent in to destroy the tribes but only resulted in counter-raids and foothill towns like Bati. Unlike the lackluster conscripts of the Ethiopian Army, the Afars were stealthy desert craftsmen, crack shots, and expert trackers, a relentless and courageous enemy with a millennium of violence behind them.

I remembered a surrealistic conversation with a visiting senior U.N. official from Geneva about the Afars. The official had a perfectly round head whose bald, pink crown shone slightly under a fluorescent light. His fingers, like his features, were oval, fat, and comfortable. His eyes, soft and permanently injured, peered from behind an obligatory pair of gold-framed glasses. He had been with the U.N. for only three months and it was clear that he was out of his depth, regretting perhaps the simpler black and white problems of his previous existence as the chief executive of an Austrian company.

In the way of these interviews we talked of this and that. I mentioned the nomads. His eyes lit up. He leaned forward. "I have just come from New York, Herr Doktor, and it is most interesting, this problem of nomads." He pronounced it "no maads." "The nomads they must be stopped. The U.N. special committee says they are responsible for deforestation and great desertification of the Sahel. It is better they are made to live in one place, resettled."

Now, watching them, the long, disciplined lines sitting quietly, cleaning their teeth, watching their children, calm on the edge of chaos, the idea of forcing them into settled collectives seemed laughable, a perverse inversion of values, a punishment for being successful. It was the nomads who should be preserved. I remembered how I had looked sharply at the U.N. official's face, but it was innocent of guile. He did not yet understand about the Benz-Mercedocracy in New York, Paris, Rome, and all the capitals of Africa.

The man with the Lee-Enfield stood quietly waiting, hand on his breast, Muslim fashion. Haile Mariam spoke in Afar, translating it into English as he went. The Red Cross, he said, did not allow guns into the camp. The man with the gun listened carefully, then detached the magazine. "They will do as you ask, they have much discipline," Deresa said.

I said to Haile Mariam, "Tell them we will look at their sick if they bring them to the hospital, but no guns, it is forbidden."

We walked toward the hospital tents. Near them Mikael had built a crude outpatient ward, a long shed with a consulting room at one end made of corrugated iron. About seven hundred people would gather there each morning to see the medical assistants or, if they were very ill, the doctors.

Very few, perhaps one hundred a day, were seriously ill; the rest were old men with aching limbs, women demanding

244 / *Myles F. Harris, M.D.*

"pills" for no clear reason, people with small boils, headaches, or colds, and a large sprinkling of the obviously healthy. Meanwhile, just outside in the growing lines of tents, lay dying children, comatose malaria cases, dead mothers, and the terminally starved. Only at the last minute, usually at the very end of the day, would the relatives of these stage a small rally. Then about twenty mothers and fathers would rush the emptying ward, each carrying an emaciated infant at the point of expiry.

The system we used in the feeding centers was the same as in Sodo. The children would be weighed, measured, and, if they fell below a certain critical figure, bracelets would be fastened to their wrists which let them into the center. Those who were fatter were given ration cards for a weekly distribution. It seemed to us, and it was the agreed practice throughout all the agencies, that the weakest had the greatest charge on our stocks of grain, flour, blankets, and medicines. Although that was not, as we found out later, how it seemed to thirty thousand peasants lying about us in the gray, muddy dust.

Over the two months the hospital had expanded to nine tents with a total of two hundred and fifty patients. Except for one small kerosene lamp, it still had no lights. The patients lay on the earth floor, attended by their parents or relatives. The worst were kept in the first tent where they could be seen first thing each morning. Whatever illness the patients had, most of them suffered as well from amebic dysentery as a result of drinking from the river. The first thing that Mikael had done on arrival was to sink a drill shaft one hundred meters through the hard shell of rock below, and now water flowed, clean and fresh twenty-four hours of the day, pumped up by the ancient Lister diesel built in England. But it was slow, and with only two taps the women and children had to line up for hours. This was often longer than the driving thirst of fever victims lying out in the desert sun could bear; they sent their children or women to the river. The water from it killed them. So we renamed the river *Mot*

Wanz, "Death River," and a man went about the camp announcing the name and the danger through a loudspeaker. It never stopped them. Each day I drove across the river past groups of women ankle deep in the lethal water, washing rags.

A new nurse, Liv Anderson, had recently arrived to take charged of the hospital. Middle-aged, comfortable, and able to speak Amharic, she had done a two-year stint in Addis some years ago in a clinic for mothers and babies. Liv was both an excellent physician and a first-class nurse. She had a sort of Jeeves-like practicality that included making the mothers encourage one another to feed their infants, organizing the food supplies from a kitchen which frequently broke down, or setting up a row of tents to take care of the elderly who had lost all their relatives. Above all she was a survivor. A week after she came I found her reading on the veranda after lunch and offered her a lift. She shook her head. The work was tough, and each week she would take a half day off. In that way she would last longer. Until then, and even afterwards, I had not been able to persuade any of the others to take even as much as an hour off. It was worrying. Inge and Tula, in charge of the feeding center, would not rest. They began work at six and finished at dusk. I watched them gradually exhaust themselves. During the first few weeks in Bati, Janet seemed to have shaken off her dysentery. She worked in the hospital organizing the mass vaccinations and supervising the medical assistants. Then one attack of dysentery after another came. Ayela found amoeba in her stools; we treated her and she recovered for a day and then it returned. Tula, near to exhaustion herself, became more and more silent and withdrawn. She did not know at the time that she herself was ill. Or if she did, she would not admit it. More of the Ethiopian nurses in the hospital went down with amebiasis, and even Ayela got it. Ali Two, another medical assistant, died and Janet worsened.

Deresa and I turned our attention to what was happening in the refugees' crowded tents. With Liv working in the hospital it was possible to spend more time in them, and more time anticipating the next moves in the political game played out about the camp.

Most of the cases in the hospital were the end result of severe malnutrition. It found its expression in weakened, sickly infants who had succumbed to TB, pneumonia, amebic dysentery, and gastroenteritis, finally becoming the swollen-bellied or wasted infants familiar in the news. They needed drips, nasogastric tubes, and constant urging of the mothers to make them drink. The tents were so crowded that often the dead lay next to the living for hours. Every common adult disease was present, including madness, and everywhere there was fear.

This morning as every morning, we began to work our way down the lines, listening to chests, sticking needles into veins, avoiding standing up suddenly because the chloroquine we took against malaria made everything spin.

The small bundles that Liv showed me had all come to lie there by exactly the same path. All these children had been driven from the breast by the birth of a new baby, then left to fend for themselves at the family pot. Unless aggressive and strong, they weakened and fell back, lost weight, lost interest, and after a few days succumbed to fever and diarrhea. The constant, chronic seepage of fluid from a parasite-infested bowel, coupled with a slow-burning fever, dried in the end even their tears. Their hair fell out, and what was left turned slightly red. Their bellies swelled, then their legs, then their faces. In a mockery of health their skin took on the shiny gleaming look that gave them the name of "sugar babies." In 1923 in Ghana a young woman missionary recognized the cause of what people there call Kwashiokor. It is a word which means "The sickness which comes to the first child when the second is born." The name stuck and is now used in the medical textbooks.

Then, often at night during the coldest time just before dawn, when the chemical fire that keeps our bodies warm flickers low, Death came and, like a verger snuffing out candles, pinched out their flames. In the morning the parents carried them to the tucul to wait their turn at the wooden trough.

The fires of some we tried to light again as soon as Death had left. Injecting sugar into their veins to start the fire, warming them with hot water bottles, wrapping them in cooking foil. Some would begin to breathe, and their color would return. But with darkness, as soon as the sun fell and the muezzin cried on Allah, they would die.

To prevent this we had divided the camp into sections of fifty tents, and each morning and evening we searched each one for those children who sat silent and still against the tent walls, or slept at midday under layers of revolting rags. These we made the mothers take to Inge at the feeding center, and we came back, once, twice, even three times a day, sometimes in half an hour, sometimes in two hours, arguing, cajoling, threatening. We talked, even shouted, in tents full of desperate, starving people, often at old people who waved trivial sores in our faces while they concealed sick and dying children behind their backs.

After we had finished in the hospital, we set out on the morning's search. In the first row of tents a thin man of about thirty stood wrapped in two blankets from our stores while at his feet an emaciated child shivered naked over the few embers of a fire. The child was so thin it magnified the size of his bones. They seemed to belong to another, much larger child.

A long harangue began. Deresa shook his head. "This man says that they are his blankets."

"And is the child his?" I asked.

"Yes, but he says that as the child is his, he can do what he wants with the blankets."

"But the child will die."

"He says, so will he if he has no blankets. Then without him all his children will die, not just one."

A very fat woman (there were even some in that place) interposed herself between Deresa and myself, gesturing with half-clenched fingers at her mouth.

We shouted at her to go away, and turned to the man's tent. It was fetid and overcrowded. Two crones sat at the far end rocking back and forth in prayer, three children slept on the floor, a woman, presumably the mother, worked at grinding a little coffee in a small mortar.

"*Yettam a male?*" asked Deresa. "Is there anybody ill?"

"*Yellum!*"—"nothing." There was the slightest of movements from a bundle of rags just behind the old woman.

Deresa walked over and picked up the rags. Underneath, a small child of about one lay dying, its face a mere skull, huge, tearless, dull eyes staring at the tent wall. A long trickle of green diarrhea mixed with blood ran slowly from its lax anus. "*Kuuffing!*" screeched the crone, waving two bony hands about her ears. Deresa told her to wrap the child in a blanket and take it to the hospital. The woman working the mortar began to cry, and all three began chanting, "*Kuufing! Kuufing!*"

When the first missionaries had come to the country, the people had noticed they always asked about "coughing." It had passed into the Amharic. To the peasants almost any childish ailment worse than a cold was a sign of the feared "kuufing" and around this disease a huge and complex demonology had grown. The fiery red eyes of a child with measles were not its own, but those of a devil. Devils died if they were exposed to the sun and so would the child.

It seemed to us abominable and selfish when we first discovered these things. Children were precious, and had a special claim to our protection because they were helpless. Were these people then savages?

With time and experience we had come to see that the desert people were not savages. They dearly loved their children and wept at the great tide of death which had engulfed them. But, despite this, they knew about survival, who should survive and how it was done, and had no illusions about what would happen if they did not preserve some over others. The entire tribe would vanish.

They knew that death comes to everyone, and it is only a matter of when. And that "when" was unimportant balanced against the fate of an entire tribe, an entire people. Ritual and custom made the choice for them.

The first that had to be saved were the adult males and females. They were the ones who carried the seeds to replace the children who would be lost. Even if all the children died the man and woman still carry their seeds until the crops revived and thus begin the cycle once again. Children could not replace themselves—adults could.

Then came the old. They treated the sick, delivered the mothers, remembered where best and when to plant the harvest, taught the children, told of the past, raised demons and myths, kept the ancient faiths, remembered the dead, foretold the future. They, like traveling libraries, carried in their heads the tribal customs and knowledge. Without them the tribe was sightless and deaf.

Lastly came the children. The oldest, in whom more love, knowledge, and effort had been invested, were the most valuable, the least those who had but recently left the protection of their mother's breast to take the first steps in a world that only rewarded survival. If they weakened they were abandoned. To the peasants our attempts to feed the weak and to stop them from giving food to the strong were terrifying and evil.

So the toddlers died first and in profusion. Each morning in the central tucul I stood with Deresa and counted the dead. Four or five of the very old, come to their time. A man perhaps, dead of malaria or typhus, and then around me eighty or more small children all between about three and six.

But while we were obsessed with death, counting it, gazing at it each day, dreaming about it at night, among the thirty thousand refugees the yeast of life continued to work. Women came into labor, delivered, and, as for centuries past, unhelped by any but their mothers and the occasional crone, survived the event or died. In the mornings we found fresh pink children in some of the tents, still fat from the calories they had harvested from their mother's blood. Most we knew, would live only as long as they remained on the breast. After that they would die.

Tula set up a delivery unit for the mothers behind the feeding center. It was spotless, always full and attended by a small eunichlike man who within four weeks acquired an unerring instinct for troublesome confinements. One woman he showed us had come to term and then, in severe pain, had failed to progress. Tula, a midwife, diagnosed an obstructed labor. Examining the woman, I knew that she would need a cesarean, not only to save the child, but to save her. We had nothing here to do it with. Deresa said, "We can send her to Dessie. They will do it there."

So we sent for the Volkswagen van that the town hospital, when it could find two gallons of fuel, used to ferry food and supplies from Dessie. It arrived, but the driver, getting out, shook his head and pointed to the gas gauge. It was empty.

"What happens now?" I asked Deresa.

"We must give him some gas and a little cash."

"What normally happens?"

"How do you mean?"

"If there is no gas?"

Deresa looked embarrassed. A nurse who had come from the clinic with the driver said with a smile. "The relatives must pay for the gas."

"And if they gave no money, or there is no gas?"

"Then nothing."

"But she would die."

"Yes." Deresa lowered his eyes and studied the gray floor.

I looked at the mother. She was about nineteen, fat despite the famine. No relatives had appeared and I wondered if the pregnancy was a wanted one. Her life depended on three pieces of paper wedged in the glove compartment of my Toyota: a permit to purchase fuel and two ten birr notes—

about four dollars. If the camp had not been here she would have only a few more hours to live.

In Western countries the death of a mother during her confinement is so rare as to rank as an unbelievable tragedy, not only to the family but to the doctor, whose career it might well ruin. Here it was a commonplace. The town hospital in Bati was in a permanent state of destitution since the missionaries who ran it had been forced out. Now it could not even provide food or water for its patients. There was nothing left to spare for gas.

We paid the driver and gave him the permit, and at about four they took her away, bumping over the rough track toward the Dessie highway. What happened to her in Dessie, whether she had her operation or the baby survived, we never knew.

There were exotic diseases as well.

Toward midday one of the stretcher bearers helped a confused, muttering man of about fifty with a high fever into the outpatient tent. He had slightly dirtier rags than most. His face was not just ill, but haggard with the crushing pain of a gargantuan headache, and his skin had a shiny waxen appearance in which there was a tinge of yellow. Giorgis said, "We should look for relapsing fever in his blood."

Relapsing fever was one of those illnesses I had half heard about in medical school, something in small print at the bottom of textbooks, taking third place to paragraphs on Tsutsugamushi disease and Balkan grippe. It could be diagnosed by examining a smear of the patient's blood on a glass slide. As we assembled the heavy Russian microscope in the yard to get the last rays of the dying sun—we had no other light source—I tried to remember what the causative agent was supposed to look like. It was carried on the jaws of the human body louse, which in biting its victim transmits the organism into his blood. For a few days nothing happens. Then without warning come hectic fevers, chills, and the characteristic headaches. Profuse bleeding from the nose, ears, mouth, vagina, and penis heralds the end. Most are dead within three days. But I still could not be sure what the organism looked like.

"It looks like a corkscrew with tails." I looked up to see Ayela grinning at me through his cheap horn-rims.

He had been in Dese looking for some more meningitis vaccine and had just got back. His black brogues were in tatters. His clothes looked even more threadbare than when I had said good-bye to him on Thursday. He lit a cigarette and gestured at the microscope under which Tabeje was fitting a slide of the patient's blood.

"Like me to have a look? We have many cases of this in Addis."

Dr. Atnafu Ayela was a strange mixture. An Ethiopian city doctor training to be a surgeon who had volunteered to work for a month in Bati with the Red Cross. He had been educated at an English public school in Addis before the revolution and when it came he had somehow been one of the fifteen hundred students in the city who survived the Red Terror. Thirty-five hundred were killed. I never knew if he was a party cadre or not. Once making a casual joke about the Party I happened to glance at him. For just a second I saw a look of intense annoyance cross his thin features. But he saw me looking at him, looked away, and lit a cigarette. He was kind to Janet when she was ill, making trips to Dese to cadge special amebicides for her from the pharmacy.

His knowledge of tropical medicine was encyclopedic and he loved medical journals and cigarettes, neither of which I ever saw him without. He was full of extraordinary tales about life in Ethiopia and taught me such arcana as how to recognize the symptoms of poisoning from chat, a stimulant drug that produces vacancy and inertia among the workers, translated odd passages of rude music from the loudspeakers mounted on the tops of buses, and knew a variety of anecdotes about the saints of the Coptic Church, including one, Teclaiman, who having stood on one leg for tens years in prayer, God rewarded by turning into a true monoped.

In company he was shy, and would concentrate on his 'tibbs and beer. He had been with us for a month, but four attacks of amebic dysentery had weakened him badly. I once suggested he should give up chain-smoking. He said, "I do not expect to live to be more than forty-five, why should I stop?"

In the evenings he would sit on the veranda with a bottle of Red Stripe beer, watching the antics of Teferi the hotel manager as he chased his pretty wife, or would talk about his experiences as a rural doctor in the Ogaden desert. Because of his schooling, his English was flawless and slightly Wodehousian, yet his experiences were all of a harsh and unforgiving society familiar with death. He had never been in the West, yet he spoke of things like scanners, radioactive isotopes, hovercraft, and computer data banks as if he had seen them. He was familiar with the idea of habeas corpus, had read Trollope, Dickens, and Shakespeare, yet knew nothing of the world or the people they described.

He came over and searched the tiny drop of blood under the lens, gave a slight grunt and stood aside, beckoning me to look. I refocused from his thick glasses. Gray filaments swam about, dead cells, some white cells, the sun slid momentarily behind a cloud, then at about one o'clock in the field I saw several corkscrew-like threads, *Borelia recurrentis*, relapsing fever, distant cousin to syphilis and yaws. We were looking at a descendant of the tiny regiments that had halted Napoleon before Borodino, destroyed the British at Sebastopol, and more certainly than the Spartans, defeated the Persians after Thermopylae. To go into one of the victim's tents was to risk catching it off the walls, or from scattered infested rags.

"He must be shaved, his clothing burned, the tent destroyed or sprayed." Ayela looked at me and smiled slightly. "White people die more quickly of typhus than black people, their arteries are not good, too stiff. If you take tetracycline you will be safe, take one or two a day."

Ayela was right. The treatment in killing the *Borellia* releases from their bodies a flood of toxins which paralyzes the arteries so that the blood pressure falls to nothing. In a young black man, brought up on a diet of sorghum and maize with only occasional meat, this would be nothing more than a fainting attack. In me, my arteries rigid with fat and calcium, such a profound state of shock could be fatal.

Marcos's narrow face appeared over the door of the postmortem room to announce the discovery of another meningitis case. We were constantly on the lookout for the variant known as meningococcal meningitis. If it got into Bati, we faced the likelihood of an epidemic sweeping away a fifth of the camp.

The patient, a young well-fed man of about twenty-five, was in a tent right on the edge of the camp. Four of his children sat crying quietly in a corner while a crone dripped water from a filthy rag between his sorde-encrusted lips. His wife, a beautiful Afar with carefully plaited hair, wept noisily, her face turned to the opposite wall. Ayela adjusted his large horn-rims with a little finger. "How long?" he asked the woman.

Two days. They had not brought him to the hospital because the soothsayer had told them the ferengi had people sick with "kuufing" there. He had given him some leaves of a certain tea. During the night the leaves had tried to shake the devil out but they were not strong enough.

It was meningitis. What the crone called "shaking the devil out" were convulsions. It was a bad sign. The man groaned slightly and tried to twist his rigid neck free of pain. In the hospital, a needle in the spine produced a slow ooze of yellow pus instead of clear rapid fluid.

"I worked with this illness in Eritrea," Ayela said. "Many died." We put the patient in a separate tent and warned the relatives to stay away from everybody. The yellow fluid was sent to Dese with a message for the laboratory to look at it. We would know in thirty-six hours. The nurses began vaccinating the contacts in the immediate tents.

I left them to it. It was twelve. As a child, the Christian

Brothers had set aside twelve to twelve-thirty for religious instruction. So each morning about this time I devoted half an hour to intrigue. Today Commissar Woubshet Tulu was expected.

Woubshet Tulu was a bad man. Even had I known he was to die two days later, I would not have changed my opinion. Not long before he had been the instigator of a most monstrous crime. It started one morning at quarter past eight.

We were standing, making idle conversation outside the kitchen among the smells of wood smoke, faffa, and wheat, when Tula suddenly pointed to the low hills around the camp. On the skyline at every hundred meters stood the silhouette of a soldier holding a machine gun or rifle. They had not been there when we arrived ten minutes before and it seemed that they had risen to a single order from behind concentration points deliberately set just below the hills. We heard the sound of powerful engines and turning toward the road from Bati saw a long convoy of army trucks heading down the narrow road toward the camp. The sanitarian and a thin Party official passed us, carrying new, powerful, loudspeakers.

Hailu had appeared, his face tense. He gestured toward the noise of the loudspeakers. "They are telling everybody to assemble in the football field, even the sick."

Slowly, over the next three hours, harangued by Party officials and soldiers in their midst, a confused horde of frightened people shuffled toward the assembly point. Those who refused to leave their tents were dragged out by the soldiers; a few who tried to escape were rounded up and taken away by some of the encircling cordon of armed troops.

By eleven o'clock nearly five thousand people stood, sat, or lay in the relentless sun, while the small gray shapes of officials moved between them selecting—on what basis we had no idea—those for resettlement. These were formed into long desperate lines. Requests to let us bring back the seriously ill were met with deliberate incomprehension. Soldiers stood between us and the assembly point. And it was not only the inmates they took, but all our trained cooks, guards, and orderlies. At noon the lines began to move into the back of the trucks. Old men eased up on insectlike limbs, squalling babies, dying children, mothers, fathers.

Three convoys were slowly formed. The first, with about two thousand refugees, began to leave after two, grinding up the hill past a heavy machine gun the soldiers had positioned on the far side of Mot, the "Death River." As they swung it about, the sun winked on the long mustache of bullets on either side of its breech. The trucks turned right along the road toward the highlands. The second, full of Afars, left an hour later. They still had their guns. Woubshet Tulu was not so foolish as to risk a shootout with them. The tribesmen looked unconcerned, even pleased. At the top of the hill the convoy turned left toward the Danakil. They were getting a free lift home.

About five hundred—nearly all men, but some women and a few children—made up the last convoy. Among them were most of our cooks and unskilled workers. But they were not going any farther than Bati; when the convoy reached the center it turned down the hill and vanished among some old school buildings invisible from the camp. Within the hour a rumor seeped across "Death River" that Tulu had set up a new camp in the town. On what criteria he had chosen its inmates—he had separated many families in doing so—there was silence. Hailu thought they might be going to an army labor brigade in the north and were waiting in Bati for the arrival of their officers. But nobody was sure how Tulu was going to feed them, provide them with water, or dispose of their waste. It was too depressing to think about.

We had found Tulu the following morning, red-eyed, taciturn, and uncommunicative, sitting on a large desk in the sanitarian's office. Abruptly he had announced that from now on the number of deaths in the camp was a military secret. He would inform us of the daily totals, but we were not to approach the tucul, count the dead, or go near the graveyard. Information like that was sensitive and could be used by the

Ethiopian government's enemies. At the word "enemies" the red eyes paused fractionally on me.

It was not worth arguing. The Red Cross supplied food to the gravediggers and the corpse washers. We would find out. I asked him if he wanted anything for the new camp. That was also a military installation, and we were not to go near it, but he would like one tent. We gave it to him.

Where were we to get new cooks and orderlies? I asked. Tulu paused for a moment and studied his elastic-sided boots. He would send an approved list tomorrow morning. They would not be the ones from the new camp.

A week later a VW minivan pulled up in front of the hospital tents. The driver got out and put his hand on the door. I do not think I can ever listen to the sound of the sliding door of a VW van without remembering. The driver pulled it back and five skeletal figures tumbled onto the sand, three lay still, barely breathing, one of them vomited. Two began to crawl on hands and knees toward the nearest tent. One made a dry gasping sound over and over again. Marcos bent down. "Water, he asks for water." They were some of the fifteen hundred men that had been held in custody in the town by the commissar.

That afternoon Gabre Mariam, the camp's chief Ethiopian Red Cross delegate, and I had gone to see him in his small room hidden among a jumble of stone offices the Italians had left behind. Outside, crowds of tribesmen, waiting for food and grain, sat in orderly rows, watched by armed soldiers. Small clusters of camels, sheltering under what trees were left, sneered at their optimism with downturned mouths and flared nostrils. Several farted. A soldier read numbers to the crowd in uncertain Amharic.

If Tulu was frightened by what had happened he gave no sign of it. But he never took his eyes off Gabre Mariam. Woubshet Tulu was a drinking man, not well educated, and advised by foolish locals who could have stepped from the pages of Gogol's *Dead Souls*. Everything frightened them: the guerrillas, the Party, the famine, the peasants, the ferengi.

Particularly Party intellectuals like Gabre Mariam, university graduates with clever words, theoreticians, lily-livered, abstemious. The camp had all the marks of a decision reached deep in the commissar's resentful cups late one night.

In Sodo I would have suspected Gabre Mariam of a power play. Here was the local commissar caught out in a spectacular mess in front of a ferengi, just the circumstances in which a lean, earnest, young Party man can demand his head and be rewarded with his job. But Bati was not like that, nor was Gabre Mariam that type of official. No Party official wanted Bati. In the last six months it had been attacked twice by guerrillas from the Danakil who had summarily executed a local Party snitch and blown the bank to pieces. The wreckage still stood—blackened beams and twisted metal girders.

After a few tense pleasantries the commissar spread two fat hands and said, "Food, we require the Red Cross to give us food."

"Can we see the camp?" He shrugged, rose, and beckoned us out to his broken-down Fiat.

It took ten minutes to weave through the back streets of the town. At the barbed-wire gates a soldier turned a key in a rusty padlock. Tulu said defiantly, "You thought you could prevent the will of the people?"

It reminded me of a Japanese prisoner-of-war camp. Barbed wire, a single hut, and as an afterthought one tent in the center set aside for the sick. At one end was a tall brick wall with a deep ditch gouged by past rains running along its base. There were a lot of people in the ditch trying to shelter from the sun. Two were dead, one rigid in the fetal position. The tent was no better. Old men, children, young women— the indifference of total starvation written on their faces—lay dying from pneumonia, measles, or dysentery. While I stood there an old man with grizzled white hair gave a slight sigh, turned over, and died.

Gabre Mariam was gray with fear and anger as he said, "We must close this place. We will need to send some nurses up to move the patients." There could be no greater contrast between Gabre Mariam and the brutal commissar. One night over coffee he had touched my arm and said, stumbling with embarrassment over the words, "I know you laugh at these things, but Lenin said, give us the organization and we will do the job." Now he was seeing a dreadful reality.

The commissar lit a roll-up and nodded his head. The sudden agreement did not surprise me. With the foreign press visiting Bati so frequently now, he stood a daily risk of his camp being discovered. If that happened the Party would show him no mercy.

But afterwards Gabre Mariam shook his head. "You know, Tulu is not a good man, and he does not want these people now because he says they are no longer fit to work—imagine this man!"

We never were able to discover how many of the inmates died, because Tulu had their bodies brought in the evenings to the mass graves and secretly buried among our own dead. It explained his orders to keep the death rate a secret from us. That had been eight weeks ago. Since then he acted only once more, to arrest Hailu. After that he spent more and more of his days immersed in the yellowing files in his small office and the nights drinking himself to extinction. But on my last day he never turned up. It was not unusual. His drinking made it difficult for him to come ever since he had once seen me looking at the slow tremor of his hands and his yellow-tinged and terrified eyes. He had cirrhosis, and I suspected the expression on my face reminded him that it was deadly. Two days after I left he was found dead in the bare room he occupied in what was once the Italian governor's residence during the Fascist occupation. He lies now on the hill with the thousands he sent on before him. Maybe God will show him mercy.

After lunch Deresa and I climbed the dusty, brown hill to the necroplis that now housed two thousand dead. In the past we had discovered discrepancies between the morning count in the House of the Dead and the numbers buried in the graveyard. We could not afford mistakes, so we came there every afternoon to count the dead. The number was the key to what was happening to the gray seething mass below us on the plain.

As usual the chat-chewing clerks were secretive and gave the same reply as they always did. They would not show us the registers. They had orders. Who from? They shrugged and scanned the distance, but two hundred yards away there were not so many open holes as yesterday and the diggers were nervous at our presence. The number of dead that day was elusive, fifty, twenty . . . they could not say. On the way back to the tent Deresa whistled at a figure sitting a few feet away from the path. We had put him there a week ago to count in secret. Deresa had said at the time, "This man is not of the ignorant classes. He will tell us the truth."

That day the official count given us by Tulu's office was eighty, but when we met the old man he wrapped his tally beads around thin, cracked fingers and said, "Fifty." Deresa told him the official figure. The old man kissed the palm of his hand then threw it out in a gesture of accusation. Deresa explained unnecessarily, "It means they lie." There had been moves lately for the RRC to take over the camp. We would have welcomed them, but in Ethiopia things are not done that way. Rumors had been spread about Addis that our death rate was rising, not falling, and Brit, phoning one day, told me there was an intrigue afoot to take Bati from us.

I looked across the valley. It was a city now, growing by hundreds a day. Smoke and dust rose from the tent lines, files of figures crossed and recrossed the gray compacted sand. I felt I was on Mars, that what was happening below me was utterly without meaning, some ritual to a God utterly incomprehensible to me. A convoy of vehicles including a large air-conditioned, green tour bus was winding its way down the hill. I felt slightly depressed, too exhausted even to try and think of the preoccupations the visitors would expect us to cater for them. Several attacks of diarrhea had left things fractionally out of focus, and I was very tired, too tired to feel.

We began to walk down the hill.

In the past six weeks we had had a lot of visitors, mainly press but lately the famous. Film stars, politicians, journalists, and of course Mengistu himself. It was said that Michael Jackson would be arriving, the Kennedys, even Margaret Thatcher. Television had transformed the camp into a public dying platform, a sacrificial pyre in front of which paid orators appeared before millions to shed a few tears and offer pious resolutions. It altered nothing.

The green bus brought the Kennedys. They were unannounced. Edward Kennedy would have made too great a prize for the Afar Liberation Front. The Senator, huge and lumbering, wearing a Red Cross front and back like a target, led a retinue of aides in the style of his President brother through the camp. They were all there: fresh-faced American girls with Jackie hairstyles, crew-cut Secret Service men who looked like Bobby, nervous political advisers. Right at the rear, dwarfing his tiny Ethiopian minders, came Kennedy's giant of a son, stumping painfully on an artificial leg. What they did, what conclusions they could possibly have drawn, were impossible to imagine. The senator was led to the sordid staff toilet, the rickety door opened and he entered, two of the crew-cuts taking up positions outside, armpits bulging conspicuously. It was bad, that toilet, a squat with a stained hole ten feet below in which thrived a festering mass of some of the worst intestinal diseases known to man. I thought of his brother, a ghost of the '60s, speaking in that high strained voice, "We will go anywhere, do anything, risk any risk . . . the new frontier."

Bati, the new frontier . . . the door opened and the presidential candidate waddled out pulling at his trousers, his face green. All he would find here was a demonstration that of all the centuries, this one, with its cruel promises of progress of the sort his brother had made, has been the worst of all.

I sat in the corner of the Kursa's dining room that evening, struggling with the monthly assessments of the nurses for Geneva. Germaine Greer, visiting the camp that day, was being noisy in one corner. Every few minutes her sharp rehearsed speech would edge into my concentration. Behind her head on the stained wall a garish portrait of Lenin reached out to embrace a swirling crowd at the Finland Station. Through the window the light faded over the hills behind the camp. A jackal howled. The mad grinning cook in the kitchen who spent so much time carefully boiling water for my wife to drink, crashed some pots in the serving hatch. Somebody said, "Yellum," nothing. In the far corner of the restaurant Gabre Mariam sat talking with the hotel manager. Ayela sipped carefully at a beer and lit another cigarette. We seemed, in that room with its chipped black-and-white tiled floor, broken coffee machine, and perpetually locked bar full of prerevolutionary drinks, to be creatures from another world. A spaceship suspended over the desert below, where in the darkness, biblical families faced total extinction. It might, I thought, be the world of the future for all of us, a semiextinct planet over which hovered a capsule with a few survivors, specimens of a lost world. It was what was so frightening about Ethiopia—given more factories, a couple of million more miles of road, and a few more years of "scientific" farming, it could happen in Europe.

Today had been no different from all the previous days, except that tomorrow I would not be going to the camp but taking Janet to Addis. She had tried to come back to work three times but had lost so much weight and felt so weak she could not keep going. Her diarrhea and vomiting were now persistent. For short periods she was all right. But sustained effort exhausted her. I had examined her again that evening. Her arms were so thin I could encircle her wrist with my thumb and forefinger. Ayela gave me an introductory note to the pathologist at the Black Lion hospital in Addis. Some tests might show what was wrong.

The next morning one of the camp drivers took us in the truck to Kembolcha. The airfield lay in a field of gray stones that sloped down toward a dry riverbed. The buildings, unpainted for years, had slowly rotted so that now the wood was black and splintered, large sections of it crumbling into soft powder under the attack of termites. A tattered poster flapped on the broken wooden door of the departure terminal, a cheerful childish airplane rising through white clouds being waved off by a fuzzy-haired man with a huge grin on his face. FLY ETHIOPIAN said the caption in English and Amharic. A sign hung above a collapsing veranda saying TICKET OFFICE, but the door was shut and padlocked, and a surly guard stood in front of it holding a Kalashnikov. Beyond, four Soviet helicopters crouched in dispersal like giant gray wasps, their rotors swinging slightly in the breeze. A huge Russian, stubble-headed and blond, walked past wearing absurd shorts like an Englishman on holiday. The soldier in front of the lounge demanded my papers, then ordered our driver to back into a car park marked out by spent concrete-filled Russian shell cases. In a square behind the terminal a squad of soldiers in field green drilled up and down beneath a line of watch-towers.

We waited, perched on a packing case. Janet drank mineral water and retched slightly. The World Vision Twin Otter was due in half an hour. The Russians began to ready one of their helicopters, and people climbed in and out of it. A pilot appeared at one of the cockpit windows. Behind it, two men pushed at a giant tortoise that had wandered onto the takeoff area, turned it over on its back, picked it up and carried it to the grass at the edge of the field. There was a buzzing sound to the north and another helicopter, flying low, secretively, and camouflaged, approached to land. Right at the far end of the runway it stopped abruptly, raised its nose, then plumped heavily onto the rough gravel. It taxied into the dispersal area and stopped, huge rotors getting lower and lower as their speed dropped. From the far side, thin, sticklike legs, bowed with famine, appeared in the gap between the fuselage and the ground. Then a file of men in gray rags, faces like skulls, each clinging with a long, thin arm to the shroud of the man in front shuffled from under the whirling blades. One or two poked the ground with long staves, but the others carried nothing, their free hand clutching their coarse rags tight about them. The first helicopter took off in a swirl of brown dust. The file of shuffling skeletons vanished into a hut on the far side of dispersal.

The Twin Otter landed short, bumping toward us with the co-pilot waving us to hurry through the already opened rear door. They were late and short of fuel.

The fifteen-seater was full. In the rear four puzzled-looking Episcopalian ministers sat among piles of mail sacks and cartons of powdered milk. I sat next to a young black man with a confident air and smooth well-fed features. Janet sat behind me. Across the aisle from her a lugubrious-faced Negro in a pith helmet stared gloomily out of the window. Through the window I watched my driver shambling back to the truck. There is a peculiar smell in the tropics on the last day you are there, a nostalgic smell like grass cuttings on an English summer's day. I smelled it as the door was slammed and knew then that I would probably not come back. We took off downhill to a tremendous rattle of stones under the wheels.

As we banked I could see below me the fortlike jail where Hailu had served his prison sentence. Behind it the road snaked over the hill toward Bati. And, before some stray wisps of cloud obscured the view, I caught a glimpse of the barrier across the summit of the pass. Small figures of policemen dotted around it like minuscule guardians at the entrance of the Inferno.

The young black turned toward me and said with an slightly complaining American accent, "Say man, where your psychic investment income coming from?"

I groped at the mixed metaphor. "How do you mean?"

He looked slightly impatient and gestured around him. Two-thirds of the seats were filled with black Americans. They all had the same well-fed look. "Well man, me and the brothers here, we here to help our African brothers in their tra-vail. I mean man, you here for what, man?"

I began to explain but he cut me short. They were a steering group for a new program that American blacks had started to help African countries find their true identity again. He talked of American Negroes coming soon to sit under the plane trees to give, brother to brother, advice to the village chiefs. Being black, he said, was something different from being white, and it was only black people who could solve black peoples' problems. I listened, hoping for another metaphor with the startling quality of his first, but he had spent his most valuable coin at the very outset of the conversation. The rest of what he said I knew to be devalued currency, long ago discarded by Aidgame, the plane-tree routine as dated as a Mary Lloyd film.

I thought about the thousands of district officers—English, Belgian, Dutch, French—who had once, in the opening moves of the game, sat under plane trees in Africa to win the confidence of the village chiefs. What had resulted from that? What had resulted from America's own colony, Liberia, the haven founded for repatriated American slaves? A month earlier Master Sergeant Doe, the president of the crumbling republic, had visited Ethiopia, deep in the councils of the OAU and Mengistu.

My neighbor had a conversational style that constantly regrouped about a new topic like an army on the run. From an explanation of the policies of the new Mayor of Chicago he moved on to Louis Farrakhan and then informed me he had once been a press secretary to a senate lobbying organization in a past administration. It had, he said, taught him a lot about public opinion.

I asked him about the other members of his party, in particular about the young man with a round, rather wistful face that seemed vaguely familiar. My neighbor jived slightly. It was, he whispered, Martin Luther King's son. I looked again, seeing now the bland round face of his father peeping from his son's features. Just in front of King, Jr., sat an elderly-looking black man with a tense face weighed down under an enormous khaki pith helmet. The man in the helmet leaned over the aisle and handed my wife, sitting behind us, a small pamphlet. She glanced at it, then pushed it at me between the seats.

After four months of Amharic the American typeset looked momentarily unfamiliar. Two lines of three-quarter-inch print announced, "Dick Gregory's Slim Face Bahamian Diet." Below it some paragraphs outlined details of a vitamin drink offered as a substitute for meals. My neighbor whispered, "Dick Gregory, the comedian." The plane bucked slightly in the turbulence.

I hunched slightly in my seat, unaccountably embarrassed, concentrating on the pilot's instruments in front of me through the open door of the cockpit. After a while I turned slightly to get another glimpse of the pamphleteer, but the elderly man sat immersed in a book, the gray curls and pith helmet overshadowing a drawn, sad face.

The co-pilot adjusted the trim and reached behind him for the approach map to Addis Ababa.

A former press secretary, a diet in the middle of a famine, and the son of one of the world's most inspired idealists, a man who once said he had had a dream, a dream of justice, equality, and freedom for the black people of the world. Now the son was seeing the dream: gray, sticklike men being bundled into huge whirling helicopters to fly over a dead land in search of a few handfuls of grain.

The Episcopalians stared out the windows at a strange un-American world through thin gold-rimmed spectacles. We landed at Addis.

15

ADDIS HILTON

WE HAD SPENT THE DAY at the Black Lion. Janet had hepatitis, something almost always overlooked and difficult to diagnose. It meant she must go home and I with her. She was not fit to travel on her own. I had spent the day waiting among furtive applicants for exit visas at the Ministry of Foreign Affairs. Over the desk in the main office an unusual smiling picture of Mengistu looked benignly down as if wishing to be remembered in the best possible light by his fleeing subjects.

After five hours, purple stamps were banged in each of the passports. A thin-fingered clerk in a threadbare sports jacket scrawled over them in red ink. We were permitted to leave the country. I took them to the airline with a huge bundle of birr notes smelling of rancid butter and Berber pepper. By dusk I had tickets, bookings, and a permit to enter the airport.

I went back to the Red Cross headquarters to sign some papers and draw money to pay for the hotel. But instead of the atmosphere I had left, one of dust, empty corridors, and a slow hopelessness, there was now a low-grade unease like a grumbling fever. People pushed past me muttering, doors were closed and locked on meetings that went on for hours. Cars drew up in the yard, hesitated, then drove off again. I went to collect some letters. In the mail room I heard somebody murmur the word cholera.

It was inevitable. Cholera, a disease that can take you from perfect health to death in twelve hours, had always threatened the camps. Large groups of people, weakened by hunger and supplied by river water, were a perfect breeding ground for it. One of the first outbreaks had been in a Red Cross camp on the Awash River, and it was feared that it would soon reach Bati. Both camps were connected by road. But that morning the government had issued an edict banning the use of the word "cholera" or taking any steps, especially vaccination or the mass movement of rehydration fluids, that would confirm the existence of the disease to the outside world. I tried to talk to Amsalu about it, but he became agitated and fearful at the very name. Those officials with more power merely shrugged. Vaccination was not that effective, it was true, but that was not the reason for the ban. If we vaccinated now the numbers of deaths would at least be diminished to some extent. But it was dangerous to meddle with the government. The best we could hope for were a few roadblocks to stop travelers getting into Bati from the infected area.

It was hopeless. I said good-bye and left. Outside on the hill above the city the statue of Menelik, the emperor who opened Ethiopia to the world, seemed to ride sideways around the old Coptic Church of St. Michael. Inside a few old men lay prostrate before the iconostasis, ancient wood-covered bibles pressed to their foreheads. Incense poured from a half-opened door and above it, among all the saints and angels, a panel depicted a youthful Haile Selassie manning a machine gun against the Italian bombers. Compared with her frequent famines, Ethiopia lost few people in that war. But maybe because famines were God's work and not man's, the church had tactfully failed to record them.

Back at the hotel, the atmosphere was pervaded by an enervating tenseness. Frantic pressmen, waiting for permits to go north, were everywhere. They stood about the lobby in terror of phone calls from their editors, got drunk in the bars and shouted their previous coups at one another or searched frantically for copy from anyone who looked remotely down-at-heel enough to have recently come in from the country.

But it was a spurious hysteria. Most of them must have been veterans of disasters as bad or worse than Ethiopia— Lebanon, Cambodia, Vietnam, Iran—and it made their frantic calls and heavy drinking suspect. In a week they would, like their readers, have forgotten Ethiopia. But while they were here, like medieval sin eaters, they had to go through the motions of atonement, guilt, and concern. Hanging about the telex office or crowding the lifts with anxious chatter about port holdups, wheat shipments, and RAF food drops.

In between they lay around the poolside in deck chairs, drinking endlessly, telling filthy stories in slow watchful tones, heavily paused to judge their effect. A reporter for *The Zimbabwe Herald*, once *The Rhodesian Herald*, face stretched with exhaustion, introduced himself, slumped into a seat opposite, lay back, and began to snore.

The public address announced a smorgasbord and video. Liberated women delegates to a black-consciousness congress, none of them Ethiopian, gave interviews from behind dark glasses to young American women reporters with innocent faces. On the grass, the children of the diplomatic corps played rough games, fat, arrogant faces frequently dissolving into tears. Waiters hurried about collecting dollar bills. A hamburger, chips, and coffee cost what a peasant earned in a week.

A tall man in an improbable Gannex raincoat stepped out of the elevator and began shouting something about his by-line. Somebody whispered *Daily Telegraph* in reverential tones. I went to my room.

I stood on the veranda, watching the flickering lights of Addis Ababa dim under the fluctuating power of its ancient electricity station. Behind me, Janet slept uneasily after a day of vomiting. We were due to fly out the following morning. It was Christmas Eve. I turned on my tiny shortwave radio and stood there listening to the choirboys of Kings College, Cambridge, singing "Adeste Fidelis" on the World Service of the BBC. Just before midnight the voice of the Archbishop of Canterbury quavered from his palace two thousand miles away.

Man, he said, had started life in the cave but had now emerged from it into the world of rational thought. Man was capable of moral decisions, of choice, of creating art. He was above all self-reflecting, he knew the difference between good and evil.

I thought of Martin Luther King's son again. I had been a student when all that had happened. When his father had been the champion of the men who, Tom Wolfe had said, walked in outsize suits through the dust of Alabama to ask for their liberty. I hadn't really understood it then; it seemed far away, and Martin Luther King just a black preacher, something to do with America and the Kennedys. But now I had begun to grasp what Wolfe had seen so clearly. The obvious monsters like Mengistu, Idi Amin, the Boers, or the quintessentialy evil Marcias Nguema of Equatorial Guinea, who liked to execute those of his subjects who could read or write —these were passing medieval freaks. The real oppression came from a white liberal guilt that threatened to lock the black man into a caricature of dependence and patronage. The laws that ruled our own societies we had come to think too strong for Africans. So, deluded, we had allowed them to develop an inverted world where murder was ignored, evil praised as enlightenment, and grotesque xenophobia billed as anti-rascism.

The results were terrifying.

We had buried three thousand six hundred and fifty-seven

people in Bati. Their names, meticulously written in a schoolboy hand by one of the assistants, lay inside the pages of a looseleaf folder on the table beside me.

I turned off the radio and got into bed. The next morning we left for London. I never saw Bati again.